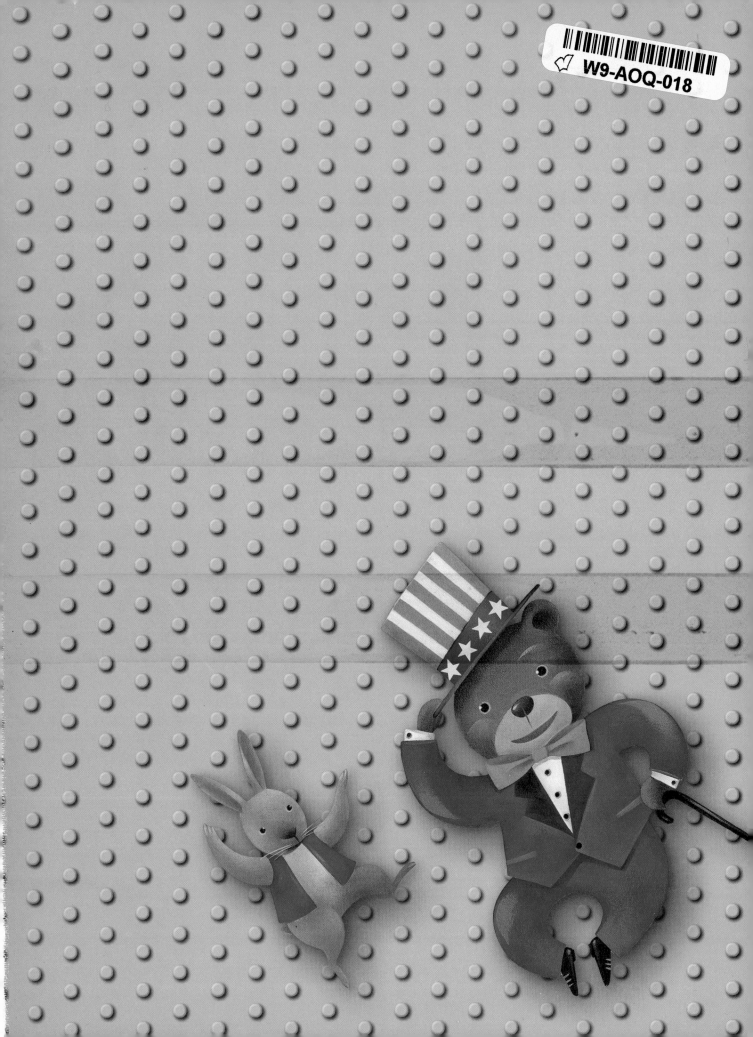

Authors

Judy Bond

René Boyer

Margaret Campbelle-Holman

Emily Crocker

Marilyn C. Davidson

Robert de Frece

Virginia Ebinger

Mary Goetze

Betsy M. Henderson

John Jacobson

Michael Jothen

Chris Judah-Lauder

Carol King

Vincent P. Lawrence

Ellen McCullough-Brabson

Janet McMillion

Nancy L. T. Miller

Ivy Rawlins

Susan Snyder

Gilberto D. Soto

Kodály Contributing Consultant

Sr. Lorna Zemke

ACKNOWLEDGMENTS

Creative Direction and Delivery: The Quarasan Group, Inc.

From the Top-On National Radio! selections are adapted from the nationally distributed public radio program, *From the Top.* CEOs/Executive Producers: Jennifer Hurley-Wales and Gerald Slavet. Authors: Ann Gregg and Joanne Robinson. © 2000, 2002, 2003 From the Top, Inc.

The Broadway Junior® logo and MTI® logo are trademarks of Music Theatre International. All rights reserved.

Grateful acknowledgment is given to the following authors, composers, and publishers. Every effort has been made to trace the ownership of all copyrighted material and to secure the necessary permissions to reprint these selections. In the case of some selections for which acknowledgment is not given, extensive research has failed to locate the copyright holders.

Songs and Speech Pieces

Apple Picker's Reel, Words and Music by Larry Hanks. Copyright © 1967 by ALPHA FILM MUSIC. International Copyright Secured. All Rights Reserved.

Artichokes, Words and Music by Malvina Reynolds. Copyright © by SCHRODER MUSIC COMPANY. International Copyright Secured. All Rights Reserved.

Baby Beluga, Words and Music by Raffi Cavourkian and D. Pike. Copyright © 1980 by Homeland Publishing, a div. of Troubadour Music, Inc. International Copyright Secured. All Rights Reserved.

Ban Dal (Half Moon), Words and Music by Keuk Young Toun. Copyright © by SEH KWANG PUBLISHING CO. International Copyright Secured. All Rights Reserved.

Bate, bate (Stir, Stir), Adapted by José-Luis Orozco. Copyright © 1989 by Arcoiris Records, Inc. International Copyright Secured. All Rights Reserved.

Bei Fang Chre (North Wind Blows), Chinese New Year Festival Song collected and transcribed by Kathy Sorensen. © 1991 Kathy B. Sorensen. All Rights Reserved.

Big Beautiful Planet, Words and Music by Raffi Cavourkian. Copyright © by Homeland Publishing, a div. of Troubadour Music, Inc. International Copyright Secured. All Rights Reserved.

Candle on the Water, from Walt Disney's PETE'S DRAGON. Words and Music by Al Kasha and Joel Hirschhorn. Copyright © 1976 Walt Disney Music Company and Wonderland Music Company, Inc. All Rights Reserved. Used by Permission.

Caranguejo (The Crab), from *Cantemos.* Brazilian Folk Song. English Words by María Luisa Muñoz. Copyright © 1962 (Renewed) by AMERICAN BOOK COMPANY. International Copyright Secured. All Rights Reserved.

Check It Out! (It's About Respect), Words and Music by John Jacobson and John Higgins. Copyright © 2001 by MUSIC EXPRESS LLC. International Copyright Secured. All Rights Reserved.

Chichipapa (The Sparrow's Singing School), Words by Katsura Shimizu. Music by Ryutaro Hirota. Collected and Translated by Hanako Fukuda. Copyright © 1965 (Renewed) by HIGHLAND MUSIC COMPANY. International Copyright Secured. All Rights Reserved.

Columbus Sailed with Three Ships, Words and Music by Margaret Campbelle-Holman. Copyright © 1981 by Margaret Campbelle-Holman. International Copyright Secured. All Rights Reserved.

Dal taro kacha (Come, Pick the Moon), Words by Suk-Joong Yoon. Music by Tae-Hyun Park. Copyright © by SEH KWANG PUBLISHING CO. International Copyright Secured. All Rights Reserved.

Dance, Dance, Dance!, Words by Ava Hogan Chapman. Music by Moses Hogan. Copyright © 2001 by MUSIC EXPRESS LLC. International Copyright Secured. All Rights Reserved.

Do-Re-Mi, from THE SOUND OF MUSIC®. Lyrics by Oscar Hammerstein II. Music by Richard Rodgers. Copyright © 1959 by Richard Rodgers and Oscar Hammerstein II. Copyright Renewed. WILLIAMSON MUSIC owner of publication and allied rights throughout the world. International Copyright Secured. All Rights Reserved. The Sound Of Music is a registered trademark used under license from The Rodgers and Hammerstein Organization on behalf of the Rodgers Family Partnership, the Estate of Oscar Hammerstein II and the heirs of Howard Lindsay and Russel Crouse.

Eating Lizards, Words and Music by Carol Huffman. Copyright © by CAROL HUFFMAN. International Copyright Secured. All Rights Reserved.

El burrito enfermo (The Sick Little Donkey), Latin American Folk Song. Adapted by José-Luis Orozco. Copyright © by José-Luis Orozco/Arcoiris Records, P.O. Box 461900, Los Angeles, CA 90046. International Copyright Secured. All Rights Reserved.

En nuestra Tierra tan linda (On Our Beautiful Planet Earth), Latin American Folk Song. Adapted by José-Luis Orozco. Copyright © 1996 by José-Luis Orozco/Arcoiris Records, P.O. Box 461900, Los Angeles, CA 90046. International Copyright Secured. All Rights Reserved.

El palomo y la paloma (The Doves), Mexican Folk Song. Adapted by José-Luis Orozco. Copyright © 1996 by José-Luis Orozco/Arcoiris Records, P.O. Box 461900, Los Angeles, CA 90046. International Copyright Secured. All Rights Reserved.

Everybody Has Music Inside, Words and Music by Greg Scelsa. Copyright © 1980 by Little House Music (ASCAP). International Copyright Secured. All Rights Reserved.

Everything Grows, Words and Music by Raffi Cavourkian and D. Pike. Copyright © 1987 by Homeland Publishing, a div. of Troubadour Music, Inc. International Copyright Secured. All Rights Reserved.

Food Song, The, Words and Music by Jackie Silberg. Copyright © 1989 by Miss Jackie Music Company. International Copyright Secured. All Rights Reserved.

continued on page 393

A

Macmillan/McGraw-Hill

Published by Macmillan/McGraw-Hill, of McGraw-Hill Education, a division of The McGraw-Hill Companies, Inc., Two Penn Plaza, New York, New York 10121.

ISBN: 978-0-02-296698-0
MHID: 0-02-296698-6
3 4 5 6 7 8 9 RJE 14 13 12 11 10

Printed in the United States of America

SPOTLIGHT on MUSIC

CONTRIBUTORS

Consultants

Brian Burnett,
Movement

Stephen Gabriel,
Technology

Magali Iglesias,
English Language Learners

Roberta Newcomer,
Special Learners/Assessment

Frank Rodríguez,
English Language Learners

Jacque Schrader,
Movement

Kathy B. Sorensen,
International Phonetic
Alphabet

Patti Windes-Bridges,
Listening Maps

Linda Worsley,
Listening/Singable
English Translations

Sr. Lorna Zemke,
Kodály Contributing
Consultant

Recordings

Executive Producer: John Higgins
Senior Music Editor/Producer: Emily Crocker
Senior Recording Producer: Mark Brymer
Recording Producers: Steve Millikan, Andy Waterman
Associate Recording Producers: Alan Billingsley, Darrell Bledsoe, Stacy Carson, Rosanna Eckert, John Egan, Chad Evans, Darlene Koldenhoven, Chris Koszuta, Don Markese, Matthew McGregor, Steve Potts, Edwin Schupman, Michael Spresser, Frank Stegall, David Vartanian, Mike Wilson, Ted Wilson
Project/Mastering Engineer: Mark Aspinall; Post-Production Engineer: Don Sternecker

Selected recordings by Buryl Red, Executive Producer; Michael Rafter, Senior Recording Producer; Bryan Louiselle and Buddy Skipper, Recording Producers; Lori Casteel and Mick Rossi, Associate Recording Producers; Jonathan Duckett, Supervising Engineer

Contributing Writers

Allison Abucewicz, Sharon Berndt, Rhona Brink, Ann Burbridge, Debbie Helm Daniel, Katherine Domingo, Kari Gilbertson, Janet Graham, Hilree Hamilton, Linda Harley, Judy Henneberger, Carol Huffman, Bernie Hynson, Jr., Sheila A. Kerley, Elizabeth Kipperman, Ellen Mendelsohn, Cristi Cary Miller, Leigh Ann Mock, Patricia O'Rourke, Barbara Resch, Soojin Kim Ritterling, Isabel Romero, Carl B. Schmidt, Debra Shearer, Ellen Mundy Shuler, Rebecca Treadway, Carol Wheeler, Sheila Woodward

Multicultural Consultants

William Anderson, Chet-Yeng Loong, Edwin Schupman, Kathy B. Sorensen, Gilberto D. Soto, Judith Cook Tucker, Dennis Waring

In the Spotlight Consultant

Willa Dunleavy

Multicultural Advisors

Brad Ahawanrathe Bonaparte (Mohawk), Emmanuel Akakpo (Ewe), Earlene Albano (Hawaiian), Luana Au (Maori), Bryan Ayakawa (Japanese), Ruby Beeston (Mandarin), Latif Bolat (Turkish), Estella Christensen (Spanish), Oussama Davis (Arabic), Mia Delguardo (Minahasa), Nolutho Ndengane Diko (Xhosa), Angela Fields (Hopi, Chemehuevi), Gary Fields (Lakota, Cree), Gilad Harel (Hebrew), Josephine Hetarihon (Bahasa Indonesian, Minahasa, and Maluko dialect), Judy Hirt-Manheimer (Hebrew), Rose Jakub (Navajo), Elizabeth Jarema (Fijian), Rita Jensen (Swedish), Malou Jewett (Visayan), Alejandro Jimenez (Hispanic), Chris Jones (Hungarian), Wendy Jyang Shamo (Mandarin), Amir Kalay (Hebrew), Michael Katsan (Greek), Silvi Madarajan (Tamil), Georgia Magpie (Comanche), Nona Mardi (Malay), Aida Mattingly (Tagalog), Mike Kanathohare McDonald (Mohawk), Vasana de Mel (Sinhala), Marion Miller (Czech), Etsuko Miskin (Japanese), Mogens Mogenson (Danish), Kenny Tahawisoren Perkins (Mohawk), Pradeep Nayyar (Punjabi, Hindi), Renu Nayyar (Punjabi), Mfanego Ngwenya (Zulu), Wil Numkena (Hopi), Samuel Owuru (Akan), Nina Padukone (Konkani), Hung Yong Park (Korean), James Parker (Finnish), Jose Pereira (Konkani), Berrit Price (Norwegian), John Rainer (Taos Pueblo, Creek), Lillian Rainer (Taos Pueblo, Creek, Apache), Arnold Richardson (Haliwa-Saponi), Ken Runnacles (German), Trudy Shenk (German), Ron Singer (Navajo), Ernest Siva (Cahuilla, Serrano [Maringa']), Bonnie Slade (Swedish), Cristina Sorrentino (Portuguese), Diane Thram (Xhosa), Elena Todorov (Bulgarian), Zlatina Todorov (Russian), Tom Toronto (Lao, Thai), Rebecca Wilberg (French, Italian), Sheila Woodward (Zulu), Keith Yackeyonny (Comanche)

Contents

Spotlight on Music Reading.........241

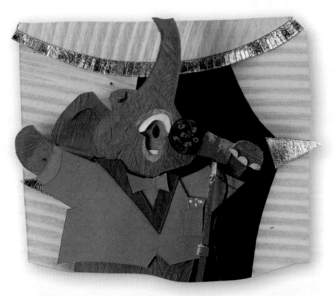

Spotlight on Performance..........273

Spotlight on Celebrations.............337

In the Spotlight

There is a light that shines
bright in the All-American sky.
It sings! It plays!
It dances like the sun!
There is a light that shines in America!
I want to step into that light!

Step into the Spotlight

Spotlight CD
Track 1

Words and Music by John Jacobson,
Emily Crocker, and John Higgins

1. Lis - ten to the world a - round you, There is
2. In a world of sound and col - or, in a

mus - ic ev - 'ry - where.__ Just step out - side__ your
rhy - thm all its own,____ It's the heart - beat of____ A -

door - way, and you can hear mus - ic in the air!__
mer - i - ca, the land we proud - ly call our home!_

From the cit - y to the farm and field,__ to the
From the cit - y to the farm and field,__ there's a

But wait … where shall we start?
Let's start at the very beginning.
It's a very good place to start!

Do-Re-Mi

from the movie *The Sound of Music*

**Spotlight CD
Track 4**

Lyrics by Oscar Hammerstein II
Music by Richard Rodgers

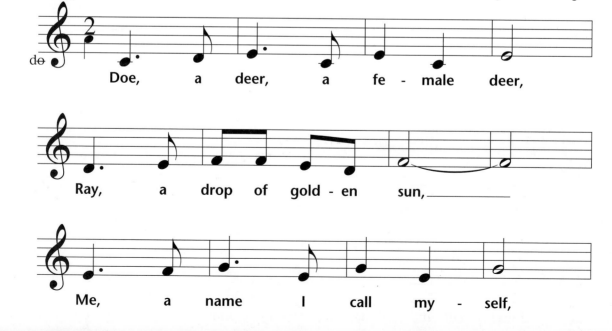

Doe,   a   deer,   a   fe - male   deer,

Ray,   a   drop   of   gold - en   sun,_____

Me,   a   name   I   call   my - self,

There is a light that shines in America.
Full of hope and pride.
I see it now!
The light that shines in America is me!

This Little Light of Mine

Spotlight CD
Track 7

Freely

African American Spiritual

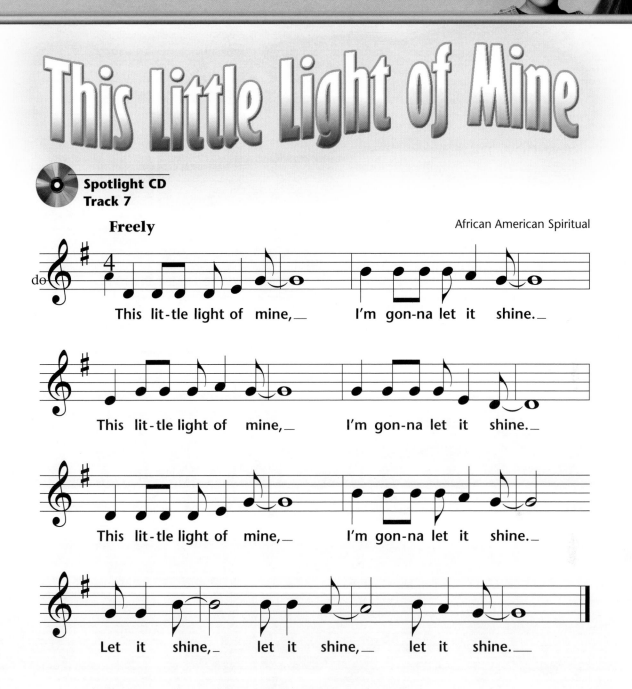

This lit-tle light of mine, __ I'm gon-na let it shine. __

This lit-tle light of mine, __ I'm gon-na let it shine. __

This lit-tle light of mine, __ I'm gon-na let it shine. __

Let it shine, __ let it shine, __ let it shine. __

2. Down in my heart, I'm gonna let it shine.
   Down in my heart, I'm gonna let it shine.
   Down in my heart, I'm gonna let it shine.
   Let it shine, let it shine, let it shine.

3. All over the world, I'm gonna let it shine.
   All over the world, I'm gonna let it shine.
   All over the world, I'm gonna let it shine.
   Let it shine, let it shine, let it shine.

When I sing the songs of
America all by myself,
I show how much
I love my country.
When we sing our songs
of America together,
we make harmony!
Then the light that shines in
America burns brighter for all!

Patriotic Medley

Spotlight CD Track 10

Words by George M. Cohan Woody Guthrie, and Katharine Lee Bates.

You're a Grand Old Flag

You're a Grand Old Flag, you're a high flyin' flag.
And forever in peace may you wave.
You're the emblem of the land I love,
The home of the free and the brave.
Ev'ry heart beats true
   for the red, white, and blue,
Where there's never a boast or brag.
But should auld acquaintance be forgot,
Keep your eye on the grand old flag.

This Land Is Your Land

This land is your land, this land is my land
From California to the New York Island.
From the redwood forest
   to the Gulf Stream waters,
This land was made for you and me.
As I was walking that ribbon of highway,
I saw above me that endless skyway.
I saw below me that golden valley.
This land was made for you and me.

America!

America! America! God shed His grace on thee.
And crown thy good with brotherhood,
From sea to shining sea! (*Repeat last two lines*)

Spotlight on Concepts

Spotlight on Concepts

Spotlight on Concepts

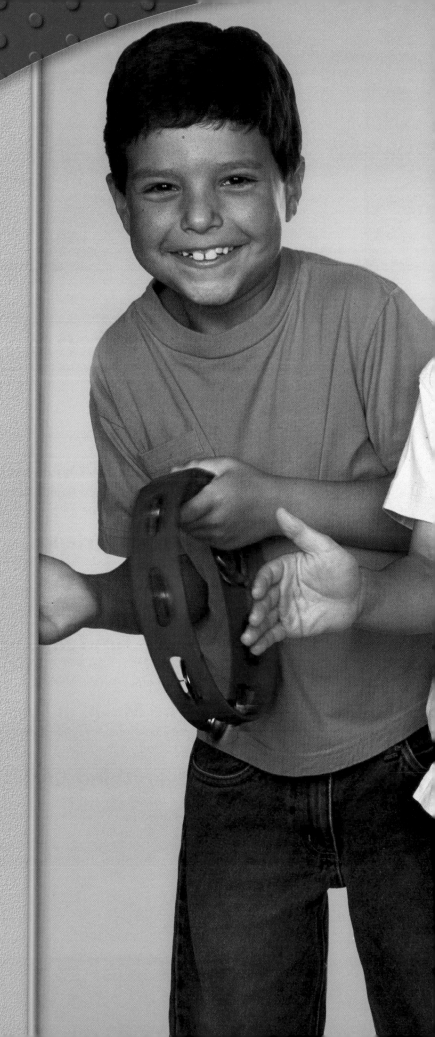

Together Through Music

How are these children making music?

Coming Attractions

Move with the beat to a jump-rope rhyme.

Play along with ballet music.

Sing about lemonade on *so* and *mi*.

Music is one way we can
work and play together.

Sing and move together with the song.

DANCE, DANCE, DANCE!

CD 1:1

Music by Moses Hogan
Words by Ava Hogan-Chapman

A

Hop, hop, hop, Hop___ to your feet. Just jump, jump, jump,

Jump___ to the beat. Let's dance, dance, dance,

Danc - ing is fun for ev' - ry - one.

B

1. Wig-gle it, *wig-gle it,* Jump it, *jump it,*
(Gr. 1) 2. Swing___ it high, _____ *(Gr. 2) swing it low, _____*

Hop it, *hop it,* Bop it, *bop it,*
Swing it fast,_ *swing it slow,_* } Move it, *move it,* Groove it, *groove it,*

(Second time to **A** *)*

'Til your bo - dy can't stop mov - in'.

5

Step to the Beat

CONCEPT
RHYTHM
SKILLS
SING, MOVE, LISTEN
LINKS
CULTURES

The steady pulse you feel in music is called **beat**. **Pat** with the beat as you learn this song. Then march to it!

Step In Time
from the movie *Mary Poppins*

CD 1:4

Words and Music by Richard M. Sherman and Robert B. Sherman

1. Kick your knees up, step in time!
2. Link your el - bows, step in time!
3. Spin a - bout and step in time!
4. 'Round the chim - ney, step in time!

Kick your knees up, step in time!
Link your el - bows, step in time!
Spin a - bout and step in time!
'Round the chim - ney, step in time!

Nev - er need a rea - son, nev - er need a rhyme,
Nev - er need a rea - son, nev - er need a rhyme,

Kick your knees up, step in time!
Link your el - bows, step in time!
Spin a - bout and step in time!
'Round the chim - ney, step in time!

5. Flap like a bird - ie, step in time!
6. Step in____ time,____ step in time!

Flap like a bird - ie, step in time!
Step in____ time,____ step in time!

Nev - er need a rea - son, nev - er need a rhyme,
Nev - er need a rea - son, nev - er need a rhyme, when you

1.
Flap like a bird - ie, step in time!

2.
step in time, you step in time.

Beat and Rhythm

When you jump rope, you jump with the beat.
Move to the beat and say this jump-rope rhyme.

**Skipping rope started a long time ago.
At first mostly boys played it. Now girls play it too.** ▶

Sheep in the Meadow

 CD 1:7

Sheep in the meadow,
Cows in the corn.
Jump in on the month
   that you were born.
*January, February, March, April,
May, June, July, August,
September, October,
November, December!*

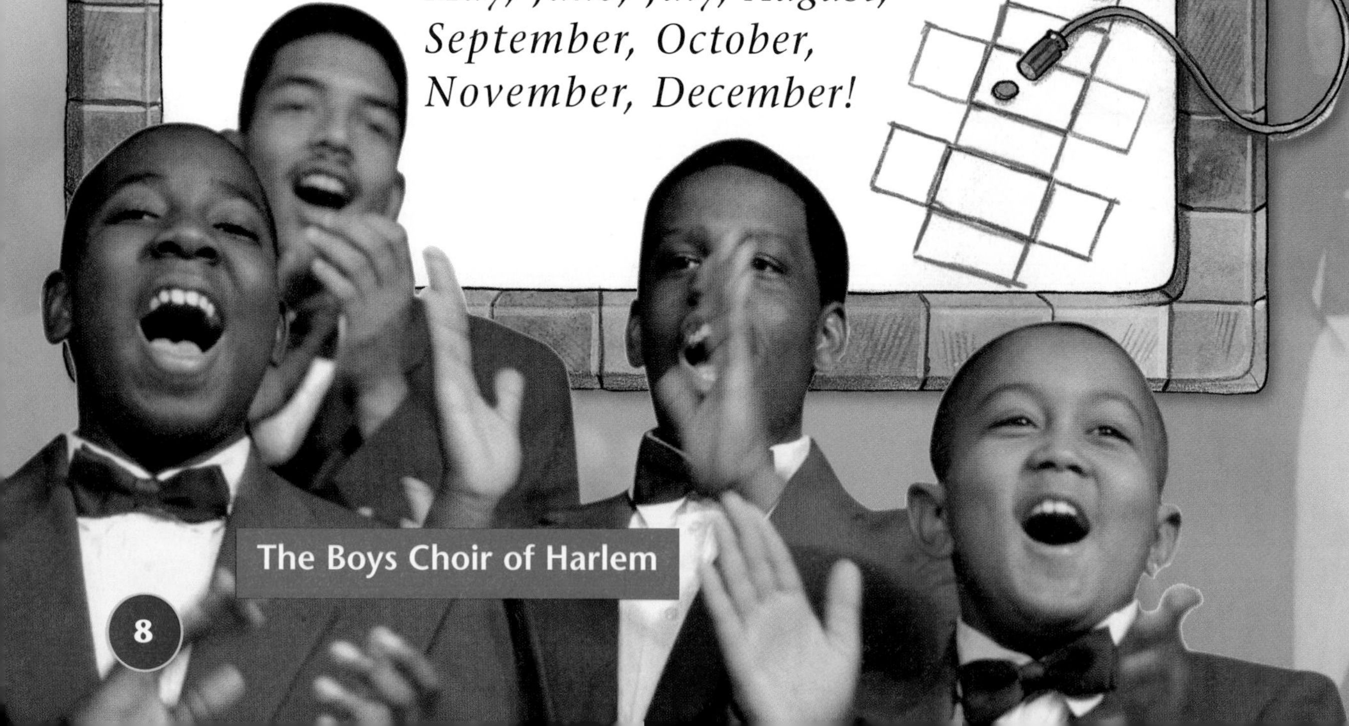

The Boys Choir of Harlem

Pat with the beat as you **listen**.

 LISTENING CD 1:10

| Little David, Play on Your Harp (African American Spiritual)

The long and short sounds in a song are called **rhythm** . Clap the rhythm.

THINK! How is rhythm different from beat?

CONCEPT
MELODY

SKILLS
SING, READ, MOVE

LINKS
SOCIAL STUDIES, FINE ART

Respect is an important part of being a good citizen. **Sing** this song about respect. Can you tell when the melody moves higher and when it moves lower?

★ Check It Out! (It's About Respect)

CD 1:14

Words and Music by
John Higgins and John Jacobson

Ⓐ

It's a - bout re - spect! Check it out! Check it out!

(Repeat Ⓐ after Ⓑ and Ⓒ)

It's a - bout re - spect! Check it out!

B Got-ta treat my friends like fam - i - ly.___ Got - ta
treat my fam - i - ly like friends.___ Treat 'em
with re - spect and they'll be there for me.___ They can
count on me in the end.___

Spoken:

 C

R! There's a reason people treat you like they do.

E! Ev'rybody take a chance.

S! It's so simple, and it all begins with you.

P! People gotta take a stand.

E! Even when you think the world isn't fair.

C! Come along and check it out!

T! Take a risk, take a ride, take a dare.

Take a breath of air and let's shout, RESPECT!

Check it out! RESPECT! Check it out!

Higher and Lower Melody

Pitch is how high or low a sound is.
A group of pitches is a **melody**.

Listen to "Engine, Engine Number Nine."
How are the pictures below like the melody?

In music, pitches are shown with **notes** on
five lines called a **staff**.

staff

note

Sing this song. Move higher and lower with the melody.

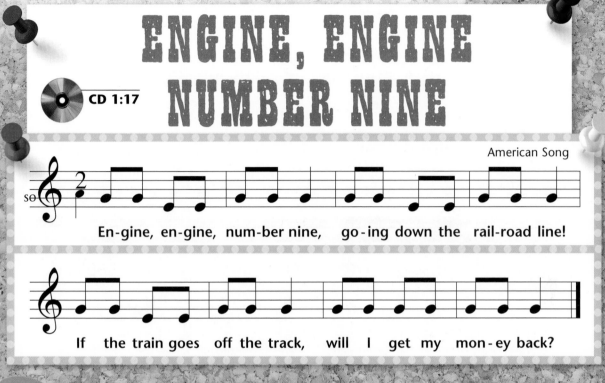

ENGINE, ENGINE NUMBER NINE

CD 1:17

American Song

En-gine, en-gine, num-ber nine, go-ing down the rail-road line!

If the train goes off the track, will I get my mon-ey back?

Art Gallery

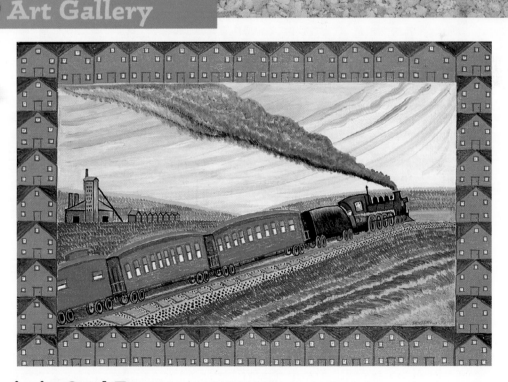

Train in Coal Town by Jack Savitsky
Jack Savitsky worked in the coal mines. He taught himself to draw and paint. He often drew on the walls of the tunnels in the coal mines.

CONCEPT
RHYTHM
SKILLS
READ, SING, PLAY
LINKS
MATH, SCIENCE, SOCIAL STUDIES

Reading ♩ ♫ ≀ Rhythms

You can show one sound to a beat with a **quarter note**.

You can show two equal sounds to a beat with two **eighth notes**.

Music has beats of silence as well as sounds. **Listen** for beats of silence in this song.

🔘 **LISTENING** CD 1:20

I Bought Me a Cat arranged by Aaron Copland

You can show a beat of silence with a **quarter rest**. Find the ≀ in the song.

I Bought Me a Cat

CD 1:21

Kentucky Mountain Folk Song

1. I bought me a cat, and the cat pleased me.

I fed my cat un-der yon-der tree.

Cat goes fid-dle-i-fee.

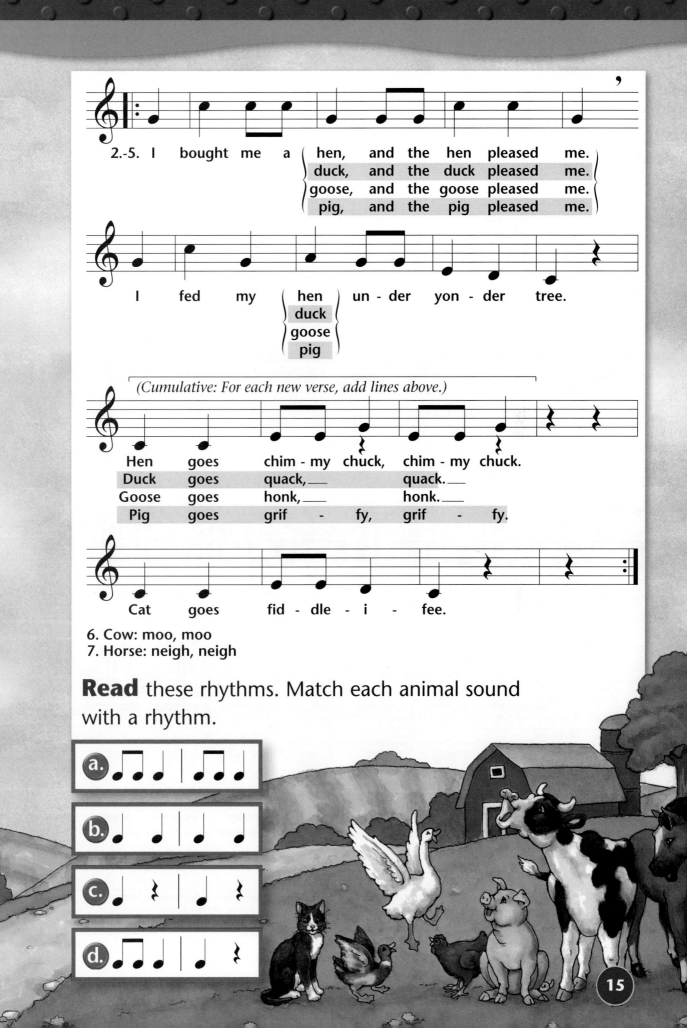

2.-5. I bought me a { hen, and the hen pleased me.
duck, and the duck pleased me.
goose, and the goose pleased me.
pig, and the pig pleased me. }

I fed my { hen / duck / goose / pig } un - der yon - der tree.

(Cumulative: For each new verse, add lines above.)

Hen goes chim - my chuck, chim - my chuck.
Duck goes quack, quack.
Goose goes honk, honk.
Pig goes grif - fy, grif - fy.

Cat goes fid - dle - i - fee.

6. Cow: moo, moo
7. Horse: neigh, neigh

Read these rhythms. Match each animal sound with a rhythm.

a.

b.

c.

d.

Playing Rhythms

Look at the Playalong. What do you think the beat bars with no instruments show?

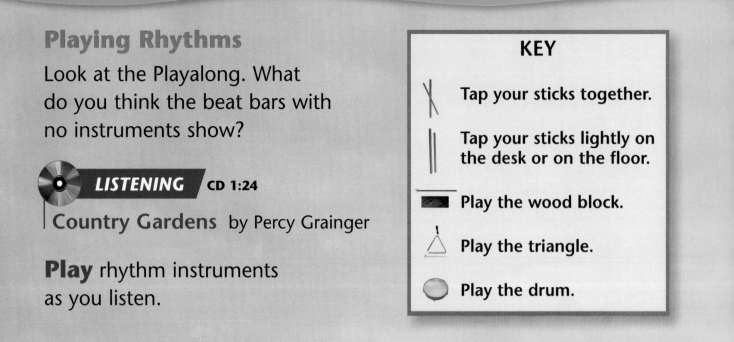

LISTENING CD 1:24

Country Gardens by Percy Grainger

Play rhythm instruments as you listen.

KEY

Tap your sticks together.

Tap your sticks lightly on the desk or on the floor.

Play the wood block.

Play the triangle.

Play the drum.

Playalong and Listening Map for *Country Gardens*

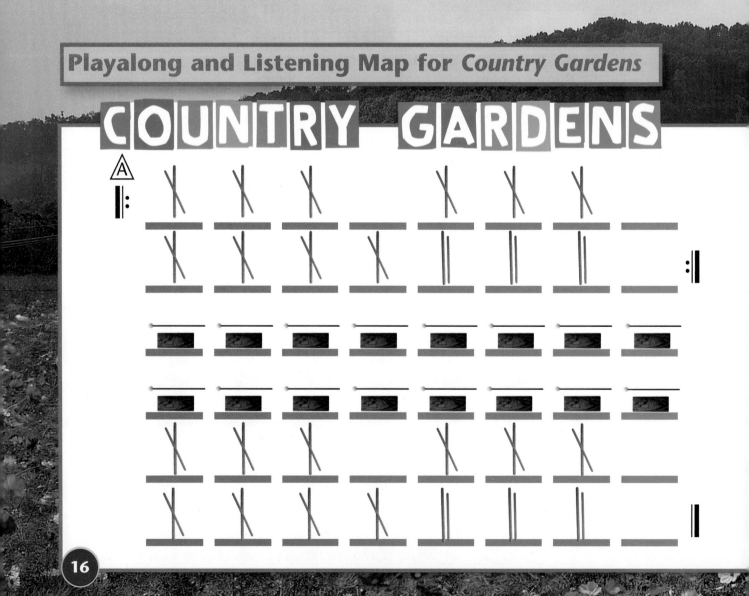

16

Meet the Musician

Percy Grainger was an Australian composer and pianist. He began playing concerts when he was ten years old. Grainger collected English folk songs. He used these songs in the music he wrote. Grainger liked to eat brown-sugar sandwiches. He did not like to carry things, so he tied his pens, pencils, and paper to his jacket with string.

THINK! How could you use ♩ and ♫ to show the rhythm for these words: *garden, flower, rose, tulip?*

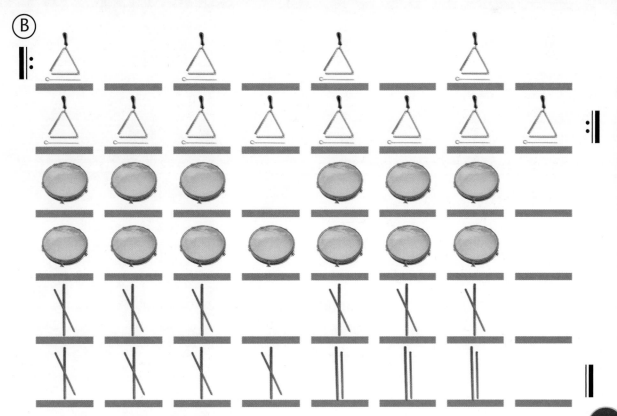

17

The pitches you have been singing are shown on this staff. The names of these two pitches are *so* and *mi*.

These are the hand signs for *so* and *mi*.

so   mi

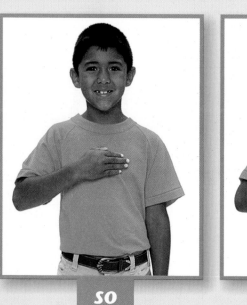

so   mi

This is called a **treble clef**. It shows that the pitches on the staff are in your voice range.

treble clef

Find *so* and *mi* in this song. Sing this song. Use hand signs.

Lemonade

CD 1:25

American Singing Game

Group 1   *Group 2*

(clap   clap)   Here we come.

Group 1   *Group 2*

(Where   from?)   New   York.

Group 1   *Group 2*

(What's your trade?)   Lem - on - ade.

Group 1   *Group 2*

(Give us some.)   Have   none.

Group 1

(Get to work and   make us some.)

THINK! How could you draw ⬭ to show the melody of "Lemonade"?

So and Mi in Latin America

There are many countries in Latin America.
Listen to this music from Latin America.

LISTENING CD 1:28

Tabu by Margarita Lecuona

Play along as you listen.

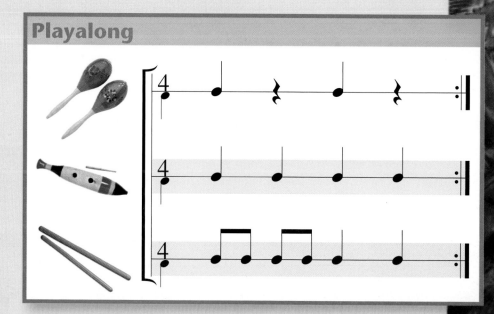

Playalong

Meet the Musician

Margarita Lecuona was born in Cuba. She was a songwriter, dancer, singer, and actress. She was one of the first women to write popular songs that became big hits in Cuba. She came from a musical family. Her uncle, Ernesto Lecuona, was an important Cuban composer and pianist.

In this song, one line has only *so* and *mi.* Can you find it?

RIQUI RAN

Sawing Song

CD 1:29

Latin American
Folk Song
English Words
by Linda Worsley

Spanish: **A - se - rrín,   a - se - rrán,**
English: **Saw - ing wood, saw - ing wood,**

los   ma - de - ros   de   San Juan,
lum - ber - men   in   old   San Juan,

co - men que - so,   co - men pan.
Eat - ing cheese and   eat - ing bread.

Los   de   Ri - que   al - fe - ñi - que,
Some of   them eat   sug - ar can - dy,

los   de   Ro - que   al - fan - do - que.
some of   them eat   gin - ger can - dy.

Ri - qui,   ri - que,   ri - qui, ran.
Ri - qui,   ri - qui,   ri - qui, ran.

Learn About Latin America

This song is well known in many places in Latin America. Latin America includes Mexico, the countries of the Caribbean, and South America.

MAP

UNITED STATES

LATIN AMERICA

Latin America is full of many wonders. It has the tallest waterfall in the world (Venezuela), the longest country (Chile), and volcanoes. In South America, people grow cacao trees, from which we get chocolate.

cacao tree ▲

21

CONCEPT
RHYTHM
SKILLS
PLAY, READ, SING
LINKS
CULTURES, DANCE, FINE ART

Play the rhythm of the sparrows' song.

Playalong

4

Chi   chi   pa   pa,   chi   pa   pa!

MAP

UNITED STATES   JAPAN

Chichipapa

CD 1:33

The Sparrows' Singing School

Music by Ryutaro Hirota
Words by Katsura Shimizu
Arranged by Kyoko Takahashi

Japanese: すずめ の がっ こう の せん せい は
English: Teach-er of the spar - rows'___ sing - ing school,

む ち を ふ り ふ り ちい ぱっ ぱ
Waves a stick to lead us sing-ing Chi pa pa.

せい と の すず め は わに なっ て
We___ stu-dents step and move to form___ a ring,

Learning about music helps us understand people around the world.

Japanese instruments from long ago are still played today. What instruments can you name that are like these?

CD-ROM

Use **World Instruments CD-ROM** to learn more about Japanese instruments.

shakuhachi ▶

samisen ▼

koto ▼

taiko drum ▶

ぢ　く　ち　を　そ　ろ　え　て　ちい　ぱっ　ぱ
And we learn to sing to-geth-er Chi pa pa.

ちい　ちい　ぱっ　ぱ　ちい　ぱっ　ぱ
Chi chi pa pa, chi pa pa!

Play Rhythm Instruments

Many musical instruments play only rhythm.
Which rhythm instruments have you played?

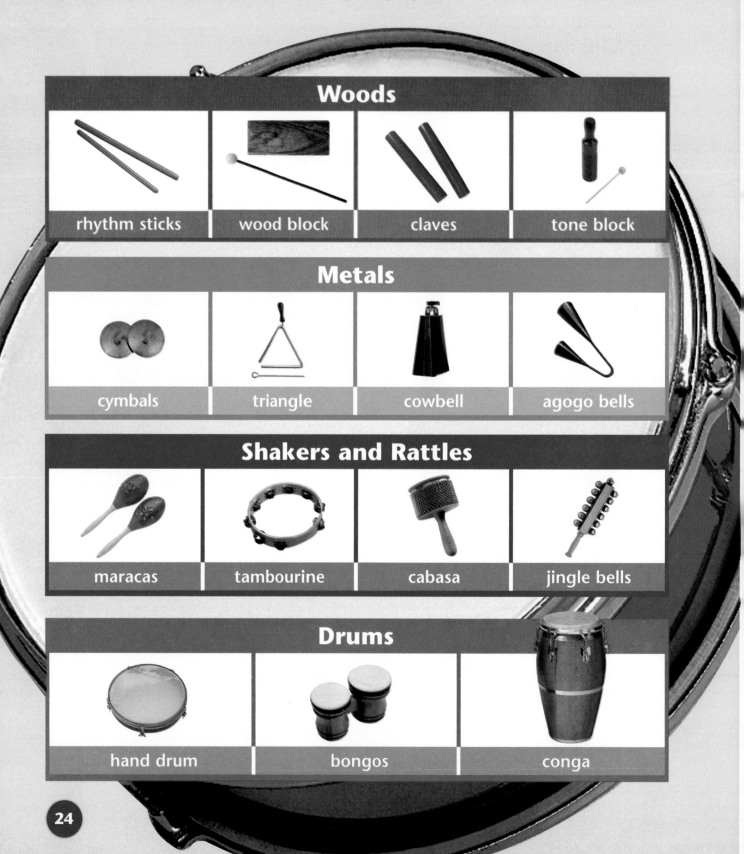

Woods

rhythm sticks | wood block | claves | tone block

Metals

cymbals | triangle | cowbell | agogo bells

Shakers and Rattles

maracas | tambourine | cabasa | jingle bells

Drums

hand drum | bongos | conga

Read this rhythm. Play it on wood instruments.

Playalong

Play the rhythm along with ballet music.

 **LISTENING**   CD 2:1

Ballet Music
by Christoph Gluck

Ballet is a type of dance. The dancers must work hard and be very strong. They wear special shoes.

New York ▶
City Ballet

Art Gallery

Little Dancer of Fourteen
by Edgar Degas

Degas loved the ballet. He spent many hours watching it. He is known for his many pictures and sculptures of ballet dancers.

Loud and Soft in Music

CONCEPT ▶
DYNAMICS
SKILLS
MOVE, SING,
PLAY
LINKS
SCIENCE,
READING

CD-ROM

Use *MIDIsaurus*
CD-ROM to practice
piano and *forte*.

Different levels of loud and soft in music are called **dynamics**. In music the word for loud is *forte*. The word for soft is *piano*.

🔵 **LISTENING**   CD 2:2

Gavotte fantastique by Amy Beach

Move to show *forte* and *piano* in this music. Use large movements to show *forte* and small movements to show *piano*.
On the music page, *f* stands for *forte* and *p* stands for *piano*. Find the *f* and *p* in the song.

Sing about a baby beluga whale. Follow the dynamics marked in the music.

🔵 CD 2:3

Words and Music by
Raffi and D. Pike

Verse   *f*

do

1. Ba - by be - lu - ga in the deep blue sea,
2. Way down__ yon - der where the dol - phins play,
3. When it's__ dark, and you're__ home and fed,

Swim so wild and you swim so free.
Where you dive and__ splash all day,
Curl up snug in your wa - ter bed.

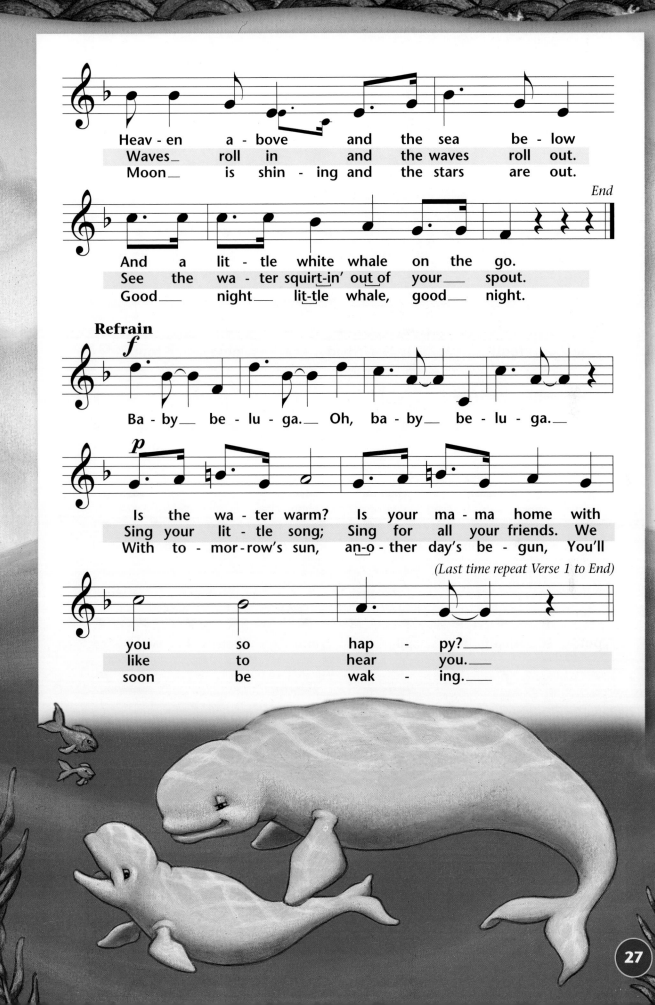

Heav - en a - bove and the sea be - low
Waves_ roll in and the waves roll out.
Moon_ is shin - ing and the stars are out.

End

And a lit - tle white whale on the go.
See the wa - ter squirt-in' out of your_ spout.
Good_ night_ lit-tle whale, good_ night.

Refrain
f

Ba - by_ be - lu - ga._ Oh, ba - by_ be - lu - ga._

p

Is the wa - ter warm? Is your ma - ma home with
Sing your lit - tle song; Sing for all your friends. We
With to - mor-row's sun, an-o - ther day's be - gun, You'll

(Last time repeat Verse 1 to End)

you so hap - py?_
like to hear you._
soon be wak - ing._

Speak and Play Louder and Softer
Say the poem with the dynamics shown.

Play these instruments when you speak these words.

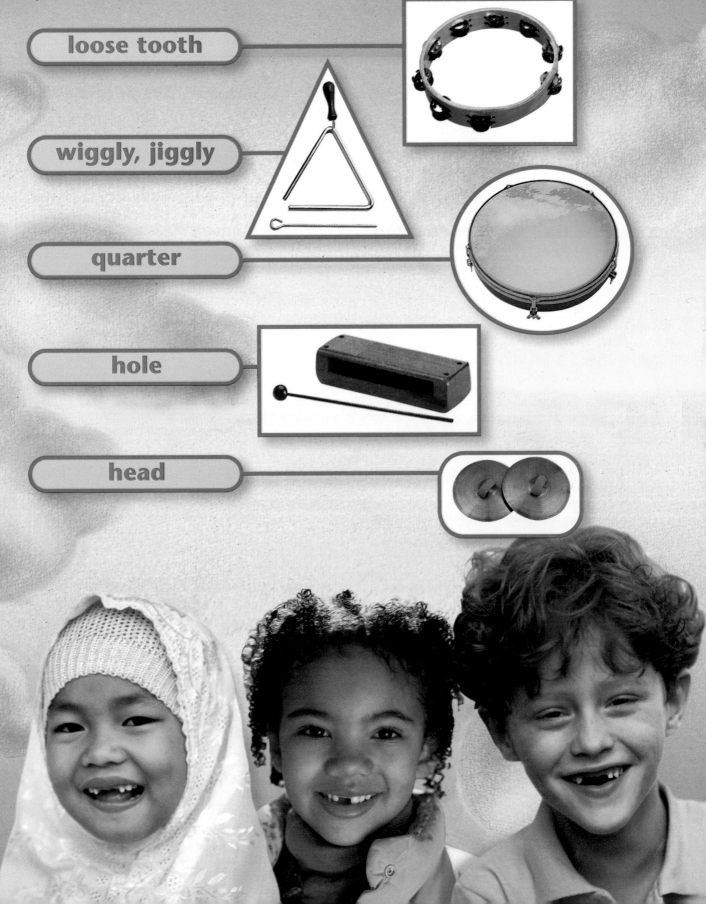

loose tooth

wiggly, jiggly

quarter

hole

head

CONCEPT
MELODY
SKILLS
READ,
IMPROVISE, PLAY
LINKS
SCIENCE

Carl Orff was a German composer and teacher. He designed these musical instruments for students.

LOG
ON

See **music.mmhschool.com** to learn more about Orff instruments.

Bass

Metallophone

Metallophone

Alto Xylophone

These instruments play different pitches.
Can you tell which is the highest? The lowest?
How do you know?

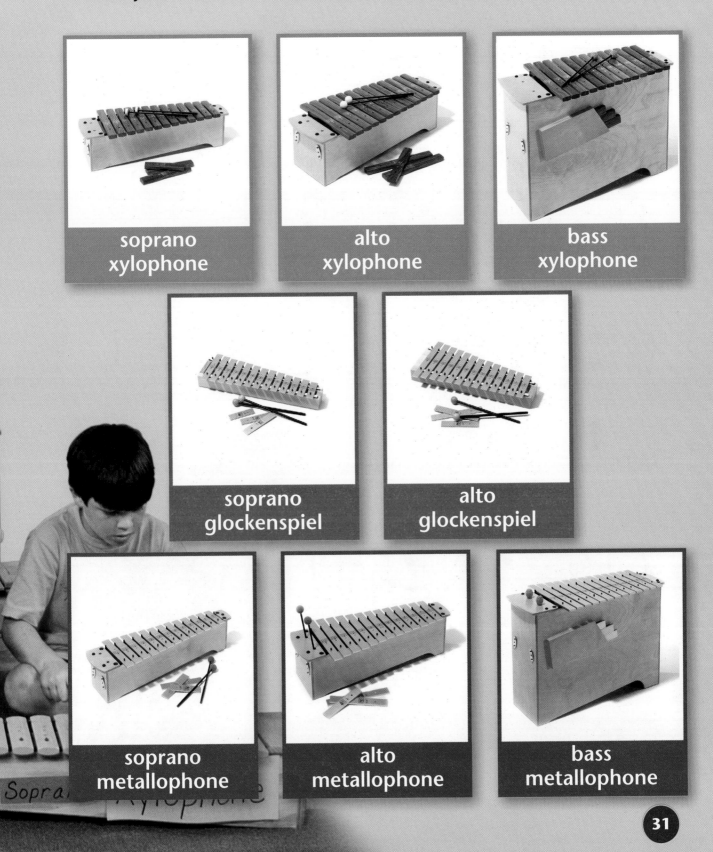

soprano
xylophone

alto
xylophone

bass
xylophone

soprano
glockenspiel

alto
glockenspiel

soprano
metallophone

alto
metallophone

bass
metallophone

Play *So and Mi*

So and *mi* can be in different places on the staff.
So is always on the line or space above *mi*.

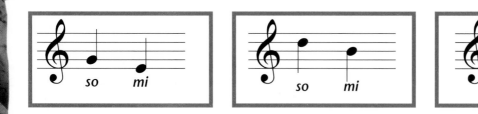

Find *so* and *mi* in "**Lemonade**."

Here we come (Where from?) New York. (What's your trade?) Lem-on-ade.

(Give us some.) Have none. (Get to work and make us some.)

Play instruments with "Lemonade."

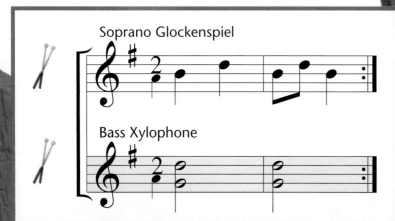

Soprano Glockenspiel

Bass Xylophone

Find *so* and *mi* in this song.
Play *so* and *mi* each time you say *"toot toot."*

She'll Be Comin' 'Round the Mountain

CD 2:9

Southern Mountain Song

1. She'll be com - in' 'round the moun-tain when she comes, *(toot toot)*
2. She'll be driv - ing six white hor - ses when she comes, *(whoa back, toot toot)*

She'll be com - in' 'round the moun-tain when she comes, *(toot toot)*
She'll be driv - ing six white hor - ses when she comes, *(whoa back, toot toot)*

She'll be com - in' 'round the moun - tain,
She'll be driv - ing six white hor - ses,

She'll be com - in' 'round the moun - tain,
She'll be driv - ing six white hor - ses,

She'll be com - in' 'round the moun-tain when she comes. *(toot toot)*
She'll be driv - ing six white hor - ses when she comes. *(whoa back, toot toot)*

3. Oh, we'll all go out to meet her . . . *(hi there, whoa back, toot toot)*
4. Oh, we'll all have chicken and dumplings . . . *(yum yum, etc.)*
5. She will have to sleep with Grandma . . . *(snoring sound, etc.)*

33

LESSON 8

What Is That Sound?

CONCEPT
TONE COLOR

SKILLS
SING, DESCRIBE, COMPOSE

LINKS
READING, CULTURES, SCIENCE

Read this poem out loud. Use your voice to show the meaning.

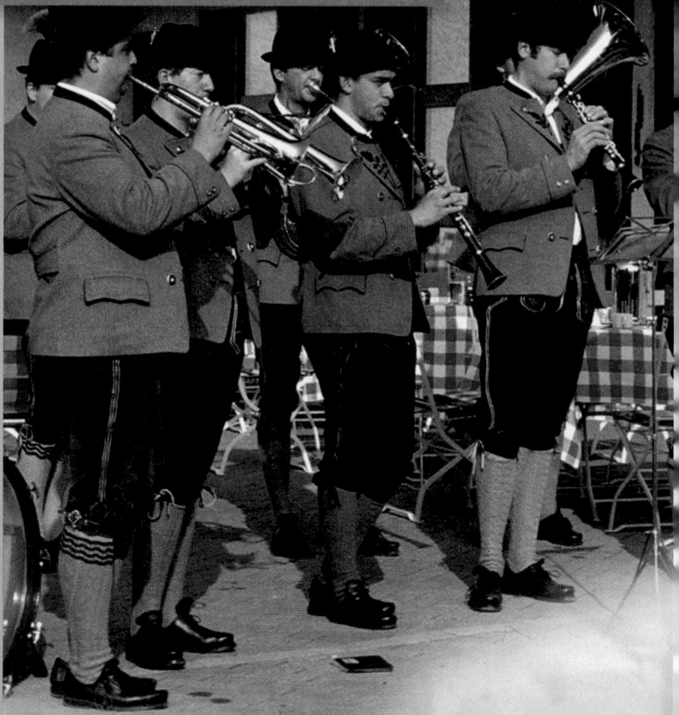

Together

Because we do
All things together,
All things improve,
Even weather.

Our daily meat
And bread taste better,
Trees are greener,
Rain is wetter.

—*Paul Engle*

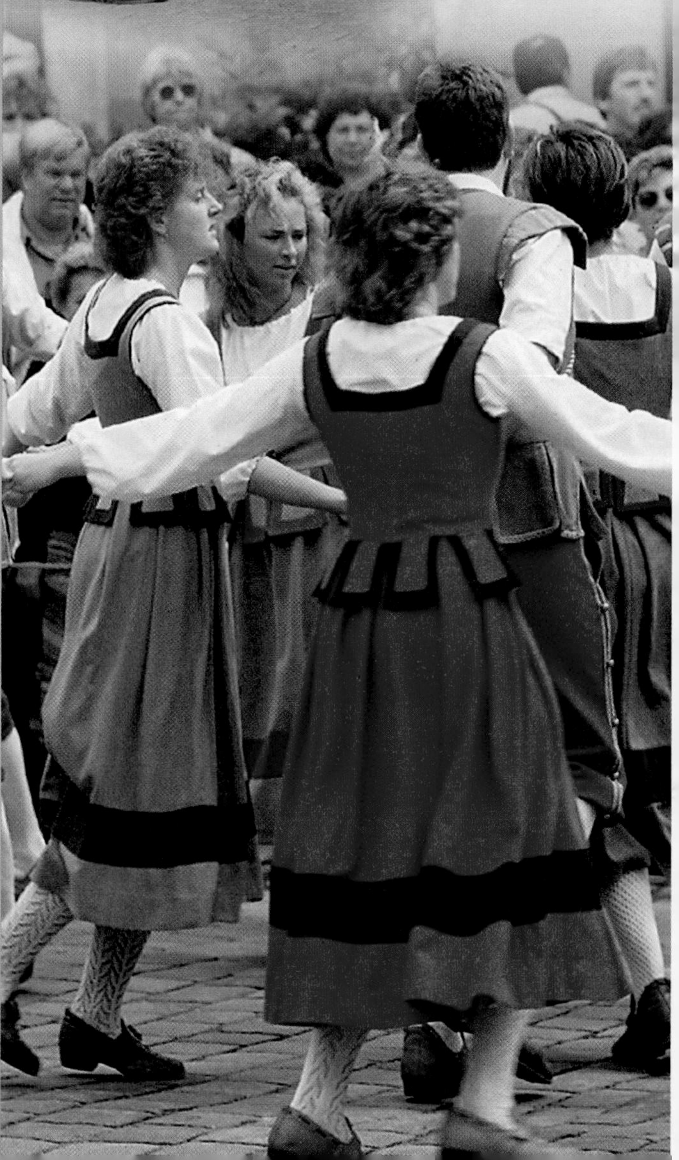

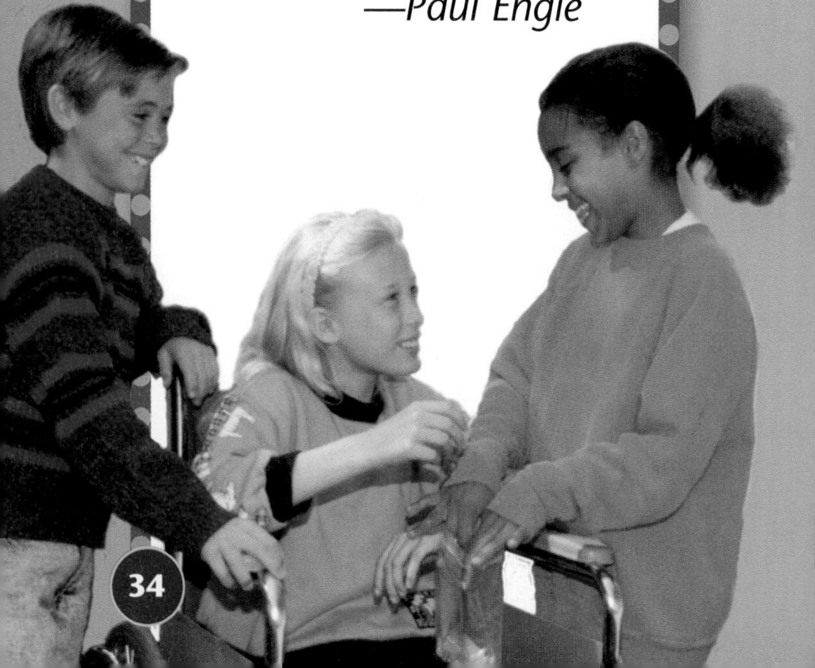

Listen to instruments playing together in this song. What type of instrument do you hear?

MAP

UNITED STATES

GERMANY

Ach, du lieber Augustin

The More We Get Together

CD 2:12

German Folk Song

German: Ach, du lie-ber Au-gus-tin, Au-gus-tin, Au-gus-tin.
English: The more we get to-geth-er, to-geth-er, to-geth-er. The

Ach, du lie-ber Au-gus-tin, Al-les ist hin!
more we get to-geth-er, the hap-pier we'll be!

Geld ist hin, Mä-dl ist hin, Al-les ist hin, Au-gus-tin.
For your friends are my friends, and my friends are your friends. The

Ach, du lie-ber Au-gus-tin, Al-les ist hin!
more we get to-geth-er, the hap-pier we'll be!

Found Sounds!

Almost anything can be a musical instrument if it is played musically!

◀ *Scrap Arts Music*
is a percussion group.
They use instruments
made from objects they
have "found."

🔘 **LISTENING** | CD 2:16

Assembly Required by Gregory Kozak

Listen to the music. Can you tell what the musicians are using for instruments?

Meet the Musician

Gregory Kozak is a Canadian musician. He writes music and makes the instruments for Scrap Arts Music to play. He uses everything from pieces of old large machines to drain pipes.

🔘 *RECORDED INTERVIEW* | CD 2:17

Listen to Gregory Kozak talk about Scrap Arts Music.

Create with Found Sounds

Find things at home to use as musical instruments. How do your instruments sound different from brass instruments?

Recycle for Sound

Create music for your found sounds.

1. Create a rhythm pattern using ♩ and ♫

2. Create a melody by adding *so* and *mi* to your pattern.

3. Play found sounds on the 𝄾

4. Perform your melody twice.

5. Say the first verse of the poem "Together" at the beginning and in between each melody.

This is really working together through music!

Spotlight Your Success!

REVIEW

1. Which word means how high or low a sound is?

   a. beat   **b.** pitch

2. Which word means the short and long sounds in a song?

   a. rhythm   **b.** beat

3. Which is the hand sign for *so*?

   a. 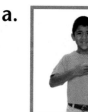   **b.**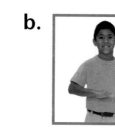

READ AND LISTEN

1. **Read** these rhythms. Then **listen**. Which rhythm do you hear?

2. **Move** to show when each melody goes up and down. Then **listen**. Which melody do you hear?

THINK!

1. How are beat and rhythm different?

2. Which instrument plays higher pitches? How do you know?

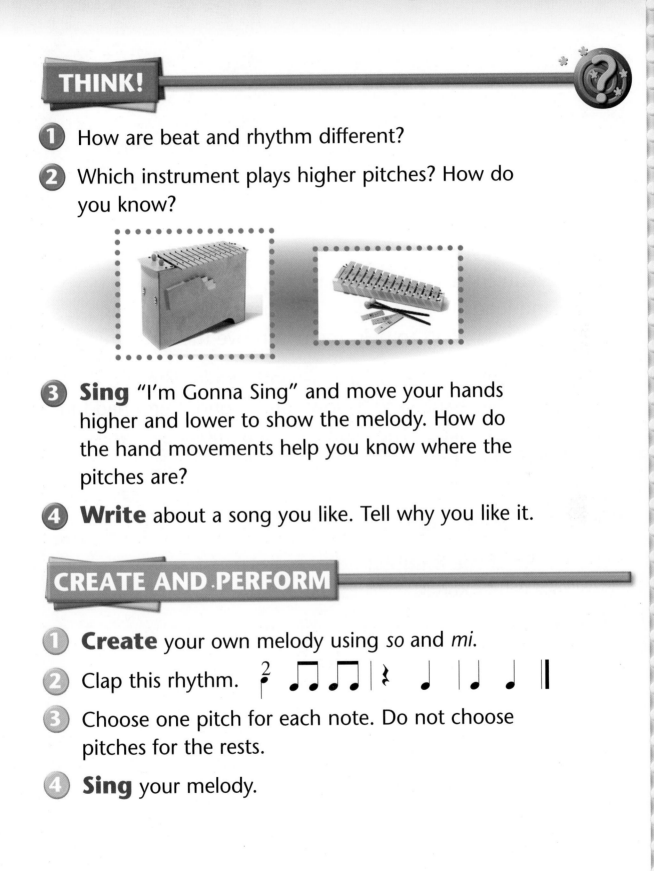

3. **Sing** "I'm Gonna Sing" and move your hands higher and lower to show the melody. How do the hand movements help you know where the pitches are?

4. **Write** about a song you like. Tell why you like it.

CREATE AND PERFORM

1. **Create** your own melody using *so* and *mi*.

2. Clap this rhythm.

3. Choose one pitch for each note. Do not choose pitches for the rests.

4. **Sing** your melody.

Music News

Meet the Musician
ON NATIONAL RADIO!

Name: Carol Jantsch   Age: 17
Instrument: Tuba
Home Town: Worthington, Ohio

It takes a lot of strength to play an instrument as big as a tuba. Seventeen-year-old Carol Jantsch says you need to have very strong lungs to play well. "Tuba players use breathing bags and special tools to help them improve their breathing."

Carol started playing the tuba in seventh grade. She chose to play tuba because she liked its low, loud sound. Carol had fun playing a piece called "The Flight of the Bumblebee" while dressed from head to toe in a giant bumblebee suit!

LISTENING   CD 2:19–20   **RECORDED INTERVIEW**

The Flight of the Bumblebee
by Nikolai Rimsky-Korsakov

Listen to Carol's performance and interview on the national radio program **From the Top.**

Spotlight on the Cello

Music has been a part of Kathy Canning's life since she started piano lessons at age five. In fourth grade she began studying the viola, and she still plays today. Ms. Canning values everything she's learned studying music, so she works to bring music to other children.

Many New York City public schools have had their music programs cut or taken away completely. Part of Ms. Canning's job is to ask for donations so schools can pay music teachers again. She also shows people how important music is.

"Kids need to learn music," she explains, because "it requires you to think and develop many skills that help you learn other subjects."

Did You Know?

The cello is one of the largest members of the string family. Because longer strings make lower sounds, a cello's pitches are deep and full.

The cello is so big that cellists have to play sitting down. They balance the instrument between their legs while playing.

LISTENING CD 2:21–22

Gavotte from Suite No. 5 for Cello
by Johann Sebastian Bach

Piano Concerto No. 2, Third Movement
by Johannes Brahms

Listen to these two pieces for cello by Bach and Brahms. Bach wrote several pieces for cello alone, without any other instruments playing along. Brahms wrote this songlike solo for cello as part of a piano concerto.

Musical Friends

Sharing music with friends is fun.

Coming Attractions

Sing in $\frac{3}{?}$ at a baseball game.

Help a doggie find his bone on *mi, so,* and *la.*

Perform a clog dance in AB form.

43

Making music can be more fun when you share it with friends.

LISTENING CD 2:23

You've Got a Friend in Me
by Randy Newman

Listen to a song about being a good friend.

Sing the song with your friends.

from the movie *Toy Story*

CD 2:24

Words and Music by Randy Newman

1. You've got a friend in me.

You've got a friend in me.

When the road_ looks rough a - head_ and you're miles_

_____ and miles_ from your nice___ warm bed,___

The Opposite of Two

What is the opposite of two?
A lonely me, a lonely you.
        —Richard Wilbur

THINK! **What are some ways you and your friends can help each other when you make music together?**

you just re-mem-ber what your old pal said.___

Son, you've___ got a friend in me.

Yeah, you've___ got a friend in me.

(Freely)
2. You've got a friend in me.
    You've got a friend in me.
    You got troubles, then I got 'em too.
    There isn't anything I wouldn't do for you.
    If we stick together we can see it through,
    'cause you've got a friend in me.
    Yeah, you've got a friend in me.

LESSON 1

CONCEPT
RHYTHM
SKILLS
PERFORM,
LISTEN, PLAY
LINKS
MATH,
CULTURES

Beats in Sets of Two

Singing can help us say how we feel.
Pat with the beat as you sing this happy song.

CD 3:1

Words and Music by Hap Palmer

Joy, I feel the joy of mu - sic.

Joy, I feel the joy of rhy - thm, and my

heart it starts sing - ing. And my bod - y starts sway - ing

ev - 'ry - time I feel the joy of mu - sic.

Beats in Sets of Two

When you sing, you pat with the beat. All beats are not the same. Some are stronger than others. Beats are usually grouped in sets of stronger and weaker beats.

Sometimes beats are grouped in sets of two.

1   **2**

🔘 **LISTENING** CD 3:4

So Glad I'm Here Arranged by Bernice Johnson Reagon, learned from Bessie Jones

Listen to Sweet Honey in The Rock sing this song.

Pat with the beat as you listen. Are the beats in sets of two?

Sweet Honey in The Rock is an African American performing group. The group sings together without any accompaniment. These singers have performed together all over the world.

47

What's the Meter?

Here is a song from a two-island nation in the Caribbean called Trinidad and Tobago. **Sing** the song. **Pat** only on beat one.

Me Stone

MAP

UNITED STATES

TRINIDAD AND TOBAGO

CD 3:5

Folk Song from Trinidad and Tobago

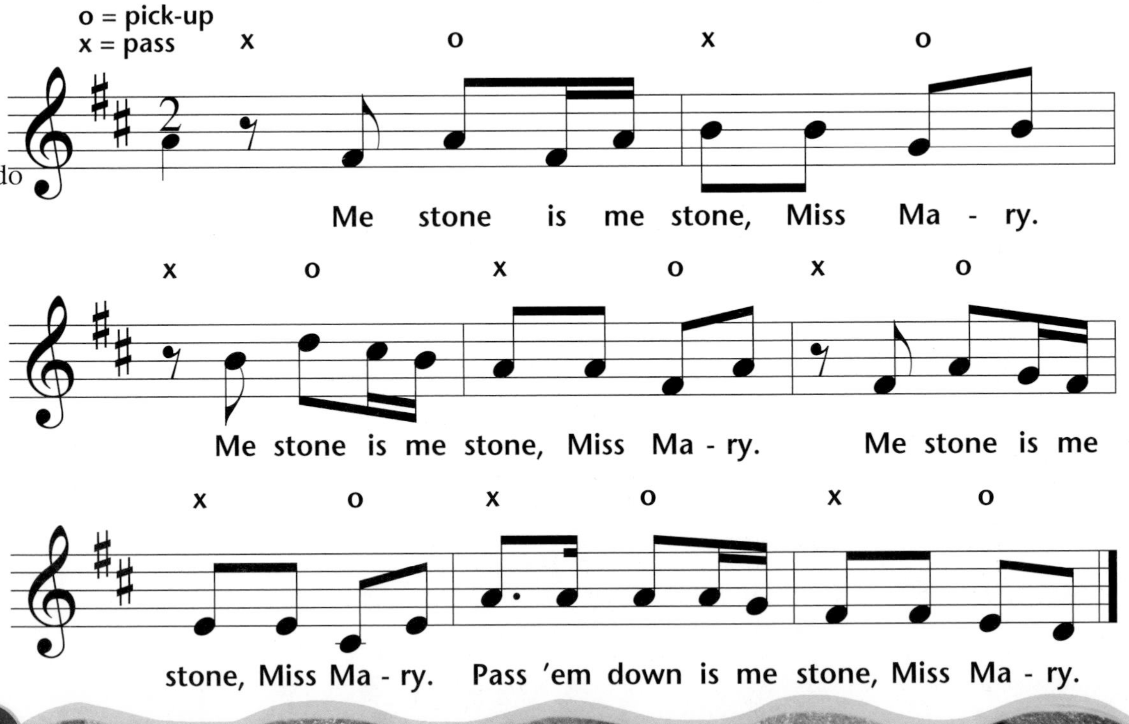

o = pick-up
x = pass

Me stone is me stone, Miss Ma - ry.

Me stone is me stone, Miss Ma - ry. Me stone is me

stone, Miss Ma - ry. Pass 'em down is me stone, Miss Ma - ry.

A **meter signature** shows how many beats are in each set. A meter signature with a 2 on top has one strong beat and one weak beat in each set.

Find the **2** meter signature at the beginning of "Me Stone." **Play** along on instruments. Play only on the strong beat.

Playalong

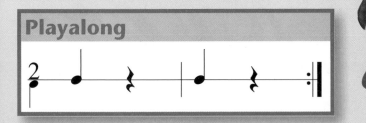

Sing the song again and play a passing game. Pass the stone only on the strong beat.

LESSON
2

CONCEPT
MELODY
SKILLS
SING, IDENTIFY,
PLAY
LINKS
CULTURES,
FINE ART

Meet a New Pitch Called *La*

Sing this funny song about a donkey named Tinga Layo. Can you find *mi* and *so* in the song?

TINGA LAYO

MAP

UNITED
STATES

WEST INDIES

CD 3:8

West Indies Calypso Song
English Words by Merrill Staton

Refrain

Spanish: **Ting - a Lay - o!** Ay, mi bu - rri - to, ven;
English: **Ting - a Lay - o!** Come, lit - tle don - key, come;

1., 2.   *(To Verse)*

Ting - a Lay - o! Ay, mi bu - rri - to, ven.
Ting - a Lay - o! Come, lit - tle don - key, come.

One of the first four notes of the song is a new pitch. **Sing** the words *Tinga Layo*. On what part of the donkey's name does the new pitch come? **Move** to show how the melody moves higher and lower.

Tin - ga Lay - o!

mi so ? so

The new pitch is **la**. It is always one step higher than *so*.

Sing "Tinga Layo" again. Use pitch syllables with hand signs instead of the donkey's name.

la

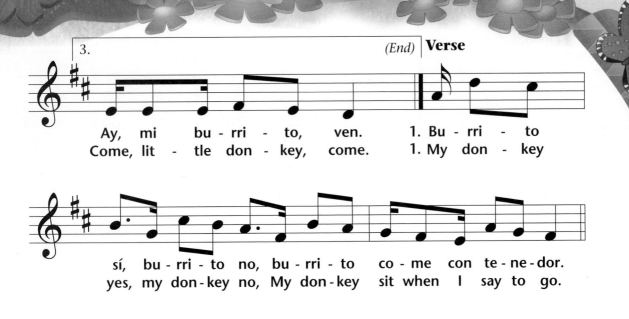

3.   (End) | **Verse**

Ay, mi bu - rri - to, ven.   1. Bu - rri - to
Come, lit - tle don - key, come.   1. My don - key

sí, bu - rri - to no, bu - rri - to   co - me con te - ne - dor.
yes, my don - key no, My don - key   sit when I say to go.

2. My donkey haw, my donkey gee,   3. My donkey balk, my donkey bray,
   My donkey don't do a thing for me.   My donkey won't hear a thing I say.
   Refrain   *Refrain*

Move with a Melody

Before we had electricity, mills were used to grind corn and flour for baking. Find *mi, so,* and *la* in this song about a mill. **Sing** the song using pitch syllables and hand signs.

The Mill Song

CD 3:12

American Singing School Song

'Round and 'round, the mill goes 'round.

As it does the corn is ground.

This pattern sounds like a mill wheel turning.
Play it on wood instruments as you sing the song.

Playalong

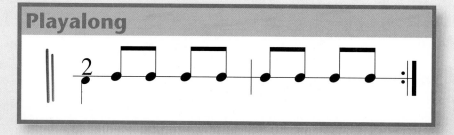

LISTENING CD 3:15

Moulinet (Polka) by Josef Strauss

A *moulinet* is a type of mill. Listen for the sounds of the mill.

Listen to "Moulinet" and follow the map.

Listening Map for *Moulinet*

Introduction A B A C A B A Coda

Art Gallery

The Mill
by Rembrandt van Rijn

Rembrandt van Rijn was a Dutch artist. He painted pictures of people and the Dutch countryside.

CONCEPT
RHYTHM
SKILLS
PERFORM,
LISTEN, SING
LINKS
PHYSICAL
EDUCATION

Have you ever seen a dragon? **Listen** to see if you can hear an instrument playing dragon music.

 **LISTENING** CD 3:16

Prelude to Act II of *Siegfried*
by Richard Wagner

Sing this song about a friendly dragon.

Puff, the Magic Dragon

CD 3:17

Verse

Words and Music by
Peter Yarrow and Leonard Lipton

1. Puff, the mag-ic drag-on, lived by the sea and

frol-icked in the au-tumn mist in a land called Hon-ah-lee.

Lit-tle Jack-ie Pa-per loved that ras-cal Puff, and

brought him strings and seal-ing wax and oth-er fan-cy stuff. Oh!

Refrain

Puff, the mag - ic drag - on, lived by the sea and frol - icked in the au - tumn mist in a land called Hon - ah - lee.

Puff, the mag - ic drag - on, lived by the sea and

1., 2., 3.
frol - icked in the au - tumn mist in a land called Hon - ah - lee. 2. To -

4.
land called Hon - ah - lee.

2. Together they would travel on a boat with billowed sail,
Jackie kept a lookout perched on Puff's gigantic tail.
Noble kings and princes would bow when'er they came.
Pirate ships would low'r their flag when Puff roared out his name. Oh!
Refrain

3. A dragon lives forever, but not so little boys;
Painted wings and giant rings make way for other toys.
One gray night it happened, Jackie Paper came no more,
And Puff, that mighty dragon, he ceased his fearless roar. Oh!
Refrain

4. His head was bent in sorrow, green scales fell like rain,
Puff no longer went to play along the cherry lane.
Without his life-long friend, Puff could not be brave,
So Puff, that mighty dragon, sadly slipped into his cave. Oh!
Refrain

An Old Favorite in ¾ Meter

Listen to this baseball song. Sway to the strong beat.

The meter signature for this song is

This means that beats are in sets of 3: **strong** = weak = weak.

Sing the song.

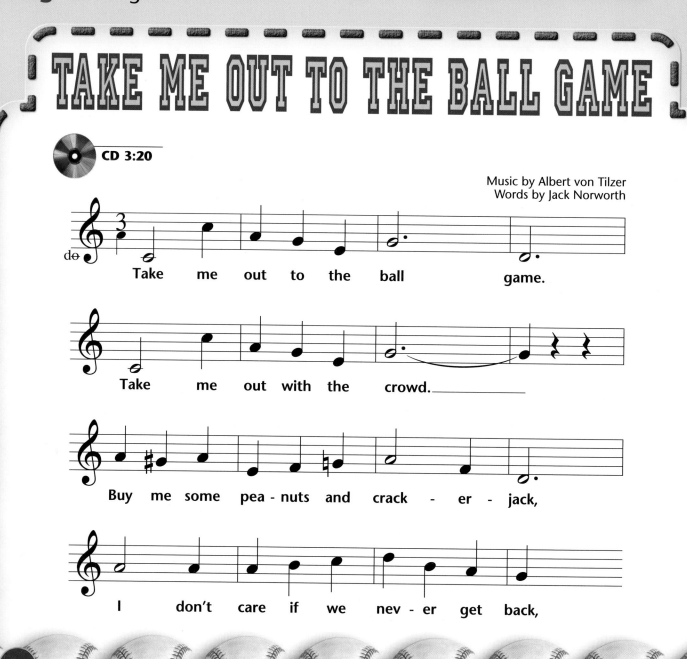

CD 3:20

Music by Albert von Tilzer
Words by Jack Norworth

TAKE ME OUT TO THE BALL GAME

Take me out to the ball game.

Take me out with the crowd._____

Buy me some pea - nuts and crack - er - jack,

I don't care if we nev - er get back,

The Little
League
World Series

Let me root, root, root for the home team,

If they don't win, it's a shame,

For it's one, two, three strikes you're out

At the old ball game.

57

CONCEPT
MELODY

SKILLS
READ, SING,
LISTEN

LINKS
READING,
SCIENCE,
CULTURES

Dogs, dogs everywhere! What is your favorite kind?

Dalmatian

The Hairy Dog

My dog's so furry I've not seen
His face for years and years:
His eyes are buried out of sight,
I only guess his ears.

When people ask me for his breed,
I do not know or care:
He has the beauty of them all
Hidden beneath his hair.

—*Herbert Asquith*

Hungarian Sheepdog (Puli)

Maybe we cannot see this dog's
eyes. We can see some of his
favorite bones! Find notes in
"Doggie, Doggie" that match
the way these bones are arranged.

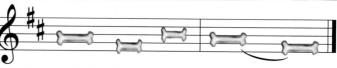

Airedale

Labrador Retriever

Beagle

Read the pitches of this song using *mi, so,* and *la.*
Sing the song with your friends.

Doggie, Doggie

CD 3:23

Singing Game

so

Dog - gie,   dog - gie,   where's   your   bone?

Some - one   stole   it   from   my   home!

Who   stole   the   bone?___   I   stole   the   bone.___

Mi, So, La in Mexico

Mariachi bands are from Mexico.
Listen to this band play.

LISTENING CD 3:26

Chango Guango
by Tinker Villarreal and Juan Ortiz

Sing this song from Mexico.

MAP

UNITED STATES

MEXICO

A la rueda de San Miguel

CD 3:27 **To the Wheel of San Miguel**

Traditional Mexican Folk Song

Spanish: 1. A la rue - da la rue - da de San Mi - guel,
English: 1. In the cir - cle, the cir - cle of San Mi - guel,

San Mi - guel, to - dos tra - en su ca - ja de miel;
San Mi - guel, Bring a box full of hon - ey to sell.

A lo ma - du - ro, a lo ma - du - ro
Wait till it ri - pens, wait till it ri - pens.

que se vol te - e Pan - cho de bu - rro.
You play the bur - ro, *Heather turn a - round now!

60 (2.) * insert any name

Meet the Musician

Carlos Chávez is an important Mexican composer. He was proud of the Indian heritage of his country. Chávez wrote *Sinfonía india* for orchestra and native Mexican instruments.

Sing this *mi so la* pattern.

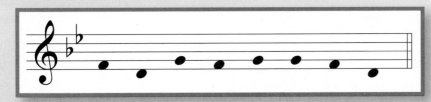

CD-ROM

Use *World Instruments* **CD-ROM** to learn more about instruments in Mexico.

Listen for the trumpet playing this pattern in the music.

LISTENING CD 3:31

Sinfonía india
by Carlos Chávez

▼ Mariachi bands travel from place to place, playing their music wherever they are invited!

Call and Response

CONCEPT
FORM

SKILLS
LISTEN, SING, PERFORM

LINKS
CULTURES, DANCE

Follow the leader in this yummy song! Learn this song by listening, without looking at the music.

Pizza, Pizza, Daddy-O

CD 4:1

African American Singing Game

Leader   *Group*

An-nie has a boy-friend, Piz - za, piz - za, dad-dy - o,

Leader   *Group*

How do you know it?   Piz - za, piz - za, dad - dy - o,

Leader   *Group*

'Cause she told me,   Piz - za, piz - za, dad - dy - o,

Pick a leader. **Sing** the song and
do the movements to the beat.

Piz - za, piz - za, dad - dy - o!

Leader   Group

Let's rope it! Rope it, rope___ it, dad - dy - o,
Let's swim it! Swim it, swim___ it, dad - dy - o,
Let's duck it! Duck it, duck___ it, dad - dy - o,

Leader   Group

Let's twist it! Twist it, twist___ it, dad - dy - o,

Leader   Group

Let's end it! End it, end___ it, dad-dy - o!

Follow the Leader

Get ready to sing and move with this song from Aotearoa, which is Maori for New Zealand.

Global Voices

New Zealand is one of a group of islands called Polynesia in the South Pacific.

Poi is the Maori word for "ball." The "long poi" is a ball tied to a long string. The string is about three feet long.

Many years ago the Maori men were known as brave warriors. They used the poi to build strength for fighting battles. Maori women also used the poi to be strong. Maori people are modern, but are proud of their traditional ways.

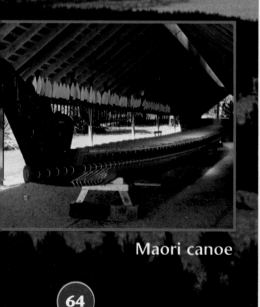

Maori canoe

Listen to this greeting song. The leader is calling everyone to get your poi ready and bring your canoe. **Sing** and move with it.

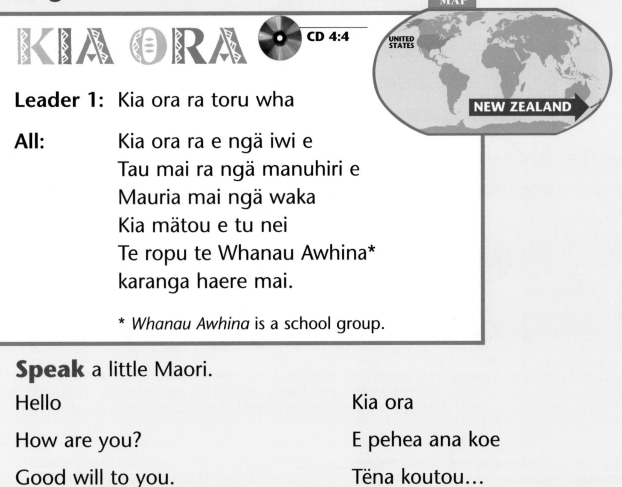

KIA ORA

CD 4:4

MAP

UNITED STATES

NEW ZEALAND

Leader 1: Kia ora ra toru wha

All: Kia ora ra e ngä iwi e
Tau mai ra ngä manuhiri e
Mauria mai ngä waka
Kia mätou e tu nei
Te ropu te Whanau Awhina*
karanga haere mai.

* *Whanau Awhina* is a school group.

Speak a little Maori.

Hello	Kia ora
How are you?	E pehea ana koe
Good will to you.	Tëna koutou…
canoe	Waka

Maori children in New Zealand practice a song.

65

CONCEPT
FORM
SKILLS
SING, IDENTIFY,
PERFORM
LINKS
FINE ART,
CULTURES

What do you think it is like to be a cowboy?
Listen to part of a cowboy song, then **sing** it.

LISTENING CD 4:5

Strawberry Roan

sung by Cowboy Ed McCurdy

American Cowboy Song

CD 4:6

Verse

do

1. I came in-to town just to spend some time,
2. "You've guessed me just right! I'm your man," I claim,
3. I jumped on his back and I held the reins,

For I had no mon-ey, not e-ven a dime;
"Do you have a wild horse you'd like me to tame?"
That straw-ber-ry horse threw me off for my pains;

Then a fel-low stepped up and he said, "I sup-pose
Well, he said that he had, and a bad one to buck,
So I climbed on a-gain to the horse-'s sur-prise,

You're a bronc-bust-ing cow-boy by the looks of your clothes."
And for throw-ing good rid-ers, the__ horse had good luck.
And he tried then to throw me right__ up to the skies.

Find the Verses and the Refrain in this song.
Verse/Refrain is the order, or **form**.
Identify the form using letters.
Listen to this music that sounds like it is
from the old West.

 **LISTENING** CD 4:9

Round-up by Elie Siegmeister

Art Gallery

Bronco Buster by Frederic Remington

Frederic Remington is an American artist.
He is famous for his Western art.

Refrain

Well, it's oh, that straw-ber-ry roan!

Oh, that straw-ber-ry roan,

That straw-ber-ry pon-y no one ev-er rode,

And the cow-boy that tries it is sure to get thrown.

Oh, that straw-ber-ry roan!

Folk Dancing in AB Form

In pioneer times, people danced to music of a string band. This style of music is called oldtime.

Clog dancing is done to oldtime music.

Perform a clog-dance step: Brush one toe forward and back. Then step firmly on that same foot. Repeat with the other foot.

 **LISTENING** **CD 4:10**

Clog (Oldtime Music)

Walk to the A section. Clog step to the B section of this music.

What is the form of this American folk song?
Sing the song and move to it.

LESSON
7

CONCEPT
TONE COLOR
SKILLS
COMPARE,
CREATE, PLAY
LINKS
CULTURES,
HISTORY

Tone Color

How does a trumpet sound different from a piano? The **tone color** of an instrument or voice is its special quality of sound. Tone quality is what makes one instrument sound different from another.

Listen for the tone color of the trumpet in this song. Many Jewish people from Eastern Europe sing this song.

Klezmer Band

MAP

UNITED
STATES

EASTERN EUROPE

CD 4:14

Chirri Bim

Traditional Yiddish Song

A

Chir - ri bim, chir - ri bom, Chir - ri

bim bom bim bom bom.___ Chir - ri bim, chir - ri

bom, chir - ri bim bom bim bom bom.

Listen to the tone color of instruments in your class. **Compare** how they are different.

Create an accompaniment for the song. Use different tone colors.

Ai chir - ri bir - ri bir - ri, ai chir - ri bir - ri bir - ri,

ai chir - ri bir - ri bir - ri, ai chir - ri bir - ri,

ai chir - ri bir - ri bir - ri, ai chir - ri bir - ri bir - ri,

chir - ri bir - ri bim bom bom.

The Color of Brass Instruments

Trumpets are made of brass tubing. A mouthpiece fits into the tubing.

Brass players buzz their lips as they blow into the mouthpiece. This makes the sound. Try buzzing to make a sound!

Brass Instruments

trumpet

French horn

trombone

euphonium

tuba

The trumpet is the smallest and highest-pitched brass instrument. It has the brightest tone color. **Listen** and compare the tone color of the other brass instruments.

THINK! Which instrument do you think plays the lowest pitches? Why?

A **concerto** is a work written to show the skill of a solo performer. Some concertos are written for two or more soloists.

Wynton Marsalis ▶

LISTENING CD 4:17

Allegro from Concerto for Two Trumpets by Antonio Vivaldi

This concerto is for two solo trumpets and an orchestra.

Point to what you hear as you **listen**.

CD-ROM

Use *Orchestral Instruments* **CD-ROM** to learn more about brass instruments.

Listening Map for *Concerto for Two Trumpets*

Meet the Musician

Antonio Vivaldi composed music for a school for orphaned girls. The school became famous for its good orchestra. Vivaldi wrote over 400 concertos.

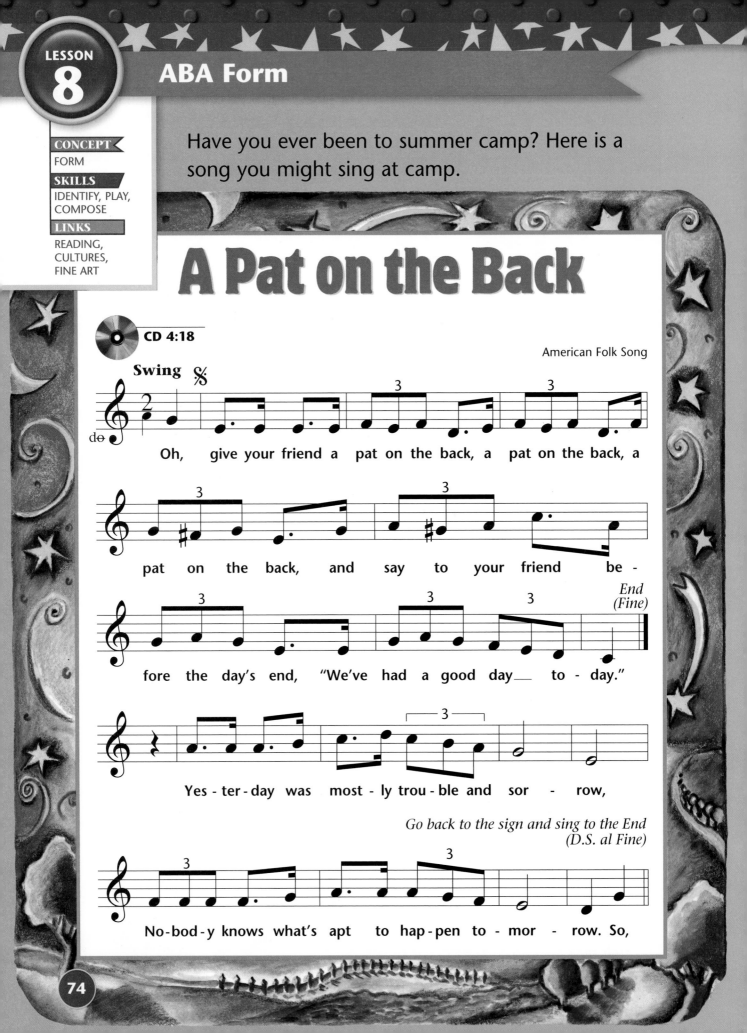

CONCEPT
FORM
SKILLS
IDENTIFY, PLAY, COMPOSE
LINKS
READING, CULTURES, FINE ART

Have you ever been to summer camp? Here is a song you might sing at camp.

A Pat on the Back

CD 4:18

American Folk Song

Swing

Oh, give your friend a pat on the back, a pat on the back, a pat on the back, and say to your friend be-fore the day's end, "We've had a good day to-day."

End (Fine)

Yes-ter-day was most-ly trou-ble and sor-row,

Go back to the sign and sing to the End (D.S. al Fine)

No-bod-y knows what's apt to hap-pen to-mor-row. So,

D.S. al Fine means to go back to the 𝄋 sign and sing until you see the word **Fine**. **Find** the terms *D.S. al Fine* and *Fine* in the song.

A song in two sections is in AB form. How many sections does this song have? Are any sections the same? This song is in ABA form.

Sing this part. Then **play** it with the A section.

See music.mmhschool.com to research American folk songs.

Compose a Melody

The moon and owls come out at night.

Finis

Night is come,
Owls are out;
Beetles hum
Round about.
Children snore
Safe in bed,
Nothing more
Need be said.

Sir Henry Newbolt

Sing this nighttime song.

Good Night, Sleep Tight

CD 4:21

Traditional

Good night, sleep tight, friends will come to-mor-row night.

Create a "nighttime" melody to the poem "Finis." Use the pitches *mi*, *so*, and *la*.
Sing your melody as the B section after you sing "Good Night, Sleep Tight."

Child Falling Asleep
by Robert Schumann

Can you tell what is happening in the music?

Art Gallery

Ara River at Akabane, 1929
by Kawase Hasui

Kawase Hasui is a Japanese artist. He is known for his pictures of night scenes and snow. He created nearly 600 prints during his lifetime.

Learn About Music That Tells a Story

Many composers like to write music that tells a story. Often the title of the music tells what it is about.

Composers might use different tone colors and melodies to paint a musical picture.

Scenes from Childhood is a book of many short piano pieces. Each piece describes a different time in a child's life.

The composer, Robert Schumann, loved to read books and poems. He also loved to play the piano. Sometimes he would compose music that was about his life and friends.

Spotlight Your Success!

Unit 2 Review

REVIEW

1 Here are *so* and *mi*. Where is *la*?

so   mi

a.   b.   c.

2 Here are *so* and *mi* in different places. Where is *la* now?

so   mi

a.   b.   c.

3 Which shows 3/4?

a.   1   2   b.   1   2   3

READ AND LISTEN

1 **Read** these melodies. Then **listen**. Which is the one with *la*?

a. do

b. do

78

2 **Listen** to this melody and pat the strong beat.
Is it in $\frac{2}{4}$ or $\frac{3}{4}$?

a. $\frac{2}{4}$ b. $\frac{3}{4}$

THINK!

1 How are beat and strong beat different?

2 How are $\frac{2}{4}$ and $\frac{3}{4}$ meters different?

3 **Write** about a song or listening selection you like. Tell what you like about the music.

CREATE AND PERFORM

1 **Create** your own melody using *mi*,
so, and *la*.

2 Use this rhythm. First, clap the rhythm.

3 Choose one pitch for each note.

4 **Sing** your melody.

Music News

Meet the Musician

ON NATIONAL RADIO!

Name: Vincent Yu   **Age: 11**
Instrument: Piano
Home Town: Longmeadow, Massachusetts

Playing piano wasn't always fun for eleven-year-old Vincent Yu. When he first started to take lessons, he didn't enjoy them at all. "My mom would have to force me to play piano," he remembers. "I wanted to watch TV!"

Before long, though, Vincent started to feel differently. Once he learned how to read music and play songs, Vincent began to like his weekly lessons. He was surprised to find that playing piano had become fun!

Playing piano is Vincent's favorite activity now. "I especially like to play pieces that make me use my imagination," he says. Learning to play piano was difficult, but Vincent is glad he stuck with it.

LISTENING   CD 4:26–27   **RECORDED INTERVIEW**

The Cat and the Mouse
by Aaron Copland

Listen to Vincent's performance and interview on the national radio program From the Top.

A Tip From the Top
"Stick with it!"
When learning something new or difficult, stick with it for a while. Vincent Yu found the piano got easier as he learned more about it, and he had fun playing it.

Spotlight on the Trumpet

Did You Know?

Trumpeters make their sound by pressing their lips against their instruments and blowing until their lips "buzz," or vibrate.

A trumpet player can fit a *mute*, or hollow cone, inside the trumpet's bell to play more quietly. Placing a mute inside a trumpet's bell softens its sound.

If you straightened out a trumpet from mouthpiece to bell, you would have a brass tube over four feet long.

Each time a trumpeter plays for a while, he or she must press the *spit valve* or *water key* to empty the water from the instrument. The wetness comes from the breath the player blows through the trumpet.

LISTENING CD 4:28–29

Prince of Denmark's March
by Jeremiah Clarke

Rondo for Lifey
by Leonard Bernstein

Jeremiah Clarke wrote his trumpet piece several hundred years ago. Back then, brass instruments were much simpler than they are today. They could only play a few notes.

Listen to the modern trumpet in the piece by Leonard Bernstein.

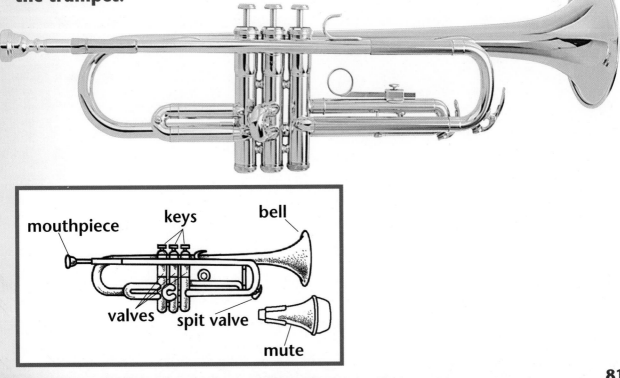

mouthpiece   keys   bell

valves   spit valve   mute

UNIT 3

Our Musical World

You are going on a musical journey in this unit. In every lesson you will visit a different continent and explore some of its music.

Coming Attractions

Move with the half note in Africa.

Play *do*, *mi*, and *so* in Korea.

Create "Ice Music" in Antarctica.

Listen to this song about our wonderful world. How does Willie Nelson sing expressively? *Expressive* singing helps us know what the song means.

 **LISTENING** CD 4:30

What a Wonderful World
by George Weiss and Bob Thiele

Sing the song expressively. Think about the words. Use dynamics and tone color to express yourself.

Willie Nelson

What a Wonderful World

CD 4:31

Words and Music by
George David Weiss and Bob Thiele

Swing (♫ = ♫)

1. I see trees of green, red ros - es too,

I see them bloom for me and you, ___

___ and I think_ to my-self What a won-der-ful world. ___

2. I see skies of blue and clouds of white,

the bright_ bles-sed day, the dark_ sac-red night,_

__ and I think_ to my-self What a won-der-ful world.__

Yes, I think to my-self, What a won-der-ful world.__

CONCEPT
RHYTHM
SKILLS
LISTEN, DESCRIBE, IDENTIFY
LINKS
CULTURES, SCIENCE, FINE ART

Celebrate our musical journey. Listen and pat the strong beat to a fanfare. A **fanfare** is a short piece of music that is played to salute someone or to celebrate.

MAP
CANADA
UNITED STATES

🔘 **LISTENING** CD 5:1

Entrance Fanfare by Robert Dickow

This fanfare is played with brass instruments. As you travel in this unit, you will learn about many instruments from different continents.

Listen to "This Is My Country" and **move** as you wave a pretend flag.

How long are your movements in each direction?

Our flag is a symbol of our country. There are symbols in music as well. The symbol for a sound two beats long is called a **half note**.

It is as long as two quarter notes put together. **Find** the half notes in this song.

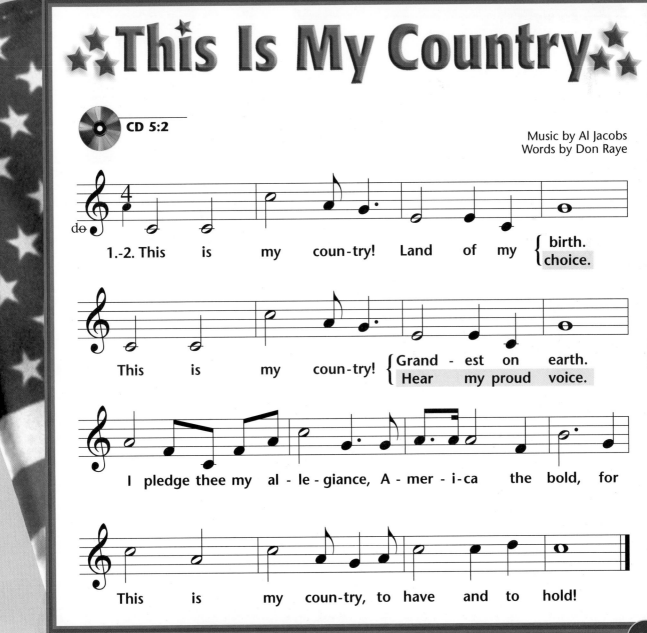

This Is My Country

CD 5:2

Music by Al Jacobs
Words by Don Raye

1.-2. This is my coun-try! Land of my { birth.
choice.

This is my coun-try! { Grand - est on earth.
Hear my proud voice.

I pledge thee my al - le - giance, A - mer - i-ca the bold, for

This is my coun-try, to have and to hold!

Sing Half Notes in Canada

This is a well-known song in our northern neighbor, Canada. The words describe the land there. Listen for, then **find** half notes in the song.

Land of the Silver Birch

CD 5:5

Canadian Folk Song

Verse

do

1. Land of the sil - ver birch, home of the bea - ver,
2. Down in the for - est, deep in the low - lands,

Where still the might - y moose wan-ders at will,
My heart cries out for thee, hills of the north,

Blue lake and rock - y shore, I will re - turn once more.
Blue lake and rock - y shore, I will re - turn once more.

Refrain

Boom de de boom boom, Boom de de boom boom,

Boom de de boom boom, Boom.

Art Gallery

Birches from Alberta, Canada
by Saelon Renkes

Saelon Renkes has taken pictures all over the world. She loves nature and traveling. She was a member of the Peace Corps.

Choose one pattern and clap as you sing "Land of the Silver Birch."

a.

b.

A New Pitch in South America

The Caribbean islands are near South America. **Listen** to *Caribbean Steel Band* play.

MAP

UNITED STATES CARIBBEAN ISANDS

PERU BRAZIL

BOLIVIA

LISTENING CD 5:8

Steel Drums Jam

Pick high, middle, and low papayas to show the melody of this song.

Shake the Papaya Down

CD 5:9

Calypso Song
Collected by W. S. Haynie

do

Ma - ma says no play, This is a work - day.

Up with the bright sun, Get all the work done.

If you will help me, Climb up the tall tree,

Shake the pa - pa - ya down.

Look at these parrots.
The highest parrot sings *so*.
The middle one sings *mi*.
The lowest parrot sings our new pitch.

The new pitch is called **do**. Here is the hand sign for *do*:

Look at these "papaya pitches."

Sing the pitches and use hand signs.
Find the "papaya pitches" in the song.

A Carnival Song with *Do*

Brazil is on the continent of South America. Every spring, the city of Rio de Janeiro has a big carnival. **Listen** as Carmen Miranda sings this popular carnival song.

 **LISTENING** CD 5:12

Mama eu quero (Brazilian Carnival Song)

Listen to the same carnival song in English.

▲ Carmen Miranda

Mama Paquita

CD 5:13

Brazilian Carnival Song
English Version by Merrill Staton

1. Ma - ma Pa - qui - ta, Ma - ma Pa - qui - ta,
2. Ma - ma Pa - qui - ta, Ma - ma Pa - qui - ta,

Ma - ma Pa - qui - ta has no mon - ey for pa - pa - yas;
Ma - ma Pa - qui - ta has no mon - ey for pa - ja - mas;

Can't buy pa - pa - yas, can't buy ba - nan - as;
Can't buy pa - ja - mas, can't buy som - bre - ros;

She can - not buy pa - pa - yas or ba - nan - as. No, ma - ma - ma - ma,
She can - not buy pa - ja - mas or som - bre - ros. No, ma - ma - ma - ma,

In this song *do* is on the
added line below the staff.

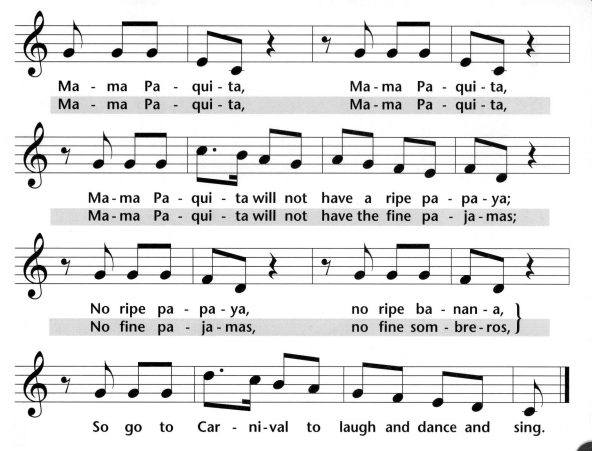

so   mi   do

Find lines in the song that
have only *do*, *mi*, and *so*.
Then sing the song.

Ma - ma Pa - qui - ta,   Ma - ma Pa - qui - ta,
Ma - ma Pa - qui - ta,   Ma - ma Pa - qui - ta,

Ma - ma Pa - qui - ta will not have a ripe pa - pa - ya;
Ma - ma Pa - qui - ta will not have the fine pa - ja - mas;

No ripe pa - pa - ya,   no ripe ba - nan - a,
No fine pa - ja - mas,   no fine som - bre - ros,

So go to Car - ni - val to laugh and dance and   sing.

93

Move to the Half Note in Africa

CONCEPT
RHYTHM
SKILLS
DESCRIBE,
LISTEN, READ
LINKS
CULTURE,
DANCE

Pata means "touch" in the Zulu and Xhosa languages. To "touch" in a dance means to put a foot or hand down lightly. **Move** to the half note as you listen to "Pata Pata."

MAP
UNITED STATES
NIGERIA
SOUTH AFRICA
ZIMBABWE

CD-ROM

Learn more about African Instruments with *World Instruments* CD-ROM.

LISTENING CD 5:16

Pata Pata by Miriam Makeba

Meet the Musician

Miriam Makeba is a very well-known South African singer. "Pata Pata" is like the songs she sang when she was a little girl.

She uses these traditional instruments in the song.

mbira

African shakers

Learn a hand dance to do with "Pata Pata."
Move with the music.

Beat 1   **Beat 2**   **Beat 3**   **Beat 4**

Beat 5   **Beat 6**   **Beat 7**   **Beat 8**

Beat 9   **Beat 10**   **Beat 11**   **Beat 12**

Beat 13   **Beat 14**   **Beat 15**   **Beat 16**

95

Half Notes in a Greeting Song

Sorida is a way to greet others in Zimbabwe.
Find the half notes in this song. Sing and move with the song.

Sorida

CD 5:17

Zimbabwe Greeting Song
as remembered and sung by Dumisani Maraire
and his wife, Mai Chi Maraire

Shona: **So - ri - da! So - ri - da, ri - da ri -**
Pronunciation: so ɾi da so ɾi da ɾi da ɾi

da, da - da-da - da, da - da-da - da, ri - da ri -
da da da da da da da da da ɾi da ɾi

da, da - da-da - da, da - da-da - da, ri - da ri - da!
da da da da da da da da da ɾi da ɾi da

Read Half Notes

Meet the Musician

Chief Fela Sowande was a tribal chief in Nigeria and a professor of music in several universities. He composed music using melodies from his country and European instruments.

Listen to the music, then learn a pattern to clap with it.

🔘 **LISTENING** CD 5:19

Akinla from *African Suite* by Fela Sowande

Read these patterns. Try them with the music.

a.

b.

This music uses only string instruments.

Learn About the String Family

The string family in an orchestra is made up of the violin, viola, cello, and double bass. Sound is produced by bowing or plucking the strings.

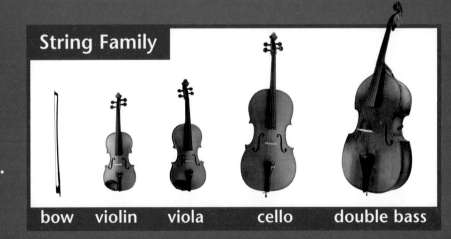

String Family

bow   violin   viola   cello   double bass

Pitches in Asia

CONCEPT
MELODY
SKILLS
PLAY, LISTEN, COMPOSE
LINKS
CULTURES, SCIENCE, FINE ART

Children in South Korea sing this song and pretend to catch the moon. **Find** *do*, *mi*, and *so* in the song.

MAP
KOREA
CHINA
UNITED STATES
INDONESIA

CD-ROM

Look at *World Instruments* **CD-ROM** to learn more about Chinese instruments.

DAL TARO KACHA

Come, Pick the Moon

CD 5:20

Music by Tae-Hyun Park
Words by Suk Joong Yoon
English Words by Linda Worsley

Korean: 애 들 아 나오 너 라 달 따 러 가 자
English: **Chil - dren come, ev - 'ry one, Come and pick the moon.**

장 대 들 고 망 태 메 고 뒷 동 산 으 로
Bring your staff and bring your knap-sack, Some-one needs it soon.

뒷 동 산 에 올 라 가 무 등 을 타 고
Climb the hill, with your staff, pick the moon to - day.

장 - 대 로 달 을 따 서 망 태 에 담 자
Now put it in your knap-sack, car - ry it a - way.

China is next to Korea. This music is about a party.

 LISTENING CD 5:24

Evening Party by He Luting

Listen for Chinese folk instruments.

erhu

Meet the Musician

He Luting was an important Chinese composer. He wrote music that mixed Chinese and European types of music. He also wrote many songs about China.

guzheng

pipa

99

Compose in Indonesia

Listen to the ducks "quack." Find *do mi so*.

CD 5:25

Itik Besenda Gurau
The Ducks

Indonesian Folk Song
English Words by Linda Worsley

Bahasa Indonesian: Kwek, kwek, kwek; Kwek, kwek, kwek! It - ik ber - ja lan ra mai.
English: Quack, quack, quack; Quack, quack, quack! Ducks go walk-ing in a line.

Kwek, kwek, kwek; Kwek, kwek, kwek! Ri - ang be - sen - da gu - rau.
Quack, quack, quack; Quack, quack, quack! Talk-ing, walk-ing, feel-ing fine.

Ha ha ha; ha ha ha! A ku ter ta wa;
Ha ha ha; ha ha ha! Laugh-ing as they go;

Ha ha ha; ha ha ha! A ku me li hat ka mu.
Ha ha ha; ha ha ha! Ducks go walk-ing in a row.

Kwek! Kwek! Kwek, kwek, kwek! Ber sa ma ra mai.
Quack! Quack! Quack, quack, quack! Hap - py, hear them say:

Kwek! Kwek! Kwek, kwek, kwek! Me nu ju su ngai! Kwek!
Quack! Quack! Quack, quack, quack! "Let's go swim to-day, Quack!"

100

Compose your own duck music!

Here are all the measures from the song that have *do*, *mi*, or *so*. Sing these measures with pitch syllables and hand signs. Then sing them with "quacks."

Using any of these measures to **compose** a four-measure melody. **Sing** your duck song.

THINK! How would you change your song if you could?

Art Gallery

Two Mandarin Ducks by Ando Hiroshige

Ando Hiroshige was born in Japan. He was a fireman, like his father, as well as a painter. He made around 5,400 pictures in his life.

CONCEPT
DYNAMICS

SKILLS
READ, DESCRIBE, LISTEN

LINKS
CULTURES, DANCE, SCIENCE

People all over the world know that work can get done faster if it is done to music. What are the steps of making wool in this song?

MAP
NORWAY
SWEDEN
UNITED STATES

Sheep Shearing

CD 5:29

Swedish Folk Song
English Words by Sam Blum

Verse

1. Go get the sheep, we're clip - ping to - day,
2. Tell Moth - er dear we're card - ing to - day,

Clip - ping their wool, yes, clip - ping their wool
Card - ing the wool, yes, card - ing the wool

So we can knit some stock - ings for you,
So we can knit a scarf for her, too,

Then we shall dance 'til morn - ing.
Then we shall dance 'til morn - ing.

When music gets gradually louder, it is called **crescendo**.

crescendo

Find the *crescendo* signs shown in the song.
Sing the song, with a *crescendo* where it is shown. **Sing** the song again, adding the movement.

pat   clap   clap

Refrain   (pat   clap   clap) (pat   clap   clap)

Surr, surr, surr, surr, surr, surr, Wheel spins a-round, hear, hear the sound;

(pat   clap   clap)

Surr, surr, surr, surr, surr, surr, Then we shall dance 'til morn-ing.

3. Tell brother John we're spinning today,
   Spinning the wool, yes, spinning the wool
   So we can knit a lace for his shoe,
   Then we shall dance 'til morning.

4. Tell sister Jane we're dyeing today,
   Dyeing the wool, yes, dyeing the wool
   So we can knit a sweater of blue,
   Then we shall dance 'til morning.

Global Voices

Music from Norway

Norway is known as the land of the Midnight Sun. In Northern Norway the sun never sets during the summer months. **Listen** to a folk song from Norway.

LISTENING CD 6:1

Såg du noko? Norwegian Folk Song

Speak the words of the song. It is about a man looking for his wife.

Såg du noko?
Norwegian Folk Song

Såg du noko til kjerringa mi?
Langt nord i lia i lia;
Svart hatt, stutt stakk;
Og lita gammal og låghalt;

Da di da di da da di do
Da da di da da di dai ja

Da di da di da da di do
Da da di da da di dai ja

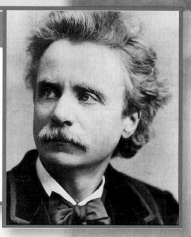

Edvard Grieg was a composer from Norway. He used folk songs from Norway in the music he composed. When he was small, he liked to stay at home and write music more than going to school.

Do you hear the folk song "Såg du noko?" in this music?

LISTENING CD 6:2

Symphonic Dances, Op. 64, No. 4 by Edvard Grieg

Listen again and **move** to show the changing dynamics.

Play Half Notes in Australia

CONCEPT
RHYTHM
SKILLS
READ, PLAY,
LISTEN
LINKS
CULTURES,
SCIENCE

Australia is called the land "down under" because it lies below the equator. There are many animals in Australia. Which ones are named in the song?

MAP

UNITED STATES

NEW ZEALAND

AUSTRALIA

LOG ON

See **music.mmhschool.com** to research musical instruments from Australia.

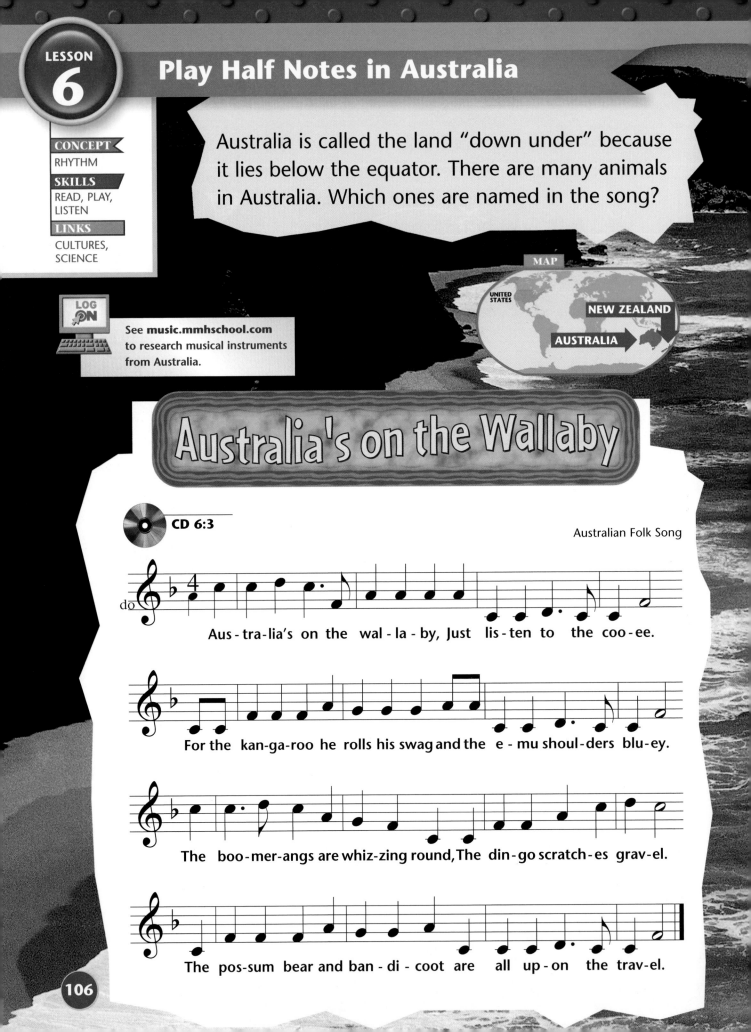

Australia's on the Wallaby

CD 6:3

Australian Folk Song

do

Aus-tra-lia's on the wal-la-by, Just lis-ten to the coo-ee.

For the kan-ga-roo he rolls his swag and the e-mu shoul-ders blu-ey.

The boo-mer-angs are whiz-zing round, The din-go scratch-es grav-el.

The pos-sum bear and ban-di-coot are all up-on the trav-el.

A rest that lasts two beats is called a half rest.

Find the half notes and half rests in this pattern.

Playalong

Choose an unpitched instrument. **Play** as you sing the song.

kangaroo

bandicoot

emu

dingo

possum bear

Play Half Notes in New Zealand

Music is special to the Maori people of New Zealand. Learn to sing the song. Play half notes on rhythm sticks with a partner.

Oma Rapeti

Run, Rabbit

CD 6:6

New Zealand Folk Song
Collected and Transcribed by Kathy B. Sorensen

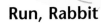

Maori: O-ma ra - pe-ti, o-ma ra - pe-ti, o-ma_ o-ma o-ma!_

Kau- a ri - ro kau-a ri - ro koe ai - a._____

Ka o - ra i - a he - i a - ha ra - pe - ti._____

O-ma ra - pe-ti, o-ma ra - pe-ti, o-ma_ o-ma o-ma!_

The *pukaea* is an early horn that is played like a trumpet. It is made from a hollow tree branch. Its sound can carry long distances. It was often used to signal a warning.

Listen for the *pukaea* in this modern music.

 **LISTENING** CD 6:10

pukaea

Pukaea by Jaz Coleman and Hinewehi Mohi

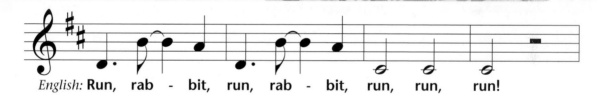

English: Run, rab - bit, run, rab - bit, run, run, run!

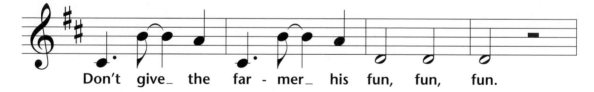

Don't give_ the far - mer_ his fun, fun, fun.

He'll get by with - out his rab - bit_ pie,

so run, rab - bit, run, rab - bit, run, run, run!

Expressive Dynamics in Antarctica

CONCEPT
DYNAMICS

SKILLS
LISTEN, COMPOSE, PLAY

LINKS
CULTURES, SCIENCE, SOCIAL STUDIES

You have been learning about many instruments. Antarctica is very cold and covered in ice. The only instrument in Antarctica is the wind itself!

Listen to music describing the Antarctic wind. Do you hear sounds of seals in the music?

LISTENING CD 6:11

Antarctica by Paul Winter

MAP

UNITED STATES

ANTARCTICA

THINK! How does the music create a feeling of being in a very cold place? If you were a composer, what different sounds would you use to create a feeling of being in a very cold place?

Crescendo means "gradually getting louder." Gradually getting softer is called **decrescendo**. Here are the symbols used in music for these two terms:

crescendo   *decrescendo*

The freezing weather creates many types of ice in Antarctica. **Create** your own "Ice Music." Choose an instrument that might sound like one of the types of ice. Use *crescendo* and *decrescendo*. **Play** your "Ice Music" along with *Antarctica*.

green growler

new frazil fibrous

pancake

pack

brash

Crescendo and Decrescendo with Penguins

Here is a funny poem about penguins. **Move** to the poem as penguins might.

Three Little Penguins

CD 6:12

Anonymous
Adapted by Marilyn Davidson

Three lit - tle pen-guins dressed in white and black.

Wad - dle, wad - dle for - ward and wad - dle right back!

End

Three lit - tle pen-guins, in a fun – ny pose,

They are wear-ing their eve – ning clothes.

Play this pattern on a triangle with the poem. Use *crescendo* and *decrescendo*.

Playalong

Their suits are black and their vests are white,

They wad-dle to the left and they wad-dle to the right.

They stand on the ice and they look ver-y neat,

Go back to the beginning and sing to the End.

As they wad-dle a - long on their lit-tle flat feet.

CONCEPT
MELODY

SKILLS
READ, PLAY, IMPROVISE

LINKS
CULTURES, SOCIAL STUDIES

Wherever we live, the earth is home for all of us. Can you name all the continents on Earth?

MAP

UNITED STATES   LATIN AMERICA

En nuestra Tierra tan linda
On Our Beautiful Planet Earth

CD 6:15

Latin American Folk Song
Adapted by José-Luis Orozco
English Words by Linda Worsley

Spanish: 1. En nues-tra Tie-rra tan lin-da _____
English: Here on our beau-ti-ful plan-et, _____

pron - to va a sa - lir el sol, _____
soon the bright sun _____ will shine, _____

pron - to va a sa - lir el sol _____
soon the bright sun _____ will shine, _____

en nues - tra Tie - rra tan lin - da. _____
here on our beau - ti - ful plan - et. _____

2. pronto va a soplar el viento

3. pronto va a caer la lluvia

4. pronto brillará una estrella

2. soon a fresh wind will blow,

3. soon a warm rain will fall

4. soon a bright star will glow

114

Sing and move to this song.

Earth   sun   wind   rain   stars

Find *do*, *mi*, and *so* in this music.
Sing it with pitch syllables and hand signs. **Play** it as you sing the song.

Improvise with *Do Mi So*

Listen to another song about our world.

For another activity with "He's Got the Whole World in His Hands," see **Spotlight on MIDI**.

LISTENING CD 6:21

He's Got the Whole World in His Hands
Sung by opera singer Leontyne Price

Find *so mi do* in this song. Sing the song.

He's Got the Whole World in His Hands

CD 6:22

Freely   Traditional Spiritual

do

1. He's got the whole world___ in His hands.___
   He's got the whole world___ in His hands.___
   He's got the whole world___ in His hands.___
   He's got the whole world in His hands.___

2. He's got the wind and the rain in His hands.
   He's got the sun and the moon in His hands.
   He's got the wind and the rain in His hands.
   He's got the whole world in His hands.

3. He's got you and me, brother, in His hands.
   He's got you and me, sister, in His hands.
   He's got you and me, brother, in His hands.
   He's got the whole world in His hands.

116

Choose a continent and write about it.
Improvise a melody using the pitches *do, mi,* and *so* to complete one of the phrases below.
Sing your melody and have others guess which continent.

Where we are we see...

Wea-ther here is of - ten...

Asia

Antarctica

Europe

Africa

North America

Australia

South America

Spotlight Your Success!

REVIEW

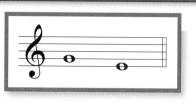

1 Here are *so* and *mi*.
Where is *do*?

   a. around the third line
   b. in the second space
   c. around the line below the staff

2 Which instrument belongs to the brass family?

a.    **b.**

READ AND LISTEN

1 **Read** these melodies. Then **listen**. Which melody uses *so mi do*?

a.

b.

Read these rhythms. Then **listen** and pat with the strong beat. Which do you hear?

a.

b.

THINK!

1 How is a half note different from a quarter note?

2 As you traveled in this unit, you learned about many instruments from different continents. Suppose you could learn to play any instrument from any country. Which instrument would you choose? Why?

3 **Write** about a song you like. Tell what you like about the music.

CREATE AND PERFORM

1 **Create** your own melody using *do, mi,* and *so.* Use this rhythm for your melody.

   1. Clap this rhythm.

   2. Choose one pitch for each note.

2 **Sing** your melody.

Meet the Musician
ON NATIONAL RADIO!

Name: Bianca Garcia
Age: 13
Instrument: Flute
Home Town: Salem, New Hampshire

Thirteen-year-old flutist Bianca Garcia likes to challenge herself. When she goes swimming, she likes to see how long she can hold her breath under water. When she goes skiing, she likes to go straight down the hill. She spent hours trying to tie her shoes before she could even walk!

Bianca also challenges herself through music. "I like to play difficult pieces the most," she says. Bianca pushes herself to be the best musician she can be.

LISTENING   CD 6:26–27   **RECORDED INTERVIEW**

Concerto for Flute and Orchestra, Allegro
by Jacques Ibert

Listen to Bianca's performance and interview on the national radio program **From the Top**.

Spotlight on the String Quartet

Did You Know?

A string quartet is made up of two violins, a viola, and a cello.

The first violin leads the group and starts the music with a signal from his or her bow.

One or both violins usually play the main melodies in a string quartet. The viola and cello play lower-sounding parts, giving the group a fuller sound.

Composers have been writing music for the string quartet since about 1750.

🎵 **LISTENING** CD 6:28–29

String Quartet No. 2 in D Minor
by Franz Josef Haydn

String Quartet No. 2
by Béla Bartók

Listen to the beautiful melody in this string quartet by Haydn. Many years after Haydn, Bartók wrote string quartets that substituted exciting sound effects for melodies.

Your Turn,
My Turn

You will get to
take turns singing,
playing, and
moving in this unit.

Your turn.

I'm next.

Coming Attractions

Sing and make shoes on *do, re, mi, so.*

Fly a kite with dotted half notes.

Move to a Round Dance.

Imagine that it is early morning and the sun is just out of sight. Let's take turns waking it up!

WAKE UP THE SUN

 CD 7:1

Words by John Jacobson
Music by Emily Crocker

Refrain

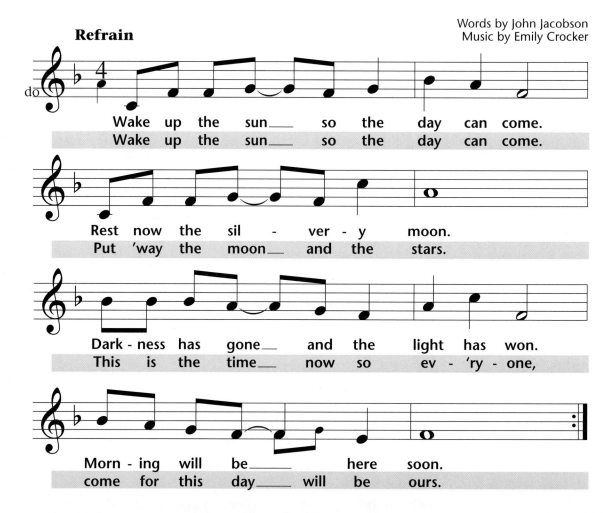

Wake up the sun___ so the day can come.
Wake up the sun___ so the day can come.

Rest now the sil - ver - y moon.
Put 'way the moon___ and the stars.

Dark - ness has gone___ and the light has won.
This is the time___ now so ev - 'ry - one,

Morn - ing will be___ here soon.
come for this day___ will be ours.

Verse

1. Shad-ows will van - ish, dew dis-ap - pear,___
2. She might be shy___ like you and I,___

the world can be - gin___ a - new.
wait - ing so long___ to grow.

Each day a new___ start, year af - ter year.___
She'll hes - i - tate,___ she'll make us wait.___

(Repeat Refrain after Verse 1)

Now let the sun shine through, for you!
Now's the time to show your glow!

Coda (last time only)

Some - bo - dy wake the sun.

125

LESSON 1

CONCEPT
RHYTHM
SKILLS
DESCRIBE,
LISTEN, PLAY
LINKS
CULTURES,
FINE ART

Celebrating with ³ Rhythm

Welcome to a party! What ways are people taking turns at this party? Take turns singing this song.

Find the meter for this song. How many beats are in one measure of ³?

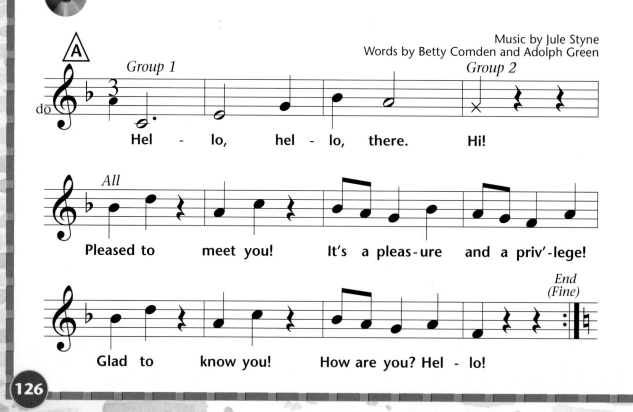

HELLO, HELLO THERE

from the musical *Bells Are Ringing*

CD 7:4

Music by Jule Styne
Words by Betty Comden and Adolph Green

Group 1
Group 2

Hel - lo, hel - lo, there.   Hi!

All

Pleased to   meet you!   It's a pleas-ure   and a priv'-lege!

End (Fine)

Glad to   know you!   How are you? Hel - lo!

126

The oboe and violin will take turns playing in this music. **Listen** for beats in sets of three. **Move** when the oboe plays.

CD-ROM

Learn more about the violin and the oboe on *Orchestral Instruments* **CD-ROM**.

LISTENING CD 7:7

Adagio from Concerto for Violin and Oboe
by Johann Sebastian Bach

(B)

Group 1

Well,   well,   what   do   you   know?

Group 2

We should have done this a   long time a - go!

Group 1

Well,   well,   is - n't   it   swell!

Go back to the beginning and sing to the End (Da Capo al Fine)

Group 2

Is - n't   it   nice   to   say:

Clap and Play to $\frac{3}{}$

Sounds lasting three beats are shown with a **dotted half note**. The dot adds one beat to the half note. **Find** the dotted half notes in this song.

MAP

UNITED STATES

MEXICO

CHIAPANECAS

Ladies of Chiapas

CD 7:8

A

Mexican Folk Song
English Version by MMH

do

Spanish: Cuan - do   la   no - che   lle - gó,   (clap clap)
English: Now that the night has ar - rived, (clap clap)

y   con   su   man - to   de a - zul   (clap clap)
un - der   a   man - tle   of   blue,   (clap clap)

El   blan - co   ran - cho   cu - brió,   (clap clap)
Un - der   the   moon shin - ing white,   (clap clap)

a - le - gre el   bai - le em - pe - zó.   (clap clap)
I   will   go   danc - ing   with   you.   (clap clap)

128

Play △ on the 𝅘𝅥𝅭 in the B section.

B

Bai - la,   mi chia - pa - ne - ca.
Dance,   now,   my *chia - pa - ne - ca.*

Bai - la,   bai - la con gar - bo.
Dance   with   grace and en - chant - ment.

1.
Bai - la,   sua - ve ra - yo de
Dance,   now,   with the moon___ shin - ing

luz._____
bright._____

2.
que en   el   bai - le rei - na e - res
Dance,   my   gen - tle one,___ You will

tú,   chia - pa - ne - ca gen - til.   (clap clap)
soon   be   the queen of the dance!   (clap clap)

129

LESSON 2

CONCEPT ▸
MELODY

SKILLS
SING, PLAY,
DESCRIBE

LINKS
SCIENCE,
LANGUAGE ARTS

Reading a New Pitch: *Re*

This woman owns a pretty pig. Find the "oinks" in the song. Move to show the shape of the "oinks" patterns. On what pitch is the last "oink"? The pitch one step higher than *do* is **re**.

OLD WOMAN AND THE PIG

CD 7:12

American Folk Song

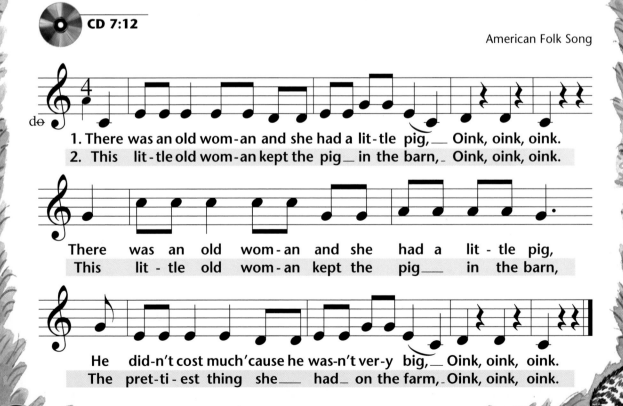

1. There was an old wom-an and she had a lit-tle pig,____ Oink, oink, oink.
2. This   lit-tle old wom-an kept the pig__ in the barn,__ Oink, oink, oink.

There   was   an   old   wom-an   and   she   had   a   lit-tle   pig,
This   lit-tle   old   wom-an   kept   the   pig___   in   the   barn,

He   did-n't cost much 'cause he was-n't ver-y big,__ Oink, oink, oink.
The   pret-ti-est   thing   she___   had_   on the farm,_Oink, oink, oink.

Here is the hand sign for *re*:

re

Sing the song. Use pitch-syllable names and hand signs instead of the "oinks."

Sing the song again and **play** the "oinks."

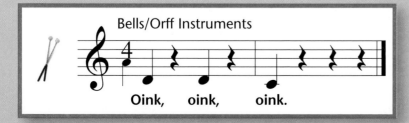

Oink,   oink,   oink.

Practice with *Do Re Mi*

This bucket has a hole in it. Listen as two people try to fix it. **Find** *do re mi* in this song.

There's a Hole in the Bucket

CD 7:15

American Dialogue Song
Traditional German Melody Liebe Hei nrich"

do

1. There's a hole in the buck-et, dear Li-za, dear Li-za,
2. Mend the hole, then, dear Geor-gie, dear Geor-gie, dear Geor-gie,
3. With__ what shall I mend it, dear Li-za, dear Li-za,
4. With a straw,_ dear Geor-gie, dear Geor-gie, dear Geor-gie,
5. The__ straw is too long,__ dear Li-za, dear Li-za,

There's a hole in the buck-et, dear Li-za, a hole.
Mend the hole, then, dear Geor-gie, dear Geor-gie, the hole.
With__ what shall I mend it, dear Li-za, with what?
With a straw,_ dear Geor-gie, dear Geor-gie, a straw.
The__ straw is too long,__ dear Li-za, too long.

Liza:

6. Cut the straw, dear Georgie,
dear Georgie, dear Georgie,
Cut the straw, dear Georgie,
dear Georgie, the straw.

8. With a knife, dear Georgie,
... a knife.

10. Then sharpen it, dear Georgie,
... then sharpen it.

Georgie:

7. With what shall I cut it,
dear Liza, dear Liza,
With what shall I cut it,
dear Liza, with what?

9. The knife is too dull,
dear Liza, ... too dull.

11. With what shall I sharpen it,
dear Liza, ... with what?

Sing these two melodies. Use pitch syllables and hand signs.

a.

b.

Listen to a funny version of "Old MacDonald Had a Farm." Which of the melodies above do you hear on "E-I-E-I-O"? What animals do you think the instruments sound like?

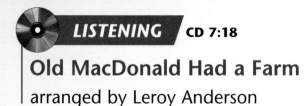

LISTENING CD 7:18

Old MacDonald Had a Farm
arranged by Leroy Anderson

12. With a stone, dear Georgie,
    ... a stone.

13. The stone is too dry,
    dear Liza, ... too dry.

14. Then wet it, dear Georgie,
    ... then wet it.

15. With what shall I wet it,
    dear Liza, ... with what?

16. With water, dear Georgie,
    ... with water.

17. In what shall I get it,
    dear Liza, ... in what?

18. In a bucket, dear Georgie,
    ... in a bucket.

19. There's a hole in the bucket,
    dear Liza, ... a hole.

Read and Play Dotted Half Notes

CONCEPT
RHYTHM

SKILLS
READ, PLAY,
LISTEN

LINKS
SCIENCE,
READING

Have you ever flown a kite? **Find** the dotted half notes in this kite song.

Let's Go Fly a Kite

from the movie *Mary Poppins*

CD 7:19

Verse

Words and Music by Richard M. Sherman
and Robert B. Sherman

1. With____ tup-pence for pa - per and strings,
2. When you send___ it fly - ing up there,

You can have your own set of wings;
All at once you're light - er than air;

With your feet on the ground you're a bird in flight
You can dance on the breeze o - ver hous - es and trees

With your fist hold - ing tight
With your fist hold - ing tight

to the string of your kite. Oh!_____
to the string of your kite. Oh!_____

Read this pattern.

Playalong

Sing the song and **play** this pattern on the Refrain.

Refrain

Let's go fly a kite, Up to the

high - est height! Let's go fly a kite,

And send it soar - ing,

Up through the at - mos - phere, Up where the

air is clear. Oh, let's go

fly a kite!

Listen and Play with the Wind

Can you see wind? **Listen** to this windy music. It is an étude. An *étude* is music that is written to help piano students build playing skill and strength.

MIDI

Use MIDIsaurus CD-ROM to practice ♩.

LISTENING CD 7:22

Étude Op. 25, No. 11, "The Winter Wind" by Frédéric Chopin

Meet the Musician

Frédéric Chopin started learning the piano at the age of four. He gave his first concerts at the age of eight. He began writing piano music in his teens. He left his home in Poland to perform and write music all over Europe.

THINK! Why do you think this music is known as "The Winter Wind Étude"?

Speak this poem about the wind.

Who Has Seen the Wind?

Who has seen the wind?
  Neither I nor you:
But when the leaves hang trembling
  The wind is passing thro'.

Who has seen the wind?
  Neither you nor I:
But when the trees bow down their heads
  The wind is passing by.

Christina Georgina Rossetti

Play this pattern as you speak the poem.
Play any pitches from C D E G A in any order.

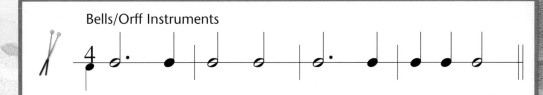

Bells/Orff Instruments

What other sounds or movement can you
add to show the wind?
Form small groups to read, play, and act
out a verse of the poem.

CONCEPT
MELODY

SKILLS
LISTEN, READ, IMPROVISE

LINKS
CULTURES, SCIENCE

Listen to music that you might hear at a street fair in New York City.

🔵 **LISTENING** CD 7:23

Somos Boricuas (We Are Puerto Rican)
by Juan Gutiérrez

Someone who repairs shoes is called a cobbler. *Zapatero* is Spanish for cobbler. **Read** this song using pitch syllables and hand signs. Form two groups and take turns singing this song.

MAP

UNITED STATES ← PUERTO RICO

EL ZAPATERO

The Cobbler

🔵 CD 7:24

Puerto Rican Folk Song

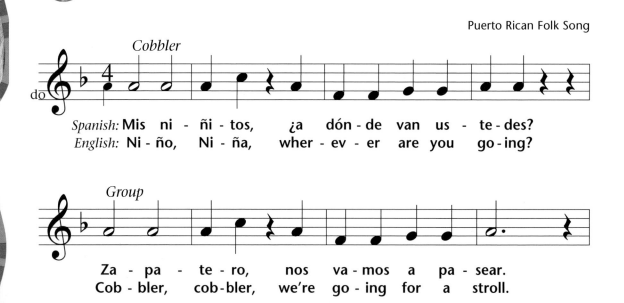

Cobbler

Spanish: Mis ni - ñi - tos,   ¿a dón - de van us - te - des?
English: Ni - ño, Ni - ña,   wher - ev - er are you go - ing?

Group

Za - pa - te - ro,   nos va - mos a pa - sear.
Cob - bler, cob - bler, we're go - ing for a stroll.

Cobbler

Mis ni - ñi - tos,   los   za - pa - tos   se   rom - pen.
Ni - ño,   Ni - ña,   you'll wear your shoes out   walk - ing.

Group

Za - pa - te - ro,   us - ted los com - pon - drá.
Cob - bler,   cob-bler,   then   will   you mend the   hole?

Reading *Re* in Wales

You are learning to read *re*. Let's see how much you remember.

1 What pitches is *re* between?

2 If *do* is in the first space, where is *re*?

3 If *do* is around the first line, where is *re*?

"Shoheen Sho" is a lullaby from Wales. **Read** this song with pitch syllables. Then **sing** it with the words.

MAP

WALES

UNITED STATES

shoheen sho

CD 7:28

Welsh Folk Song
Verse 1 Traditional Welsh Words
Verses 2 and 3 by Margaret Campbelle-duGard

1. Sho - heen   sho,   ba - by   boy,
   Bird - ie   sleeps   in   the   nest,

Fa - ther's   pride,   Moth - er's   joy.
Sun   doth   sink   in   the   West.

2. Shoheen sho, baby girl,
   Father's pride, Mother's pearl.
   Birdie sleeps in the nest,
   Sun doth sink in the West.

3. Shoheen sho, little dove,
   Fill my heart full of love.
   Birdie sleeps in the nest,
   Sun doth sink in the West.

Learn About Wales

Wales is known for its mountains, its castles, its rugby, and its singing.

Some of the greatest opera singers, such as Bryn Terfel, are proud to be Welsh.

Welsh choirs are famous all over the world.

Listen to the Welsh National anthem sung by Welsh men's choirs.

LISTENING CD 7:31

Hen wlad fy nhadau (The Land of my Fathers)
Morriston Orpheus Choir and the Welsh Guards

Welsh boys playing rugby

Morriston Orpheus Choir at Carnegie Hall, New York

Harlech Castle in Wales, Great Britain

CONCEPT
RHYTHM
SKILLS
DESCRIBE,
PLAY, LISTEN
LINKS
HISTORY, FINE
ART, DANCE

A hat with three corners is called a *tricorn* hat. Tricorn hats were worn more than 200 years ago. Because of their shape, they would not blow off your head easily. This was useful since many people rode horses at that time.

Mein Hut

My Hat

CD 7:32

German Folk Song

German: **Mein Hut** er hat drei Eck - en,
English: My hat it has three cor - ners,

Drei Eck - en hat mein Hut,
Three cor - ners has my hat,

Und hätt er nicht drei Eck - en,
And had it not three cor - ners,

Dann ist er nicht mein Hut.
It would not be my hat.

Move as you sing the song. Leave out one action word on each repeat.

My

hat

three

corners

Play this pattern as you sing the song.

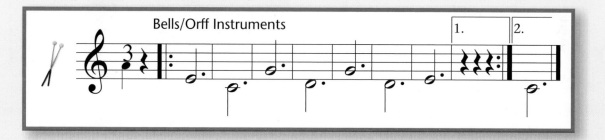

Bells/Orff Instruments

Move and Play with a Minuet

The minuet was a dance popular in the late 1700s. *Minuet* means "little steps."

Art Gallery

Minuet by Giovanni Domenico Tiepolo

Giovanni Domenico Tiepolo was an Italian painter during the 1700s. His father was a great painter and his teacher as well

Play each pattern lightly. Find these patterns in the listening map.

① 3

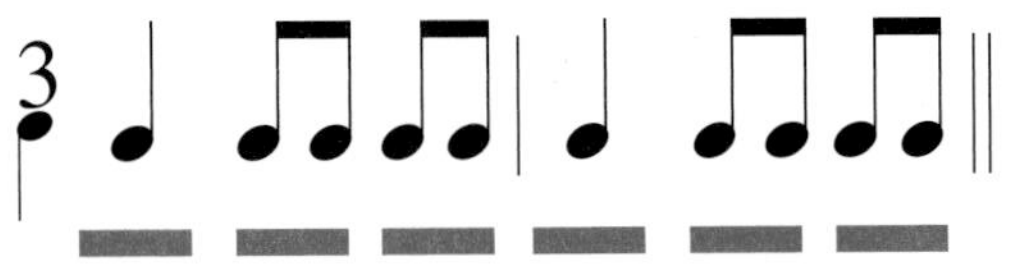

② 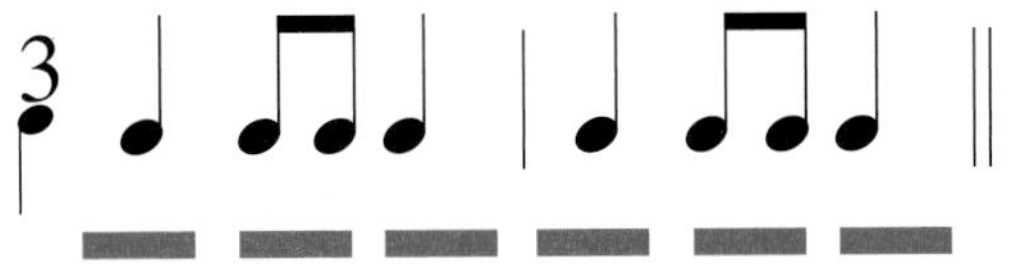 3

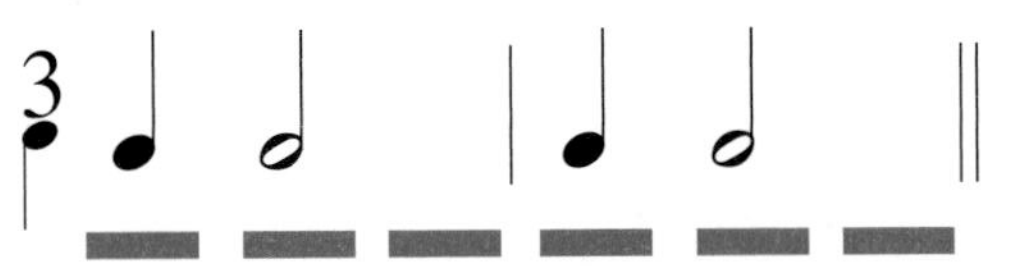

③ 3

④ 3

⑤ 3

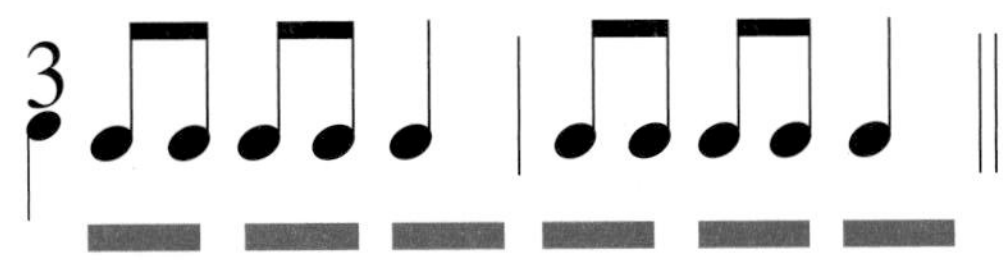

Learn some minuet steps with a partner.
Play the patterns and move with minuet steps.

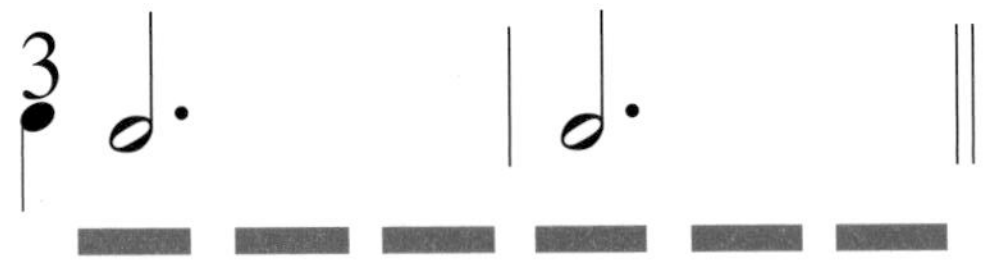

144

This minuet is music from a play.

LISTENING CD 8:1

Minuet from *Abdelazar*

by Henry Purcell

Follow the listening map. **Listen** for the different brass instruments taking turns on the melody.

Listening Map for Minuet

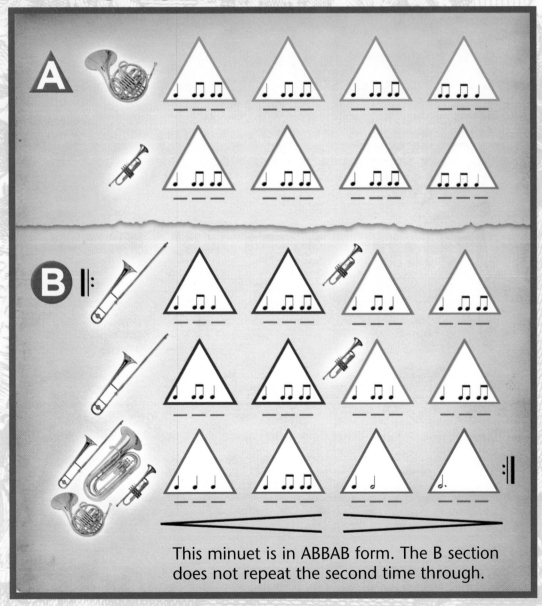

This minuet is in ABBAB form. The B section does not repeat the second time through.

Sing and Play *Do Re Mi So*

CONCEPT
MELODY
SKILLS
READ, CREATE, PLAY
LINKS
SOCIAL STUDIES

Board the boat!

Many years ago people traveled to America by boat. This song is about people boarding the boat.

Find *do* in this song. **Read** the song with pitch syllables.

Sammy Sackett

CD 8:2

American Folk Song

do Sam - my Sack - ett, hold on to my jack - et,

Hold on to my coat. That's the way we board the boat.

146

Sing the song and play the game for "Sammy Sackett." When the leader taps you, everyone sings your name instead of "Sammy."

Find these patterns in "Sammy Sackett." **Create** a new melody by putting the patterns in order. **Play** and sing your melody.

Question and Answer

When you ask a question, someone gives an answer. In music there are questions and answers, too.

The question ends "up in the air." It does not end on *do*. The answer has a "final" feeling because it ends on *do*.

Read this melody.

THINK! Why does the melody above sounds like a musical question?

Play the question.

Create an answer by ending on *do*. Change only the last three notes.

Listen for a melody that sounds like the one you just played. Raise your hand when you hear it. This music is played by the U.S. Marine Drum and Bugle Corps.

U.S. Marine Drum and Bugle Corps ▲

LISTENING CD 8:5

We're Looking Good

by John Williams

▼ **Philippine Marine Drum and Bugle Team performing in Makati City, Philippines**

LESSON 7

CONCEPT
STYLE

SKILLS
SING, DESCRIBE, LISTEN

LINKS
SCIENCE, FINE ART

Folk Songs and Opera

The rabbit in this song has mighty long ears. What do you notice about the verses of the song? Form two groups and **sing** the song.

Mister Rabbit, Mister Rabbit

CD 8:6

Southern Folk Song

Verse

Friend

1. Mis-ter Rab-bit, Mis-ter Rab-bit, your ears' might-y long!
2. Mis-ter Rab-bit, Mis-ter Rab-bit, your coat's might-y gray!
3. Mis-ter Rab-bit, Mis-ter Rab-bit, your tail's might-y white!

Rabbit

Yes in - deed, they're put on wrong._
Yes in - deed, 'twas made that way.___
Yes in - deed, I'm go-ing out of sight.__

Refrain

All

Ev' - ry lit - tle soul must shine, shine, shine._

Ev' - ry lit - tle soul must shine,_ shine, shine.

Young Hare
by Albrecht Dürer

A **folk song** is a song by an unknown composer. It has been passed on from one person to another for many years.

Find where the music tells you that "Mister Rabbit, Mister Rabbit" is a folk song.

Can you find other folk songs in this book?

LOG ON

Use **music.mmhschool.com** to research folk songs on the web.

Going to the Opera

This music is from an opera. An **opera** is a story told through music.

A solo by a singer in an opera is called an *aria*. Music with two people singing is called a *duet*. Sometimes the two singers take turns. Sometimes they both sing at the same time.

LISTENING CD 8:9

Papagena! Papagena! Papagena! from *The Magic Flute* by Wolfgang Amadeus Mozart

Listen to the duet between Papageno and Papagena. It is from the opera *The Magic Flute*. Hold up your right hand when you hear Papageno, the man. Hold up your left hand when you hear Papagena, the woman.

Papageno and Papagena in *The Magic Flute* ▶

Opera has singing, acting, scenery, costumes, and sometimes dancing.

Wolfgang Amadeus Mozart was from Austria. He began to play the harpsichord, which is an early keyboard instrument, when he was 3 years old. By the age of 6, he was composing his own music. When he was 11, his first opera was performed.

THINK! How are "Mister Rabbit, Mister Rabbit" and "Papagena! Papagena! Papagena!" from *The Magic Flute* alike?

153

Read and Play *Do, Re, Mi,* and *So*

CONCEPT
MELODY
SKILLS
READ, LISTEN, PLAY
LINKS
CULTURES, SOCIAL STUDIES, FINE ART

This song is a Native American lullaby from the Muscogee Creek Nation of Oklahoma. It is about a mother who has gone to hunt for turtles.

Listen to "Baby Nodja." Then sing the song.

CD 8:10

Muscogee Creek Lullaby
As Sung by Lillian Rainer

Creek: Ba - by No - dja

No - dja No - dja

la - dja ho - ho gan ai - yang - si

ma - ki - to wa - la - ka - his

ma - ki - to ai - yang - si

Ba - by No - dja

154

Taos Village is in northern New Mexico. It has been the home of the Taos Native Americans for more than 800 years.

This round dance is performed by the Taos people. Form a circle and step with the beat as you listen.

🎵 **LISTENING** CD 8:12

Taos Round Dance (Traditional)

The village where the Taos people live is called a *pueblo. Pueblo* is the Spanish word for "town."

A pueblo is made up of houses with many floors around a central square. The houses are made of adobe, which is a brick made of mud and straw.

Art Gallery

Taos July by Joseph Amadeus Fleck

Adobe buildings in Taos Pueblo, New Mexico

155

Take Turns Playing
Name some ways you can take turns in music.

You'll Sing a Song and I'll Sing a Song

CD 8:13

Words and Music by Ella Jenkins

You'll sing a song, and I'll sing a song,

and we'll sing a song to - geth - er.

You'll sing a song, and I'll sing a song,

in warm or win - try weath - er.

156

Meet the Musician

Ella Jenkins grew up in Chicago. She performs with and teaches children around the world. She has been to all seven continents including Antarctica. Much of the music she writes helps us to get to know people from other countries. Ella was awarded the "Grammy 2004 Lifetime Achievement Award" for her work in music.

Listen as Ella speaks about writing songs.

RECORDED INTERVIEW CD 8:16

Sing the song again. **Play** this bell part with the song.

Bells/Orff Instruments
Play 3 times

Ella Jenkins with students from ▼
Middleton Elementary School;
Skokie, Illinois

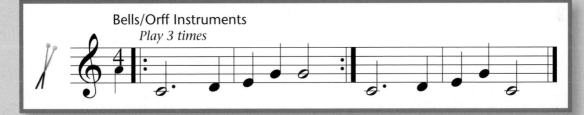

Spotlight Your Success!

REVIEW

1 How many beats does a dotted half note last for in $\frac{3}{4}$?

    a. 1   **b.** 2   **c.** 3   **d.** 4

2 Which is the hand sign for *re*?

    a.    **b.**

READ AND LISTEN

Read these patterns. Then **listen**.
Which do you hear?

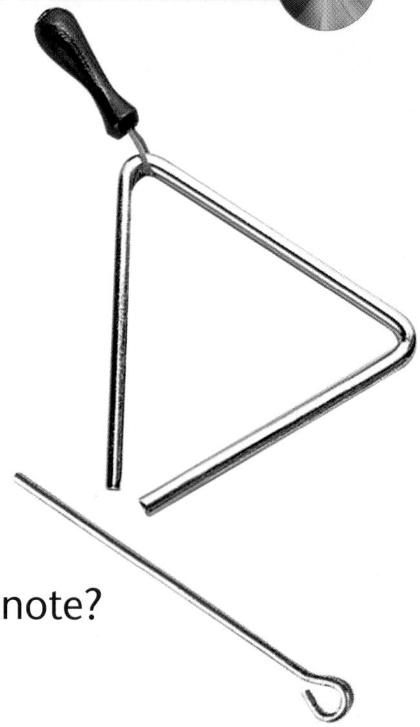

1 Which pattern has only *do, re,* and *mi*?

    a.

    b.

2 Which rhythm pattern has a dotted half note?

    a.

    b.

THINK!

1 Which of these songs are folk songs? How do you know?

Hello, Hello, There
Chiapanecas
Old Woman and the Pig

2 **Write** about a song or listening you like. Tell why you like it.

CREATE AND PERFORM

Question:

Answer:

1 **Read** and clap the rhythms for the question and the answer with a partner.

2 **Create** a melody using *do*, *re*, *mi*, and *so* for each part. End the question on *so*. End the answer on *do*.

3 **Perform** your question and answer, taking turns.

Meet the Musician

FROM THE TOP

ON NATIONAL RADIO!

Name: Trevor Ochieng
Age: 14
Instrument: Violin
Home Town: Wyandanch, New York

Trevor Ochieng was only three years old the first time he played the violin onstage. He remembers feeling scared. "My teacher brought me onto the stage, but once she left, I was too nervous to start playing," he says.

Trevor's teacher decided to stand next to him to help him feel better. Trevor began to play his violin, but when his teacher tried to leave the stage again, Trevor stopped and tried to follow her. Again and again his teacher tried to walk offstage, but Trevor would only play when she stood nearby. "My teacher had to stay right by my side the whole time!" says Trevor.

Since then, Trevor has performed onstage many times. Luckily, he doesn't get "stage fright" anymore!

LISTENING **CD 8:18–19** **RECORDED INTERVIEW**

Scherzo and Tarantella by Henryk Wieniawski

Listen to Trevor's performance and interview on the national radio program **From the Top**.

Spotlight on the Clarinet

Did You Know?

The clarinet's inventor thought its high notes sounded like a trumpet or "clarino," so he named it after that instrument.

The clarinet is a single-reed instrument. Sound is produced when the player blows across a thin strip of wood, called a *reed*, to make it vibrate.

The clarinet's body is made up of five separate pieces that fit together.

The clarinet has changed little since it was invented, about 300 years ago.

 **LISTENING** CD 8:20–21

Peter and the Wolf by Sergei Prokofiev

Dance Preludes for Clarinet and Piano, No. 3 by Witold Lutoslawski

Listen to these pieces for clarinet. The Prokofiev clarinet part is heard when the cat appears in the story of "Peter and the Wolf." In the piece by Lutoslawski, you can hear the very high, brilliant sound of the clarinet.

UNIT 5

The Music in Us!

You will find many ways that people make music in this unit. Maybe you will find some new ways to make music yourself!

Coming Attractions

Play pentatonic with a donkey.

Help an elephant find its trunk in $\frac{2}{4}$.

Listen and ride a motorcycle with a trombone.

You can make music, even if you are not
a virtuoso. A *virtuoso* is a very good musician.

Sing a song about how we all have music inside us.

Everybody Has Music Inside

CD 8:22

Swing(♫ = ♩♪)

Words and Music by Greg Scelsa

Ev-'ry-bod-y has mu-sic in - side__ es - pe-cial - ly for you.

Don't be a - fraid__ to let it out,__ it is-n't hard to do. __

You don't have to be a vir - tu - o - so,

it does - n't mat - ter if you sing just "so - so."

It's a feel-ing down in-side your soul, so come on, you can do_ it!

Ev-'ry-bod-y has mu-sic in - side,__ so let a song ring out.__

Just let it come right from your heart, that's what it's all a - bout.

Mu - sic is the sound of life reach-ing out for love.

Ev - 'ry - bod - y has mu - sic, Ev - 'ry - bod - y has mu - sic, Ev - 'ry - bod - y has mu - sic in - side.

Read these patterns. Which pattern goes with the verse and which goes with the refrain?

1 barn   barn   dance in the   barn

2 barn   barn   in the   barn

In $\frac{2}{\bullet}$ meter there are two beats to a measure. The **dotted quarter note** gets the beat in this meter.

A dot after a note makes the note longer. The ♩. is as long as three eighth notes ♫♪

Here are the patterns you clapped above.

Refrain

Verse

Play the patterns with the song.

167

Move and Play with Elephants

This $\frac{2}{\cdot}$ music is about an elephant named Effie who goes folk dancing! The solo instrument is the lowest-pitched brass instrument, called the *tuba*.

tuba

Gradually getting slower in music is called **ritardando**. Gradually getting faster is called **accelerando**.

Listen for the tuba in the music. **Move** like an elephant with the beat. Watch out for the *ritardando* and the *accelerando*!

LISTENING CD 8:28

Effie Goes Folk Dancing by Alec Wilder

168

Read this poem in $\frac{2}{4}$ meter.

The Elephant Carries a Great Big Trunk

The elephant carries a great big trunk;
He never packs it with clothes;
It has no lock and it has no key,
But he takes it wherever he goes.

Anonymous

Sometimes the same word can mean two things.
What trunk is the poem talking about?

Read this pattern. Play the pattern with the poem:

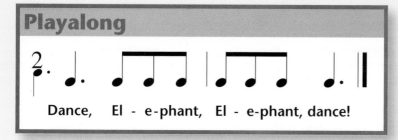

Playalong

Dance,   El - e-phant,   El - e-phant, dance!

Play the pattern with "Effie Goes Folk Dancing."

169

CONCEPT
MELODY

SKILLS
SING, READ, PLAY

LINKS
FINE ART, READING

Pull up the anchor and set sail on this ship.
Sing the *response* after the captain *calls*.

Away for Rio

CD 8:29

American Sea Chantey

Verse

Call

1. Oh, the an-chor is weighed and the sails they are set,
2. We've a jol-ly good ship and a jol-ly good crew,
3. Oh,— say, were you ev-er in Ri - o Grande?

Response

A - way⎯⎯ for Ri - o!

Call

The friends that we're leav-ing we'll nev-er for-get,
A jol-ly good mate and a good skip-per too,
It's there that the riv-ers run down gold-en sand,

Response

For we're bound for Ri - o Grande!

U.S.S. Constitution
by Myron Clark

The U.S.S. Constitution was a ship that was made of wood. The wooden sides were so thick that in a battle in 1812, the cannon balls bounced off. The ship then became known as "Old Ironsides."

The pitches in the crew's responses are *do re mi so* and *la*.

do re mi so la

When these five pitches are placed in order, they create a scale. A five-tone scale is called **pentatonic**.

Sing the responses of the song. Use pitch syllables and hand signs.

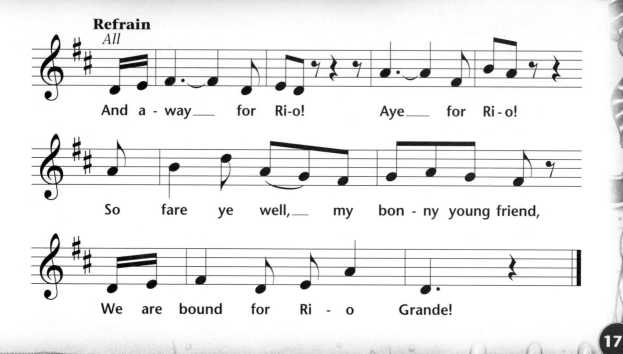

Refrain
All

And a-way___ for Ri-o! Aye___ for Ri-o!

So fare ye well,___ my bon-ny young friend,

We are bound for Ri - o Grande!

Sing and Play in Pentatonic

Cookie and his friend are talking. Find out what is missing. Pick a part and **sing** the song.

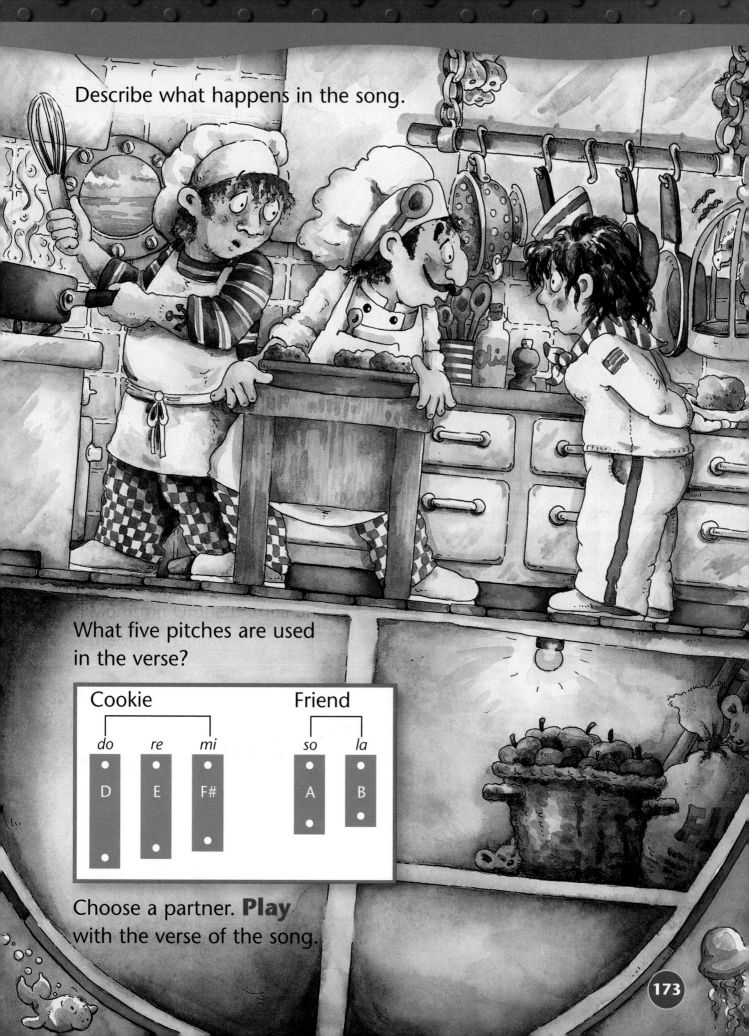

Describe what happens in the song.

What five pitches are used in the verse?

Cookie   Friend

do   re   mi   so   la

D   E   F#   A   B

Choose a partner. **Play** with the verse of the song.

173

LESSON
3

CONCEPT
RHYTHM
SKILLS
LISTEN,
SING, READ
LINKS
CULTURES,
FINE ART

Game Songs in 2/4 and 2/2

Global Voices

MAP

UNITED STATES   CYPRUS

Cyprus is an island near Turkey. Look at the pictures of Cyprus. Compare it with the place you live. How is it the same? How is it different?

Cyprus is known for its olives, wine, and fruit. It is also known for beautiful artwork, such as pottery, baskets, and weaving.

Art Gallery

Pilgrim Flask

This piece of pottery is from Cyprus. It was made many years ago.

Listen to this song from Cyprus in $\frac{2}{\bullet.}$

POUN TO, POUN TO

CD 9:1   **Where Is It? Where Is It?**
Greek & Cypriot Children's game song

Πού 'ν' το, πού 'ν' το, το δακτυλίδι
Ψάξε, ψάξε, δεν θα το βρεις.
Δεν θα το βρεις, δεν θα το βρεις,
Το δακτυλίδι πον ζητείς.

Where is it, where is (it), the ring
Look for it, look for it, you will not find it.
You will not find it, you will not find it
The ring that you are looking (asking) for.

In $\frac{2}{\bullet.}$ meter you will often find this rhythm: ♩♪

$\frac{2}{\bullet.}$ ♩ ♩ ♩ ♪ |

poun   to   poun   to

Listen to the song. Identify the words in the song that have this rhythm. **Clap** the rhythm as you sing it.

175

Read a Song in 2/

Who is wearing buttons today? Tell what the meter is of this song. **Read** and clap the rhythm.

Button, You Must Wander

CD 9:2

American Singing Game

do

But - ton, you must wan - der, wan - der, wan - der,

But - ton, you must wan - der ev' - ry - where.

Bright eyes will find you, sharp eyes will find you.

But - ton, you must wan - der ev' - ry - where.

Sing the song and play the game.

MIDI

For another activity with "Button, You Must Wander," see *Spotlight on MIDI*.

176

This music has four French horns in it. The French horn is a member of the brass family.

"Pass" the beat as you **listen**. Gallop and then walk with the music. Which fits best? Is this music in $\frac{2}{4}$ or $\frac{2}{4}$?

LISTENING CD 9:5

La Choisy by Michel Corrette

THINK!

"Poun to, Poun to" and La Choisy are both in $\frac{2}{4}$ meter and use similar rhythms. How are they different?

CONCEPT
MELODY

SKILLS
LISTEN, READ,
IMPROVISE

LINKS
CULTURES,
READING

Read and Play Pentatonic

Zydeco is a kind of folk music found in southern Louisiana. It often uses pentatonic melodies. **Play** rhythm instruments with the beat as you listen.

 **LISTENING** CD 9:6

Bon Chien by Clifton Chenier

Some people work on shrimp boats along the coast of Louisiana. When the boats come in from the sea, people like to go to the dock to meet them.

Listen to this song about going to meet the shrimp boats.

LISTENING CD 9:7

Shrimp Boats by Paul Howard and Paul Weston

zydeco band ▼

Which lines in this song are alike?
Identify pitches in lines 3 and 4. **Read**
them with pitch syllables and hand signs.

SHRIMP BOATS

CD 9:8

Words and Music by
Paul Howard and Paul Weston

do

Shrimp boats is a - com - in', their sails are in sight.

Shrimp boats is a - com - in', there's danc - in' to - night.

Why don't you hur - ry, hur - ry, hur - ry home?

Why don't you hur - ry, hur - ry, hur - ry home!

Shrimp boats is a - com - in', there's danc - in' to - night.

A Song in Pentatonic

This little donkey is not feeling well. Can you help him? How many pitches are in this song?

MAP
UNITED STATES
LATIN AMERICA

El burrito enfermo

The Sick Little Donkey

CD 9:11

Latin American Folk Song
Arranged by José-Luis Orozco
English Words by Linda Worsley

do

Spanish: A mi bu - rro, a mi bu - rro
English: Lit - tle don - key, my don - key,

le due - le la ca - be - za,
my don - key has a head - ache.

y el mé - di - co le man - da
The doc - tor came and gave him

[Cumulative: for each new verse, add previous line]

u - na go - rri - ta ne - gra, [u - na go - rri - ta ne - gra]
a black cap for his head - ache, [a blackcap for his head - ache.]

y mue - ve las pa - ti - tas *(tap, tap, tap, tap).*
And now his lit - tle hooves go *(tap, tap, tap, tap).*

180

Read this bell part. Use pitch syllables and hand signs.

Play the bell part as you sing the song.

2. A mi burro, a mi burro
le duele la garganta,
y el médico le manda
una bufanda blanca,
una bufanda blanca,
una gorrita negra
y mueve las patitas
(tap, tap, tap, tap).

Little donkey, my donkey,
my donkey has a sore throat.
The doctor came and gave him
a white scarf for his sore throat,
a white scarf for his sore throat,
a black cap for his headache.
And now his little hooves go
(tap, tap, tap, tap).

3. A mi burro, a mi burro
ya no le duele nada,
y el médico le manda
trocitos de manzana,
trocitos de manzana,
una bufanda blanca,
una gorrita negra
y mueve las patitas
(tap, tap, tap, tap).

Little donkey, my donkey,
my donkey's feeling better.
The doctor came and gave him
some little bits of apple,
some little bits of apple,
a white scarf for his sore throat,
a black cap for his headache.
And now his little hooves go
(tap, tap, tap, tap).

Learn and Play Orff Instruments

CONCEPT
TONE COLOR
SKILLS
DESCRIBE, LISTEN, PLAY
LINKS
CULTURES, FINE ART

There are three kinds of Orff instruments. Each is made from a different material, so it has a different sound.

Carl Orff designed them. He wanted them to represent sounds from different parts of the world. He chose the xylophone from Africa. The metallophone came from Indonesia. He chose the glockenspiel from his own country, Austria. Look at the pictures and name the three types of Orff instruments.

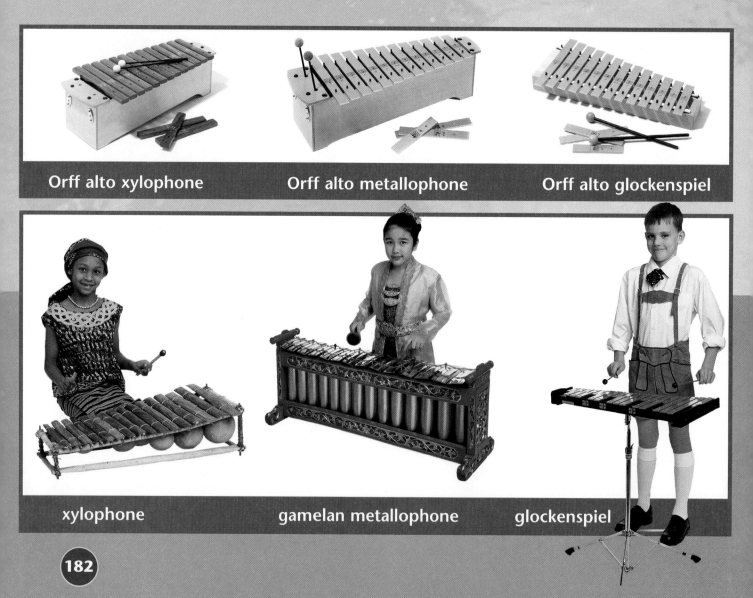

Orff alto xylophone   Orff alto metallophone   Orff alto glockenspiel

xylophone   gamelan metallophone   glockenspiel

Speak this to learn the names of Orff instruments.

By Donna Otto and Janet Graham

A Orff in - stru - ments! Orff in - stru - ments!

Learn a - bout each name, Then you can play a game!

B Xy - lo - phones have wood-en bars, wood-en bars, wood-en bars,

Xy - lo - phones have wood-en bars, Rose - wood bars. bars.

C Met - al - lo - phones have met - al bars, met - al bars, met - al bars,

Met - al - lo - phones have met-al bars, Gray met-al bars. bars.

D Glock - en - spiels have ti - ny bars, ti - ny bars, shi - ny bars,

Go back to A and repeat.

Glock - en - spiels have ti - ny bars, ti - ny, shi - ny bars.

Play with a Lullaby

A lullaby is soft music that can help you fall asleep. A *berceuse* is a kind of lullaby.

Listen to this berceuse. **Pat** the beat as you listen to feel the $\frac{2}{4}$ meter.

LISTENING   CD 9:21

Berceuse by Gunild Keetman

Meet the Musician

Gunild Keetman was a dancer and composer. She worked with Carl Orff. She enjoyed teaching music to children. Her knowledge of dance helped her find ways to use movement to learn.

Gunild Keetman with students ▼

Choose an instrument. **Play** this pattern softly with "Berceuse."

Playalong

THINK! What are things to think about when choosing an instrument to play with this music?

Art Gallery

Mother and Child
by Mary Cassatt

Mary Cassatt loved to paint mothers and children. Born in Pennsylvania, she studied painting in Europe. She became one of the most important American painters of her time.

CONCEPT
MELODY
SKILLS
READ, IMPROVISE, PLAY
LINKS
CULTURES

The frog in this song is from China. **Read** the first line of the song. Use pitch syllables and hand signs.

MAP

UNITED STATES   CHINA

I Chih Ching Wa
Frogs

CD 9:22

Chinese Folk Song
English Words by Linda Worsley

Chinese: 一 只 青 蛙 一 张 嘴 两 只 眼 睛 四 条 腿
English: Frog-gy has one mouth, you see. And two eyes, four legs has he.

乒 乒 乒 乒 跳 下 水 呀 青 蛙 不 吃 水
pin pong pin pong Jump_down, frog. The Frog-gy will not drink,

太 平 年 青 蛙 不 吃 水 太 平 年
When it's_ calm, Frog-gy will not drink. When it's_ calm,

青 蛙 向 水 里 跳 洗 个 痛 快 的 澡。
he will take a bath. Frog jumped in! Have a hap-py bath, Mis-ter Frog!

186

Improvise a melody to go with this frog poem. Use pentatonic pitches.

Do you want my little frog?
Could you please house and feed him?
It isn't that he isn't nice.
I guess I just don't need him!

Hazel Copeland

The instruments are from China.
Do they look like any you know?

CD-ROM

Use *World Instruments* **CD-ROM** to learn more about instruments in China.

yangquin ▶

◀ dizi

gu ▶

187

Play a Descant

Have you ever seen a wolf put his socks on?
Name the actions of the wolf in this song.
Practice the actions while speaking the Spanish
words. **Sing** the song.

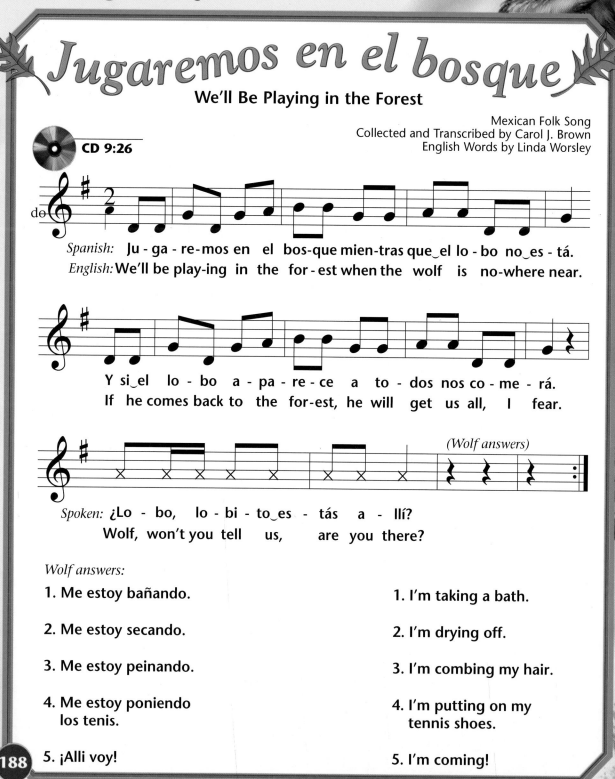

Jugaremos en el bosque
We'll Be Playing in the Forest

Mexican Folk Song
Collected and Transcribed by Carol J. Brown
English Words by Linda Worsley

CD 9:26

Spanish: Ju - ga - re - mos en el bos-que mien-tras que el lo - bo no es - tá.

English: We'll be play-ing in the for - est when the wolf is no-where near.

Y si el lo - bo a - pa - re - ce a to - dos nos co - me - rá.

If he comes back to the for-est, he will get us all, I fear.

(Wolf answers)

Spoken: ¿Lo - bo, lo - bi - to es - tás a - llí?

Wolf, won't you tell us, are you there?

Wolf answers:

1. Me estoy bañando.

2. Me estoy secando.

3. Me estoy peinando.

4. Me estoy poniendo
   los tenis.

5. ¡Alli voy!

1. I'm taking a bath.

2. I'm drying off.

3. I'm combing my hair.

4. I'm putting on my
   tennis shoes.

5. I'm coming!

188

A *descant* is a higher part that goes along with a melody. Name the pitches in this descant. **Play** the descant with the song.

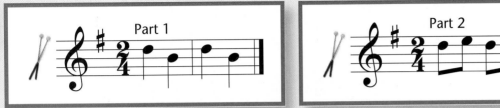

Part 1

Part 2

CONCEPT
INSTRUMENTAL
TONE COLOR
SKILLS
SING, LISTEN,
DESCRIBE
LINKS
HISTORY

Dela is wearing something special
in this song. What is it?

What Did Delaware?

CD 9:32

American Folk Song

1. What did Del - a - ware? Oh, what did Del - a - ware?
   wore her New Jer - sey. She wore her New Jer - sey. She

What did Del - a - ware? Oh, what did Del - a - ware?
wore her New Jer - sey. She wore her New Jer - sey. She

What did Del - a - ware? Oh, what did Del - a - ware? I
wore her New Jer - sey. She wore her New Jer - sey. I

ask you as a friend of mine. What did Del - a - ware? She
tell you as a friend of mine. She wore her New Jer - sey.

2. Why did Caliphone ya?   She phoned to say "Hawaya."
   Why did Caliphone? . . .   Phoned to say "Hawaya." . . .
   I ask you as a friend of mine, I tell you as a friend of mine.
   Why did Caliphone?   She phoned to say "Hawaya."

To slide up or down very fast in music is called *glissando*.

Listen for glissandos in this music. Pretend you are playing a trombone as you listen.

🔘 **LISTENING** CD 10:1

Lassus Trombone by Henry Fillmore

Meet the Musician

Henry Fillmore was a composer from Cincinnati, Ohio. He wrote a lot of band music. He liked the slide trombone. He even played it with a circus at one time.

Dixieland band ▼

Learn About Dixieland Bands

Dixieland music is an early type of jazz. It started in the African American communities of New Orleans. Dixieland was played for parties, parades, weddings, and even funerals.

The musicians improvise, or make up, melodies and rhythms while they are playing. Most bands have a cornet, a clarinet, a trombone, a tuba, and drums. Other instruments such as a banjo, a saxophone, a string bass, and a piano are also often used.

191

Ride with a Trombone

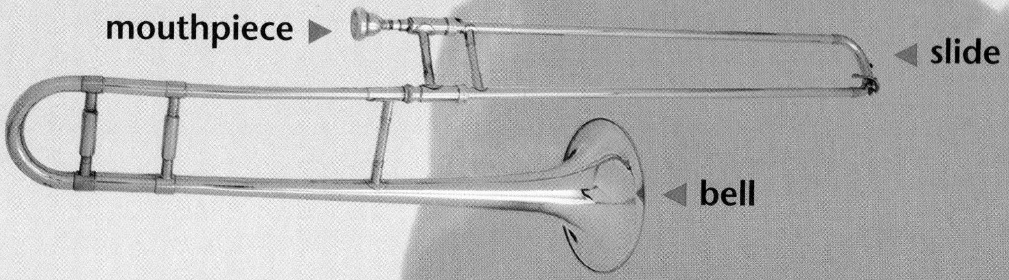

mouthpiece ▶   ◀ slide

◀ bell

The trombone is a large brass instrument. Only the tuba sounds lower than the trombone.

Different pitches can be created by making the lips tighter or looser. Different pitches are also created by moving the slide to different positions.

You are about to hear the trombone in a concerto. First, **listen** to this music and learn how to ride!

LISTENING   **CD 10:2**

Motorcycle Ride by Bruce Haack and Esther Nelson

Listen to hear what makes
this music unusual.

CD-ROM

Use *Orchestral Instruments*
CD-ROM to learn more
about the trombone and
other brass instruments.

LISTENING CD 10:3

Motorbike Concerto
by Jan Sandström

Listen and follow the map.

Listening Map for *Motorbike Concerto*

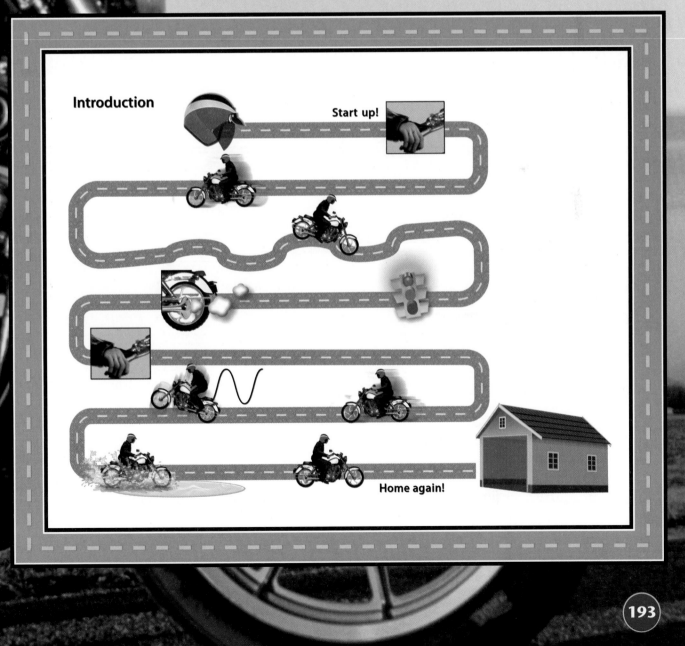

Introduction

Start up!

Home again!

Read and Move to *Do Re Mi So La*

CONCEPT
MELODY

SKILLS
READ, SING

LINKS
DANCE, READING

What does it mean to "jim along"? Let's jim, tiptoe, jog, and jump along with this song. **Read** the first four lines of this song. Use pitch syllables and hand signs.

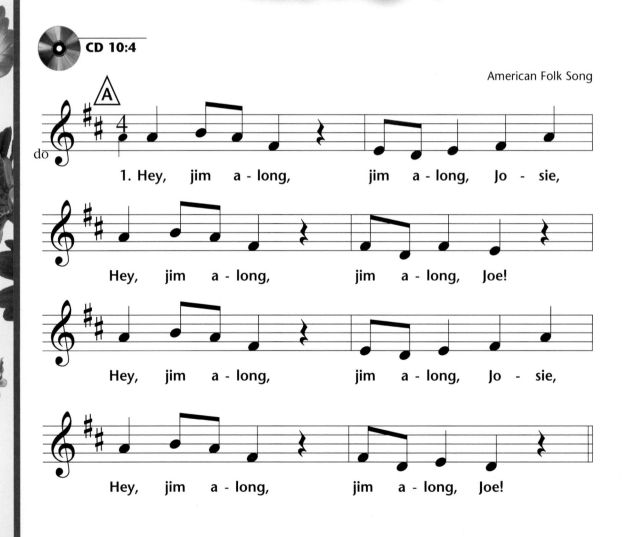

Jim Along, Josie

CD 10:4

American Folk Song

1. Hey, jim a - long, jim a - long, Jo - sie,

Hey, jim a - long, jim a - long, Joe!

Hey, jim a - long, jim a - long, Jo - sie,

Hey, jim a - long, jim a - long, Joe!

Sing the song and move to it.

A Section ▼

B Section ▲

Read the poem. Then **compose** a melody for the poem using *do, re, mi, so,* and *la.* End the first two lines on *so* for the musical question. End the last two lines on *do* for the musical answer.

Happy Thoughts

The world is so full
  of a number of things,
I'm sure we should all be
  as happy as kings.

Robert Louis Stevenson

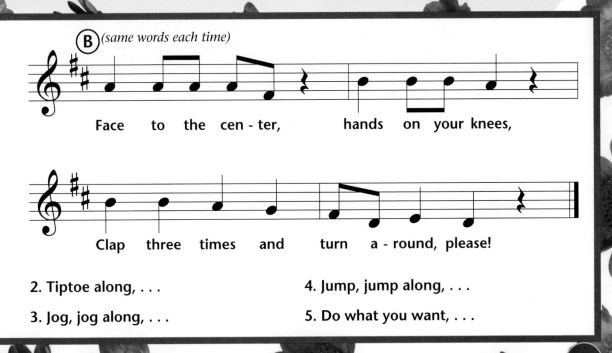

B *(same words each time)*

Face to the cen-ter, hands on your knees,

Clap three times and turn a-round, please!

2. Tiptoe along, . . .

3. Jog, jog along, . . .

4. Jump, jump along, . . .

5. Do what you want, . . .

Sing with Pitch Syllables

Singing can brighten any day.

Sing! Sing! Sing!

CD 10:7

Music and Words by Branice McKenzie

Swing

Verse

1. I'm talk-ing to the trees and birds, things a - round the u - ni-verse.
2. I'm walk-ing, skip-ping, run-ning free, el - e-phants can talk to me.

Sing, Sing, Sing.—

Clouds and flow - ers rain - y days,
My heart and mind can al - ways see,

love them all___ just the same.
all the good things here in me.

Sing, Sing, Sing.—

When-
It

ev - er I am feel-ing low, I take my smile and go, go, go.
is - n't just a luck - y chance___ that the peo-ple want to dance.

Sing, Sing, Sing.—

Ne - ver will I be a - fraid,
Re-mem-ber can and ne - ver can't,

Sing the pitches for each *Sing, Sing, Sing* from the song. Are the pitches always the same each time? Sing the song. Use pitch syllables and hand signs for each *Sing, Sing, Sing*.

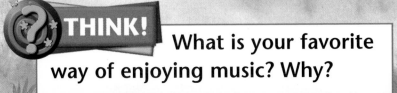

THINK! What is your favorite way of enjoying music? Why?

mu - sic I can al - ways make. }
spread your wings and ne - ver land. } Sing, Sing, Sing.___

Refrain

Let's all just sing, make me mu - sic, make me hap - py.___

Let's all just sing, make me ma - gic.___ Sing, Sing, Sing.___

197

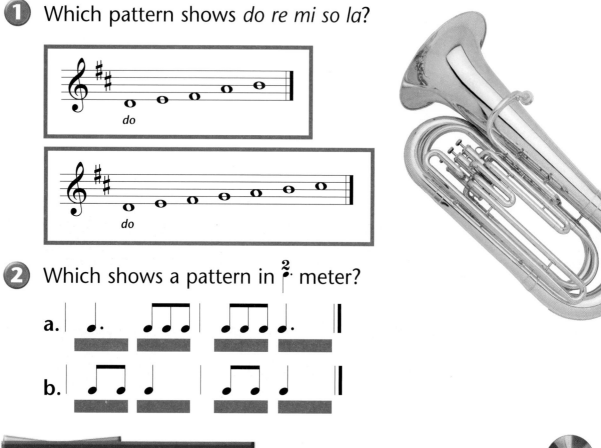

Spotlight Your Success!

REVIEW

1 Which pattern shows *do re mi so la*?

do

do

2 Which shows a pattern in ²/⁴· meter?

a.

b.

READ AND LISTEN

Read these patterns, then **listen** to identify.

1 Which pattern is in ²/⁴· meter?

a.

b.

2 Which pattern uses *do re mi so la*?

a.

b.

THINK!

1 If you composed a melody about a galloping pony, would you use $\frac{2}{4}$ or $\frac{2}{4}.$ meter? Why? What brass instrument would you choose to play your melody about the pony? Why?

2 List the favorite music and songs in this unit. Create a class graph that shows how many chose each piece. **Write** about the favorite piece and why you think it was chosen.

CREATE AND PERFORM

In groups, **create** a performance of "The Elephant Carries a Great Big Trunk" with a narrator, movement, and instruments.

Tell:
- Your choice of rhythms.
- Your choice of instruments.
- Things you did well and those that need work.

Perform your piece.

Music News

Meet the Musician
ON NATIONAL RADIO!

Name: Rebecca Brown
Age: 9
Instrument: Guitar
Home Town: Chicago, Illinois

Nine-year-old Rebecca Brown loves to practice her guitar. "I practice in the morning, after school, and before I go to bed," she says. "I play guitar if I'm happy or sad, frustrated or glad!"

Rebecca learns to play a song first by listening to it on a recording. Then she tries to play the song on her guitar. Rebecca's teacher works with her to correct any mistakes.

Playing guitar is Rebecca's favorite thing to do, but she also likes to read books and draw pictures. She has won her school's spelling bee two years in a row!

LISTENING CD 10:11–14 *RECORDED INTERVIEW*

Packington's Pound (Anonymous)
and **Allegro** by Mauro Giuliani

Listen to Rebecca's performance and interview on the national radio program **From the Top**.

"Singing together makes us reach deeply into our hearts and lets us know these feelings will stay there for our whole lives," explains Peter Yarrow.

Mr. Yarrow has been singing folk music for many years with his friends Paul Stookey and Mary Travers. In 1963 they sang "Blowin' in the Wind" at the Civil Rights March on Washington, D.C. They told the world that America's unfairness to African Americans had to end.

Today Mr. Yarrow works on "Project Respect," a program to help children grow up in a safe world without name-calling and mean-spirited teasing. The song "Don't Laugh at Me" is the program's anthem. It reminds people to care for and respect one another. Mr. Yarrow knows that songs of truth can make the world a more peaceful place.

Spotlight on the Bass Drum

Did You Know?

Drums have been around for more than 6,000 years.

The bass drum can sometimes be as large as the person playing it.

When a bass drum is played in an orchestra, it stands on its side on a rack. The player strikes the head with a large stick, or *beater*.

LISTENING   CD 10:15–16

Batik by Linda Worsley

The Rite of Spring by Igor Stravinsky

Listen for the bass drum. It is played softly in "Batik" except when new instruments are added. In "*The Rite of Spring*," eleven very loud sounds are played on the bass drum before a wild dance begins.

Everything Grows

You can grow
in many ways,
including playing,
listening, composing,
and singing music.

Coming Attractions

Sing in a moon boat in pentatonic.

Create a rondo with hand jive.

Step, skip, and leap with animals from a rain forest.

Everyone and everything grows.
Find things on the page that grow.
Find them in the song.

What is the form of the song?

Everything Grows

CD 10:17

Music by Raffi
Words by Raffi and D. Pike

Ev - 'ry-thing grows and grows._____

Ba - bies do, an - i - mals too. Ev - 'ry-thing grows.

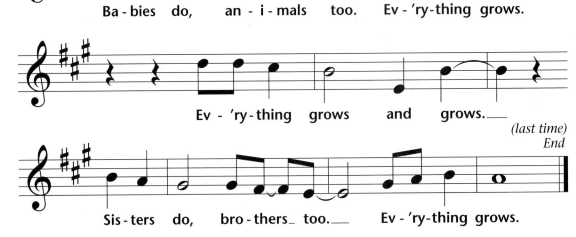

Ev - 'ry-thing grows and grows._____

(last time)
End

Sis - ters do, bro - thers_ too._____ Ev - 'ry-thing grows.

Verse

1. A blade of grass,___ fin-gers and toes,___
2. Food on the farm,___ fish in the sea,___

Hair on___ my head, a red, red rose.
Birds in___ the air, leaves on the tree.

Go back to the beginning and sing to the End.

Ev-'ry-thing grows, an-y-one knows_ that's_ how_ it goes.

Rhythm in the Seasons!

CONCEPT
RHYTHM
SKILLS
NOTATE, CREATE, SING
LINKS
SCIENCE, FINE ART

Fall, winter, spring, summer!
Which is your favorite season?

Sing about a seed's journey.
What is the meter of this song?

Seeds and Seasons

CD 10:20

Words and Music by Jim Walters

Verse

do

1. When a show - er breaks o - ver the mea - dow,
2. And the wa - ter will whis - per the se - cret,
3. Then a shoot will grow in - to the sun - shine,

And the thun - der is heard on the plain,
It is time for the seed - ling to grow.
Reach - ing up for the heat and the light.

Ev - 'ry seed that in win - ter was sleep - ing
Ti - ny roots will reach down to the wa - ter,
Through the stem it will lift up the wa - ter,

Will a - wak - en and swell in the rain.
Tak - ing life from the warm earth be - low.
So the leaves will grow stur - dy and bright.

Read this poem. Pick four vegetables from the poem and **write** their rhythms.

from LITTLE SEEDS

Little seeds we sow in spring,
growing while the robins sing,
give us carrots, peas and beans,
tomatoes, pumpkins, squash and greens.

Else Holmelund Minarik

Refrain

And the sea-son will cir-cle, will cir-cle a-round,

And the sea-son will cir-cle a-round.

4. And the leaves blow and dance in the summer,
   Growing hardy and strong in the sun,
   Using nutrients, sunlight, and water,
   To make food until summer is done.
   Refrain

5. In the summer there may come a blossom,
   Where the bees find the nectar they need,
   Never knowing they carry the pollen,
   So the blossom can make a new seed.
   Refrain

6. Then at last when the leaves begin changing,
   Then the seed will fall into the ground.
   It will sleep in the meadow all winter,
   To awake when the spring comes around.
   Refrain

A Gardening Song in 2

Have you ever eaten a tortilla? Tortillas are flat bread. They are served at most meals in Mexico. This song is about growing corn to make tortillas. **Read** the rhythm. Practice the actions in the song.

MAP
UNITED STATES
MEXICO

LA BELLA HORTELANA

The Beautiful Gardener

CD 10:23

Traditional Mexican Song
English Words by Linda Worsley

Verse

do

Spanish: Cuan - do siem - bra, la be - lla hor - te - la - na,
English: When she goes sow - ing, the beau - ti - ful farm - er,

cuan - do siem - bra, siem - bra a - sí.
When she goes sow - ing, she sows just like this.

A - sí siem - bra po - co a po - co,
She sows the seeds,_____ lit - tle by lit - tle,

Cumulative

lue - go po - ne las ma - nos a - sí
then she holds both her hands just like this,

Siem - bra a - sí
Sow - ing like this.

Peasants by Diego Rivera

Diego Rivera was an artist from Mexico. He painted many pictures that show life in Mexico. The men in this picture are farming.

Clap these rhythms.

Name vegetables that match each rhythm.
Create a two-beat rhythm pattern using two of these vegetables. Clap your pattern during the Refrain of the song.

End

Lue - go po - ne las ma - nos a - sí.
Then she holds both her hands just like this.

Refrain

La, la, la, la, la, la, la, la, la.

Go back to the beginning and sing to the End.

La, la, la, la, la, la, la, la, la.

2. Cuando riega ...
3. Cuando corta ...
4. Cuando muele ...
5. Cuando come ...

2. When she goes watering
3. When she goes reaping
4. When she is grinding
5. When she is eating

CONCEPT
MELODY
SKILLS
READ,
LISTEN
LINKS
SCIENCE, FINE
ART, READING

Almost everyone enjoys seeing flowers growing wild. Yellow buttercups bloom in the spring in many parts of North America.

Art Gallery

Ranunculus by Charles Belle

Charles Belle is a French artist who likes to paint things found in nature. Ranunculus is the name of a group of flowers. One type is the buttercup.

Read this song. Use pitch syllables and hand signs.

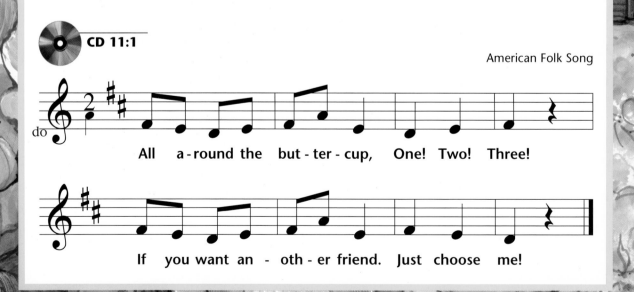

ALL AROUND THE BUTTERCUP

CD 11:1

American Folk Song

All a-round the but-ter-cup, One! Two! Three!

If you want an-oth-er friend. Just choose me!

Sing each part with pitch syllables.
Play both patterns as you sing the song.

This music is about a day on a farm. **Listen** and tell what you think is happening on the farm.

LISTENING CD 11:4

The Farm

by Eugene Zador

Tell a Story on *Do Re Mi So*

Read this poem about a loyal friend.
Who is the friend?

Bliss

Let me fetch sticks,
Let me fetch stones,
Throw me your bones,
Teach me your tricks.

When you go ride,
Let me go run,
You in the sun,
Me at your side;

When you go swim,
Let me go too
Both lost in blue
Up to the brim;

Let me do this,
Let me do that—
What you are at,
That is my bliss.

Eleanor Farjeon

What do you think the boy is
saying to the dog?

Art Gallery

A Boy and His Dog
by Norman Rockwell

**Norman Rockwell is a well-known
American artist. He painted
scenes of everyday American life.**

Read the pitches in this song. Who is Blue?

OLD BLUE

CD 11:5

Southern Mountain Song

1. I had a dog and his name was Blue,
2. Chased that___ pos-sum up a hol - low tree,
3. Caught that___ pos-sum up a hol - low tree,
4. Baked that___ pos - sum___ good and brown,

I had a dog and his name was Blue,
Chased that___ pos-sum up a hol - low tree,
Caught that___ pos-sum up a hol - low tree,
Baked that___ pos - sum___ good and brown,

I had a dog and his name was Blue, and I
Chased that___ pos-sum up a hol - low tree,_____
Caught that___ pos-sum up a hol - low tree,_____
Baked that___ pos - sum___ good and brown,_____

bet - cha five dol - lars he's a good dog, too.
Best___ hunt-in' dog___ you___ ev-er did see.
Best___ hunt-in' dog___ you___ ev-er did see.
Laid___ sweet po-ta - ters___ all a - round.

Here, Blue, you good dog, you.

213

LESSON
3

CONCEPT
RHYTHM
SKILLS
READ,
PLAY
LINKS
READING,
SOCIAL STUDIES

Read and Play with a ♩ Bounce!

Skip and gallop to this song.
Be your favorite animal!

Animal Fair

CD 11:8

American Folk Song

I went to the an - i - mal fair,

The birds and the beasts were there.

The big ba - boon, by the light of the moon,

was comb - ing his au - burn hair.

Read the pattern below using animal names.
Play the pattern on any rhythm instrument as you sing the song.

Playalong

You ought to have seen the monk;

He climbed up the el - e - phant's trunk.

The el - e - phant sneezed and fell on her knees,

and what be - came of the monk?

At Sea and at the Barber's in ²₄

Have you ever gone to sea?

Read the rhythm of this song. Find the words that rhyme.

Play this pattern ♫♫ ♩. on *sea*, *me*, and *three* as you sing the song.

Going Over the Sea

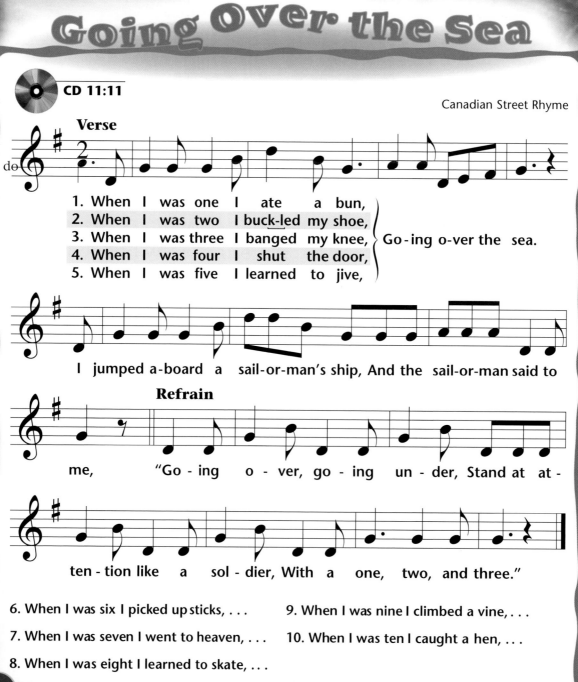

CD 11:11

Canadian Street Rhyme

Verse

1. When I was one I ate a bun,
2. When I was two I buck-led my shoe,
3. When I was three I banged my knee, } Go-ing o-ver the sea.
4. When I was four I shut the door,
5. When I was five I learned to jive,

I jumped a-board a sail-or-man's ship, And the sail-or-man said to

Refrain

me, "Go - ing o - ver, go - ing un - der, Stand at at -

ten - tion like a sol - dier, With a one, two, and three."

6. When I was six I picked up sticks, . . .   9. When I was nine I climbed a vine, . . .

7. When I was seven I went to heaven, . . .   10. When I was ten I caught a hen, . . .

8. When I was eight I learned to skate, . . .

What does a barber do? *The Barber of Seville* is an opera about a smart and funny barber. His name is Figaro.

When one person sings a solo in an opera, it is called an **aria**. In this aria Figaro sings about how busy he is. People are always ordering him around.

Figaro in
The Barber of Seville

Fi - ga - ro quà
Fi - ga - ro here

Read this pattern. Raise your hand when you hear this rhythm pattern in the aria.

 LISTENING CD 11:14

Largo al factotum from
Il Barbiere di Siviglia
(The Barber of Seville)
by Gioachino Rossini

See music.mmhschool.com to research opera.

CONCEPT
MELODY
SKILLS
IMPROVISE,
NOTATE, SING
LINKS
SCIENCE,
CULTURES, DANCE

The moon can look different at different times of the month. Some people think the moon looks like a boat.

Read this poem. Speak it again as you **play**. **Improvise** using *do re mi so* and *la*.

LOG ON
See music.mmhschool.com to research Korean music.

Moon Boat

Moon Boat, little, brave and bright,
Tossed upon the seas of night,
One day when I'm free to roam,
I'll climb aboard and steer you home.

Charlotte Pomerantz

Art Gallery

The Sun Rises While the Moon Sleeps
by Peter Davidson

This song describes the way a crescent moon in Korea looks like a boat sailing in the sky.

MAP

UNITED STATES   KOREA

BAN DAL

Half Moon

CD 11:15

Words and Music by Keuk Young Youn
English Words by Linda Worsley

Korean: 푸른 하늘 은 — 하 수 하얀 쪽 배 엔
English: Sky of blue, and glit-ter-ing moon, Lit - tle boat so white;__

계 수 나 무 한 — 나 무 토 끼 한 마 리
On your hull a cin-na-mon tree, sail-ing through the night.__

돛 대 도 아 니 달 고 삿 대 도 없 이
On your bow, a rab-bit runs, lit-tle boat so high,__

가 기 도 잘 도 간 다 서 — 쪽 나 라 로
With-out a sail or rud-der, tra-vel-ing through the sky.___

219

Step Back with *Do Re Mi So* and *La*

Move down the "alley" as you sing this song.
What pitches are in this song? Write them.

Here Comes Sally

CD 11:19

African American Folk Song

With a gentle swing

do

1. Here comes Sal - ly, Sal - ly, Sal - ly,
2. Step back Sal - ly, Sal - ly, Sal - ly,
3. Com-ing down the al - ley, al - ley, al - ley,
4. Here comes an-oth-er one, just___ like the oth-er one,

Here comes Sal - ly all___ night long.
Step back Sal - ly all___ night long.
Com-ing down the al - ley all___ night long.
Here comes an-oth-er one, all___ night long.

1 **Sing** and **move** with the song. Pick a partner and form an "alley." Swing your arms with the beat on the first verse.

2 Step back and clap with the beat on the second verse. One person moves down the alley.

3 Continue clapping and singing. The other partner moves down the alley on the third verse.

CONCEPT
FORM
SKILLS
ANALYZE,
SING, LISTEN
LINKS
SCIENCE

Shoo the flies away as you **listen** to this song.
What is the form of the song?

In music a **fermata** tells you to hold
the note longer.

Find the ⌢ in the song. **Sing** the song.

CD 11:22

American Folk Song

Shoo, fly,   don't both - er me,   Shoo, fly,   don't both - er me,

Shoo, fly,   don't both - er me, For   I   be-long to some-bod-y.

I   feel, I feel, I   feel,   I   feel like a morn-ing star,

I   feel, I feel, I   feel, I feel, I   feel like a morn-ing star.

Some music has different sections between each A section. The name of this form is **rondo**. One kind of rondo form is ABACA.

The form of "Shoo Fly" is ABA. **Create** a rondo by adding a C section to "Shoo, Fly." **Perform** a speech piece with a hand jive to create a new C section.

Hand Jive

1st	2nd	3rd	4th
cool wave	hitch hike	champ cheer	catch a fly

THEN...

1 CATCH A FLY.

2 LOOK AT IT.

3 LET IT GO.

4 WAVE GOODBYE.

A Oh, Shoo, fly, don't both - er me, Shoo, fly, don't both - er me,

Shoo, fly, don't both - er me, For I be - long to some-bod-y.

Piano Music in Rondo Form

You have to practice many hours to become a great musician. Evgeny Kissin is a very talented classical pianist.

Meet the Musician

Evgeny Kissin was born in Moscow, Russia, in 1971. He began to play the piano when he was two years old. He has performed all over the world.

RECORDED INTERVIEW CD 11:25

Listen to Evgeny Kissin talk about playing the piano.

THINK! What do you think helped Evgeny Kissin become a great pianist?

Did you ever get really angry over losing something? In this music someone is angry because he or she lost a penny. This music is in rondo form.

 **LISTENING** CD 11:26

Rondo a capriccio (Rage over a Lost Penny) by Ludwig van Beethoven

Follow the map as you **listen**.

Listening Map for Rondo a Capriccio

A   B   A   C   A

Listen again. **Move** to show the different sections of ABACA form.

Meet the Musician

Ludwig van Beethoven is considered one of the greatest composers who ever lived. Beethoven's father was a singer and musician and was Ludwig's first teacher. Beethoven was only 12 when he wrote and published his first music. He began to lose his hearing when he was 30. Even though he could not hear his pieces performed, Beethoven could hear the music in his head. He composed some of his greatest works after he was completely deaf.

CONCEPT
INSTRUMENTAL TONE COLOR

SKILLS
ANALYZE, SING, LISTEN

LINKS
CULTURES

You can find many instruments at the market in San Juan, Puerto Rico.

What instruments do you hear in this song? How is the sound of each instrument different?
Sing the song.

MAP

UNITED STATES   PUERTO RICO

En la feria de San Juan

In the Market of San Juan

CD 11:27

Puerto Rican Folk Song
English Version by MMH

Verse

Spanish: En la fe - ria de San Juan, yo com - pré un pi -
English: In the mar - ket of San Juan, I_____ bought my - self a

Cumulative

tí - o, pi - ti, pi - ti, pi - ti, el pi - tí - o.
whis - tle, *(whistle the melody)*———————— the whis - tle.

Refrain

Ven - ga_u - sted, ven - ga_u - sted, a la fe - ria de San Juan,
Come with me, come with me, to the mar - ket of San Juan.

Ven - ga u - sted,   ven - ga u - sted,   a   la   fe - ria   de   San   Juan.
Come with me,   come with   me,   to   the   mar-ket   of   San   Juan.

2. En la feria de San Juan
   yo compré un tambor.
   Ton, ton, ton, el tambor, . . .

   In the market of San Juan
   I bought myself a drum.
   Tum, tum, tum, tum, the drum . . .

4. yo compré un violín,
   Lin, lin, lin, el violín, . . .

   I bought a violin,
   Lin, lin, lin, the violin, . . .

3. yo compré una guitarra,
   tara, tara, tara, la guitarra . . .

   I bought a guitar,
   tara, tara, tara, the guitar . . .

Meet the Orchestral Instrument Families

The instruments of the orchestra are grouped in families. The families are **woodwinds**, **brass**, **strings**, and **percussion**. **Listen** to instruments from each family. Point to each instrument when you hear it.

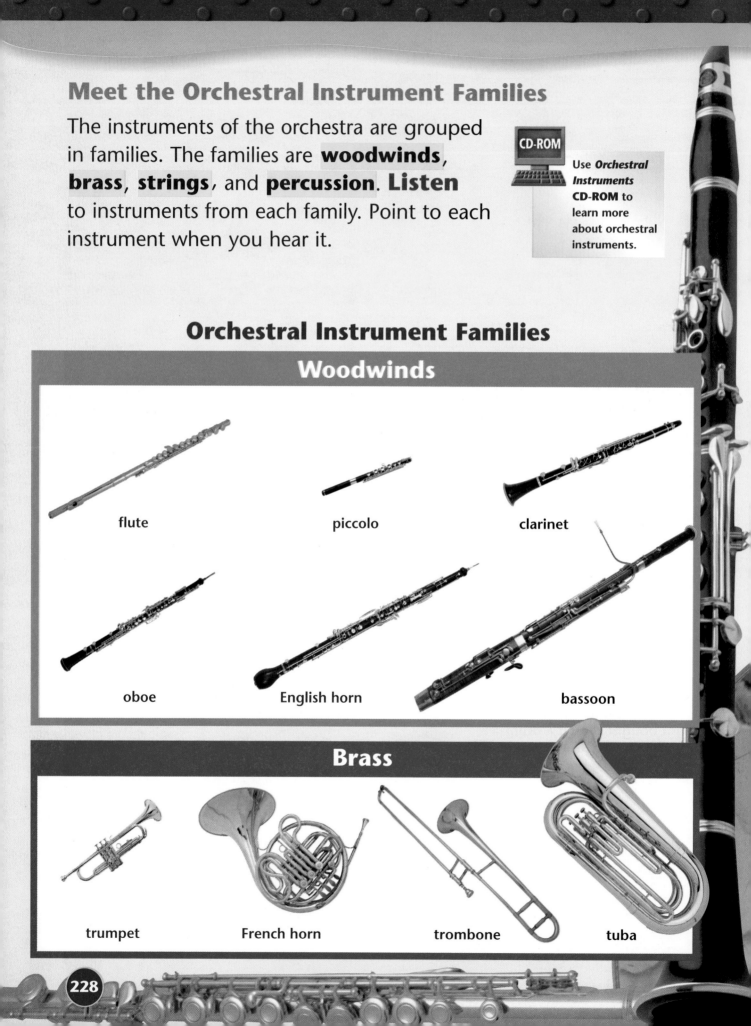

CD-ROM

Use *Orchestral Instruments* **CD-ROM** to learn more about orchestral instruments.

Orchestral Instrument Families

Woodwinds

flute

piccolo

clarinet

oboe

English horn

bassoon

Brass

trumpet

French horn

trombone

tuba

Find each instrument family on these pages as you **listen** to this music.

LISTENING CD 12:1

Young Person's Guide to the Orchestra
by Benjamin Britten

THINK! How are the instruments in each family alike? How are they different?

Strings

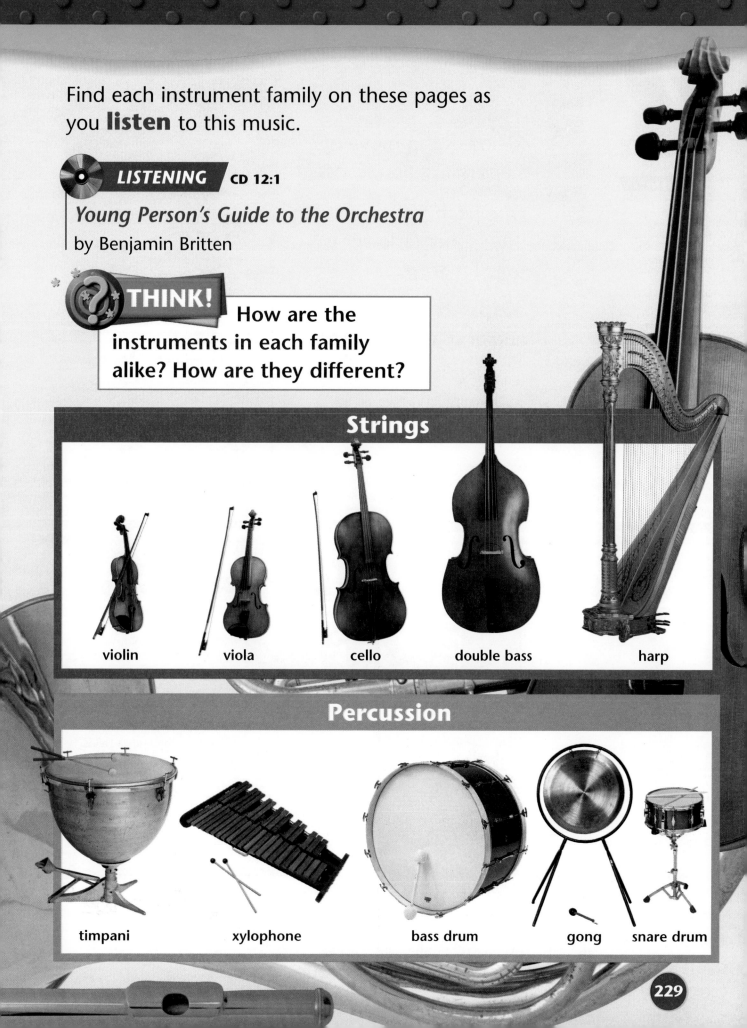

violin   viola   cello   double bass   harp

Percussion

timpani   xylophone   bass drum   gong   snare drum

229

Steps, Skips, and Leaps

CONCEPT
MELODY

SKILLS
LISTEN, SING, CREATE

LINKS
CULTURES, READING, SCIENCE

Melodies can move by steps, skips, and leaps.

One pitch to the next one higher or lower is called a **step**.

Skips are from line to line or space to space.

Any jump larger than a skip can be called a **leap**.

Find a step, skip, and leap in this Native American song. **Sing** the song.

NIKOSI

Bluebirds

 CD 12:2

Hopi Children's Song
As Sung by Angela Fields

Hopi: **ah   ah   ni - ko - si   ah   ah   ni - ko - si**

At the end of 2nd time song is sung in the story, pitches are spoken, in a faster tempo.

ah   ah   ni - ko - si   ah - ah   ni - ko - si   ah   ah   ah   ah   ah

This song is part of the Hopi story "Coyote and the Bluebirds." **Listen** to the story and **sing** the song.

LISTENING CD 12:4

Coyote and the Bluebirds Hopi Children's Story as told by Angela Fields

Follow the story pictures as you listen.

Learn About the Hopi Nation

The Hopi are a group of Native Americans who live in northern Arizona. They have always lived in the dry land of Arizona and farming is an important part of their lives.

The Hopi are well known for making beautiful woven baskets, pottery, paintings, and silver jewelry.

Skips and Leaps in the Rain

Rain forests are very thick, wet forests. It rains almost all the time in rain forests. Rain forests are filled with trees, plants, and animals.

"La lluvia" means "the rain" in Spanish. **Listen** to two main melodic ideas in this music. Which moves in leaps and which moves in steps?

a.

b.

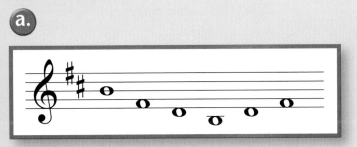

Listen to *La lluvia*. Tell what you hear.

🔘 **LISTENING** CD 12:5

La lluvia by Stephen Hatfield

Listen to the music again. **Move** as a rain-forest animal with steps, skips, or leaps.

Meet the Musician

Stephen Hatfield is a composer from British Columbia, Canada. He was raised near a rain forest. This music is about a rain forest.

Sing this song about rain.

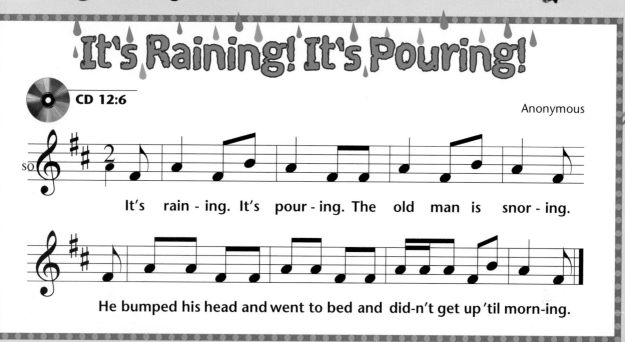

It's Raining! It's Pouring!

CD 12:6

Anonymous

It's rain-ing. It's pour-ing. The old man is snor-ing.

He bumped his head and went to bed and did-n't get up 'til morn-ing.

Create a "Rain Rondo." Use "It's Raining! It's Pouring!" for the A section. Choose one song below for the B section and one song for the C section.

1

Alto Xylophone

Rain on the green grass and rain on the tree.

Rain on the house-tops, but not on me!

2

Bass Xylophone

Rain be - fore sev - en will

clear by e - lev - en.

Play instruments and sing your "Rain Rondo."

The Shape of the Melody

CONCEPT
MELODY
SKILLS
LISTEN,
DESCRIBE, SING
LINKS
CULTURES,
SCIENCE,
READING

Global Voices

This is a song that children in Ghana, Africa, like to sing. "Tue Tue" is the name of a rice dish. **Listen** and **move** to show the shape of this music.

MAP

UNITED STATES   GHANA   UGANDA

LISTENING CD 12:9

Tue Tue collected by Akosua Addo

Tue Tue Maria Tue Tue
Tue Tue Maria Tue Tue
Abosom daa, Ama na wa ye
Tue Tue
Abosom daa, Ama na wa ye
Tue Tue la la la

Learn to speak Akan:

Good morning.	Mema wo akye.
Good-bye.	Nante yie.
My name is ...	Me din de ...
Thank you.	Meda wo ase.
You are welcome.	Yenni aseda.

This song is from Uganda, Africa. **Move** to show the shape of the melody as you listen.

🔘 **LISTENING** CD 12:10

Mwiji Mwena

Traditional African spiritual sung by the African Children's Choir

Clap with the beat as you **listen** again. Clap four beats to the right, then four beats to the left.

African Children's Choir

The Shape of Growing Things

Have you ever planted a flower garden? Are the lines in this painting of flowers curved or straight?

Art Gallery

Irises by Vincent van Gogh

Vincent van Gogh was a painter from the Netherlands. He painted this picture of irises in a flower garden in France.

Sing this song about a garden. **Show** the shape of the melody with your hands.

Garden Song

CD 12:11

Words and Music by David Mallett

1. Inch by inch, row by row,___
2. Pull - in' weeds and pick - in' stones,_
3. Plant your rows straight and long,___

Gon - na make this gar - den grow,___
We are made of dreams and bones,
Temp - er them with prayer and song,

All it takes is a rake and a hoe
Feel the need to___ grow my___ own
Moth - er Earth will___ make you___ strong,

and a piece of fer - tile ground.___
'cause the time is close at hand.___
if you give her love and care.___

Inch by inch, row by row,___
Grain for grain, sun and rain,___
Old crow watch-ing hun - gri - ly___

Some - one bless the seeds I sow,
Find my way in na - ture's chain,
From his perch in yon - der tree.

Some - one warm them from be - low___
Tune my bod - y and my brain___
In my gar - den I'm as free___

'til the rain comes tum - bl - ing down.
to the mu - sic from___ the land.
as that feath - ered thief___ up there.

Spotlight Your Success!

1 Which shows the pitches in a pentatonic scale?

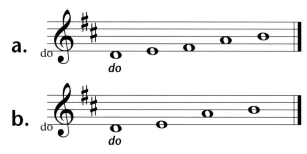

a.

b.

2 Which rhythm shows three sounds to a beat in $\frac{2}{}$?

a. ♩ ♩ ♩   b. ♪ ♪ ♪   c. 𝅗𝅥 𝅗𝅥 𝅗𝅥

READ AND LISTEN

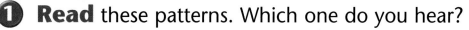

1 **Read** these patterns. Which one do you hear?

a.

b.

2 **Read** these patterns. Which one do you hear?

a.

b.

THINK!

1. Tell what an aria is and how it is different from a folk song.

2. Name the four instrument families. Pick two and tell how they are alike and different.

3. **Choose** a song you liked in this unit. Write about why you liked it.

CREATE AND PERFORM

1. Create a pattern two measures long.

   • Write in $\frac{2}{4}$ meter.

   • Use only *so* and *la*.

2. **Play** your pattern as you sing "All Around the Buttercup."

Spotlight on Music Reading

Spotlight on Music Reading

Spotlight on Music Reading

Quarter Notes and Eighth Notes

Read the rhythm. Play a game about stirring chocolate.

MAP

UNITED STATES

MEXICO

Bate, Bate

Stir, Stir

CD 12:15

Mexican Game

Spanish: **Ba** - te, ba - te, cho - co - la - te,

Con ar - roz y con to - ma - te.

U - no, dos, tres, { CHO, CO,

U - no, dos, tres, { LA, TE,

Cho - co - la - te, cho - co - la - te,

Cho - co - la - te, cho - co - la - te.

So and *Mi*

Sing these pitches. Follow the hands up and down.

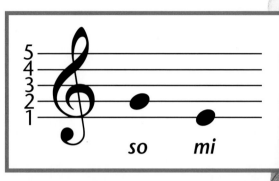

so   mi

Read the whole song with pitch names.
Sing it with the words.

so   so

mi   mi

so   so

mi

SAY YOUR NAME

CD 12:19

Music by Marilyn Copeland Davidson
Words by Sue Snyder

Say your name and when you do,

We will say it back to you.

Play the game!

Read and Listen for *So* and *Mi*

Sing *so* and *mi* in this song in a new place.

Cuck-   oo,   where are you?   Here I   am,   where are you?

Cuckoo, Where Are You?

CD 12:22

American Singing Game
Words Adapted by MMH

Group   *Solo*

so

Cuck - oo,   where are you?   Here   I   am,   where are you?

LISTENING   CD 12:25

Im Krapfenwaldl (In Krapfen Woods), Op. 336
by Johann Strauss, Jr.

Listen and point to each section as you hear it.
Move when you hear the cuckoo call, *so-mi*.

so mi

A   B   A

Start   a b a   c d   Start again   a b a   Coda

244

UNIT 1 READING

CONCEPT
MELODY
SKILLS
READ, SING

So-Mi Games and the Silent Beat

Read these pitches.
Sing each song and play the games.

Hey, Hey, Look at Me

CD 12:26

American Singing Game
Words Adapted by MMH

Hey, hey, look at me, Make your-self look just like me.

so   mi   so so   mi

In and Out

CD 12:29

American Folk Song

In and out, 'Round a - bout.

O - U - T and that spells out!

Listen for *So* and *Mi*

Name three of your favorite outdoor games.
Read these melodies from "Children's Dance."

Play a game! Let's play a game now!

Come, play! Come and play with me!

Like to play Hide and Seek!

How are the melodies alike?
How are they different?
Give each melody a game name.
Listen to the three melodies.
Identify each melody as you listen by
pretending to play that game.

 **LISTENING** CD 12:32

"Children's Dance" from *Merry Mount*
by Howard Hanson

Listen for these melodies in "Children's Dance."

Identify games in the painting.

Art Gallery

Games

Hand Stands
Blind Man's Bluff
Hoop Game
Riding Barrels
Leap Frog
Get the Hat
Tug-of-War
Odds and Evens

Children's Games by Pieter Brueghel

Pieter Brueghel liked to paint everyday people having fun. Some of the games in this painting are listed here.

Read these game rhythms.

Leap Frog, Tug-of-War, Odds and E-vens, Hoop Game.

Choose games from the list.
Create a song using *so* and *mi*.

UNIT
2 READING

CONCEPT
MELODY
SKILLS
READ, SING

Sing with *La*

Find *la* in this song.

so

la

la

Read the pitches of this song.
Sing the song with the words.

Plainsies, Clapsies

CD 12:33

American Folk Song

so

Plain - sies,   clap - sies,   twirl a - round to   back - sies,

Right hand,   left hand, stretch it high,   stoop it   low,

Touch your knee, touch your toe, touch your heel and 'round you go.

Sing the *mi-la* leaps in these songs.

Red Rover

CD 12:36

American Singing Game

mi la   *mi la*

Ro - ver, Red Ro - ver,   Send { 1. Ja - son / 2. Jen - nie } o - ver.

Little Sally Water

CD 12:39

African American Folk Song

Lit - tle Sal - ly Wa - ter,   sit - ting in a   sau - cer,

Rise Sal - ly, rise Sal - ly, wipe a - way your tears, Sal - ly.

Turn to the east, Sal - ly, Turn to the west, Sal - ly.

Turn to the one that you love the best, Sal - ly.

Beats with No Sound

Find the beats with no sound.
Read the rhythm of the song.
Say "yum-my" for ♫
Say "treat" for ♩

Sing the song.

Eating Lizards

CD 12:42

Words and Music by Carol Huffman

Bil - ly Iz - zard ate some liz - ards. Tossed their tails in

gar - bage pails. Bil - ly's broth - er ate an - oth - er.

Got in trou - ble with his moth - er.

No more liz - ards for the Iz - zards!

Find ⅀ in the song.
Sing the song and solve the riddles.

Riddle Song

CD 12:45

Words and Music by
Marilyn Copeland Davidson

Refrain

Rid - dles   are such fun!   Can   you   tell me one?

Verse

1. I   have   let - ters,   one   two   three,
2. 'Til   I'm   meas - ured,   I'm   not   known,

Add   two   more   and   few - er there will   be.
But   you'll   miss   me   when a - way I've flown.

Step the rhythm of the first line of "Riddle Song."
Bend forward on measures 1 and 3.
Bend back on measures 2 and 4.

Now you know part of a folk dance from Bolivia.

LISTENING CD 13:1

Carnavalito (Bolivian folk dance) performed
by the Shenanigans

Move your feet as you listen to "Carnavalito."
Stay still on each ⅀

251

CONCEPT
MELODY
SKILLS
READ, SING

Sing with *Do*

Do, mi, and *so* all sit on lines or in spaces.

do

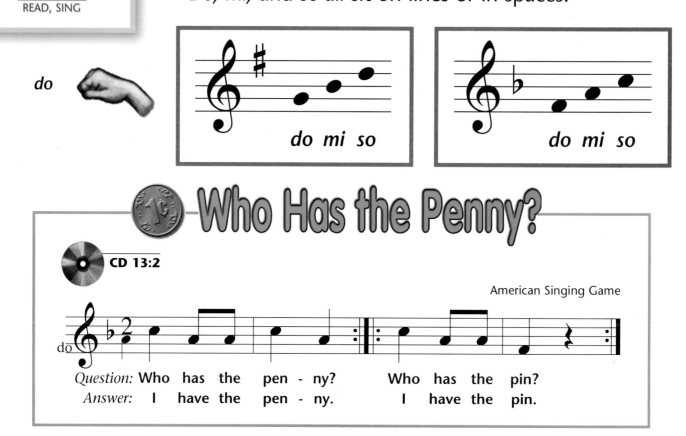

do mi so

do mi so

CD 13:2

American Singing Game

Question: Who has the pen - ny? Who has the pin?
Answer: I have the pen - ny. I have the pin.

CD 13:5

American Folk Song

Heigh ho, here we go,

Up and down and high and low. We're

rid - ing on a see - saw.

Sing a *mi-do* cuckoo call.

mi   do

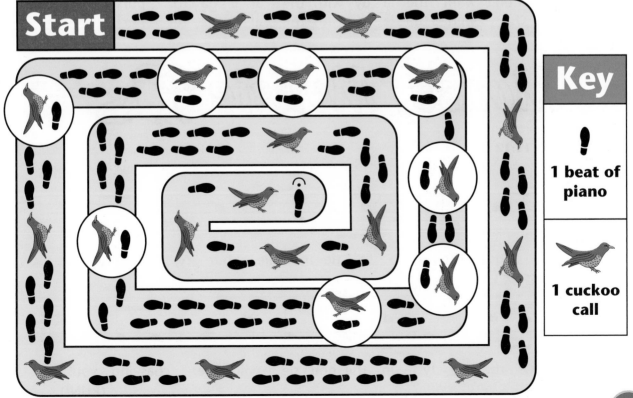

🔘 **LISTENING**   CD 13:8

Cuckoo in the Heart of the Woods from
Carnival of the Animals by Camille Saint-Saëns

Listen to "Cuckoo in the Heart of the Woods."

Tap each footprint and cuckoo to follow the path.

Listening Map for
Cuckoo in the Heart of the Woods

Start

Key

1 beat of piano

1 cuckoo call

More Practice with *Do*

Both of these songs have *so, mi,* and *do.*

Read *so, mi,* and *do* then sing the songs.

Mother, Mother

CD 13:9

Swing (♫ = ♫)

American Jump Rope Game

do

1. Moth - er, Moth - er, I am sick.
2. In came the doc - tor, In came the nurse,
3. I don't want the doc - tor, I don't want the nurse,
4. Out went the doc - tor, Out went the nurse,

Call for the doc - tor Quick, quick, quick!
In came the la - dy with the al - li - ga - tor purse.
I don't want the la - dy with the al - li - ga - tor purse.
Out went the la - dy with the al - li - ga - tor purse.

Mouse, Mousie

CD 13:12

Hungarian Folk Song

do

Mouse, Mou - sie, lit - tle mou - sie, hur - ry, hur - ry do!

Or the kit - ty in the hou - sie will be chas - ing you!
(RUN!)

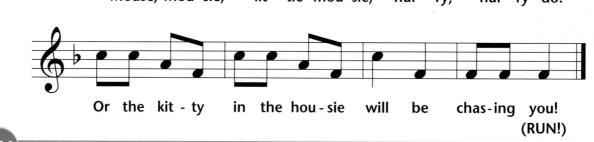

UNIT
3
READING

CONCEPT
MELODY
SKILLS
READ, SING

Sing with *La*

Find *la* on the staff, on the stairs, and in the song.
Read the pitches in this song.
Sing the song and play the game.

do   mi   so   la

la

la
so
mi
do

CD 13:15

American Singing Game

Daisy Chain

Chain,   chain,   dai - sy chain,   All the pret - ty   flow - ers,

One for you, and   one for me, and   one for Jen - ny   Bow - ers.

255

Read and Sing Half Notes

A half note ♩ is a sound that lasts for two beats.
♩♩ = ♩

Find the half notes in this song.
Read all of the rhythms and pitches.
Sing the song with the words.

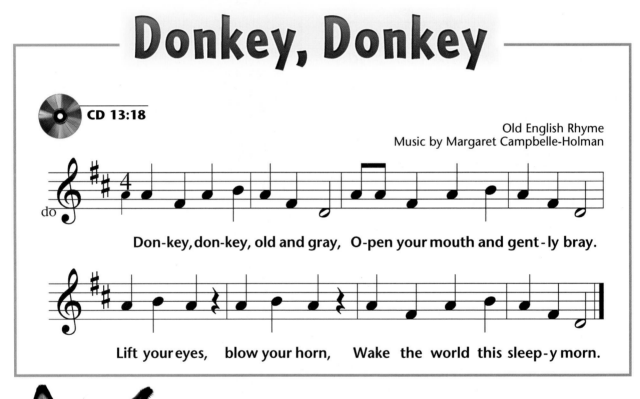

Donkey, Donkey

CD 13:18

Old English Rhyme
Music by Margaret Campbelle-Holman

Don-key, don-key, old and gray, O-pen your mouth and gent-ly bray.

Lift your eyes, blow your horn, Wake the world this sleep-y morn.

Say this pattern as others sing the song.

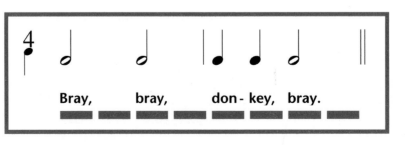

Bray, bray, don-key, bray.

Create your own donkey song using these rhythms and *do mi so la*.

UNIT 3 READING

CONCEPT
MELODY
SKILLS
READ, SING

Practice Reading *Do Mi So La*

Read the pitches. Sing these songs.

King's Land

CD 13:21

American Folk Song

do

I'm on the king's land, the king is not at home.

He's gone to Bos - ton, to buy his wife a comb.

MR. FROG

CD 13:24

American Singing Game

do

On a log, Mis - ter Frog sang a song the whole day long,

Glumph, Glumph, Glumph.

Sing with *Re*

Re is between *mi* and *do*. **Find** and sing the yellow *mi re do* patterns. **Read** the pitches and sing both songs.

re

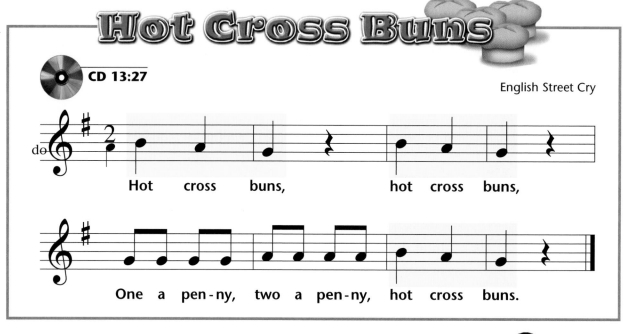

Hot Cross Buns

CD 13:27

English Street Cry

Hot   cross   buns,   hot   cross   buns,

One a pen-ny, two a pen-ny, hot cross buns.

Hop, Old Squirrel

CD 13:30

Virginia Folk Song

Hop,   old   squirrel,   Ei - dle dum,   ei - dle dum,

Hop, old squirrel,   Ei - dle dum, dee!   Ei - dle dum, dee!

Read *Mi Re Do*

This Japanese song is about a bottomless pot.
Read and sing these pitches and rhythms.

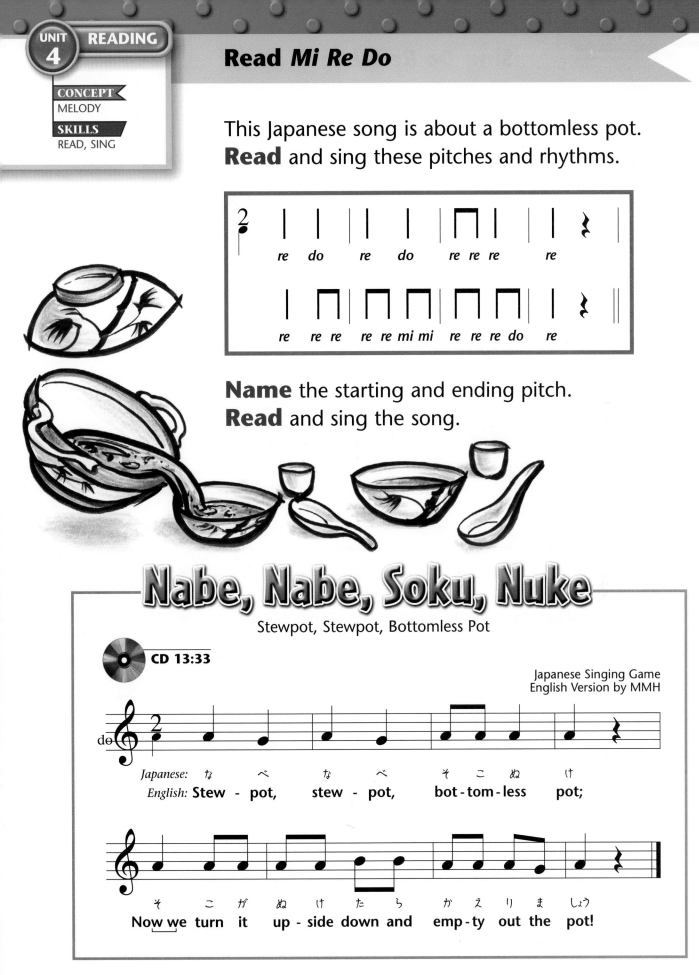

re do re do re re re re

re re re re re mi mi re re re do re

Name the starting and ending pitch.
Read and sing the song.

Nabe, Nabe, Soku, Nuke

Stewpot, Stewpot, Bottomless Pot

CD 13:33

Japanese Singing Game
English Version by MMH

Japanese: な べ な べ そ こ ぬ け
English: Stew - pot, stew - pot, bot - tom - less pot;

そ こ が ぬ け た ら か え り ま しょう
Now we turn it up - side down and emp - ty out the pot!

Sing *Do Re Mi So*

"Rover" is a dog's name.

Sing *do re mi so* up and down the stairs.

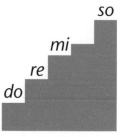

Find the half note.
Read the song with syllables then sing it.

Rover

CD 13:37

Music by Denise Bacon
Traditional English Rhyme

1. I have a dog, and his name is Ro - ver.
2. When he is good, he is good all o - ver.

He is the one I love the best.
When he is bad, he is just a pest.

Think of another name for a pet. Use it to sing the song again.

Sing *Do Re Mi So* Game Songs

Find *do re mi so* in both songs.

Find the half notes in the first song.

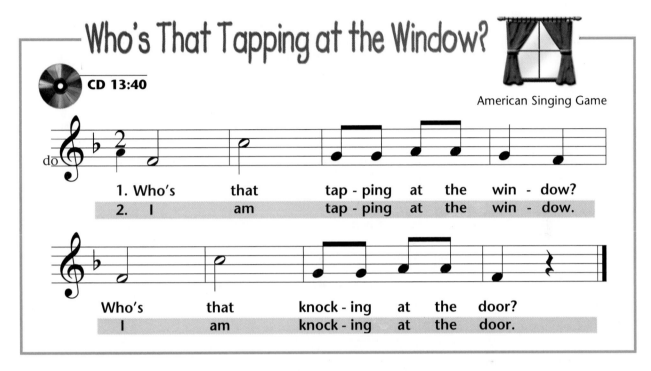

2. Quiero marchar, . . .
   I want to march, . . .

3. Quiero correr, . . .
   I want to run, . . .

261

Dotted Half Notes

𝅗𝅥. is a sound that lasts for 3 beats. ♩♩♩ = 𝅗𝅥.

Find the 𝅗𝅥. in this song. How many are there?

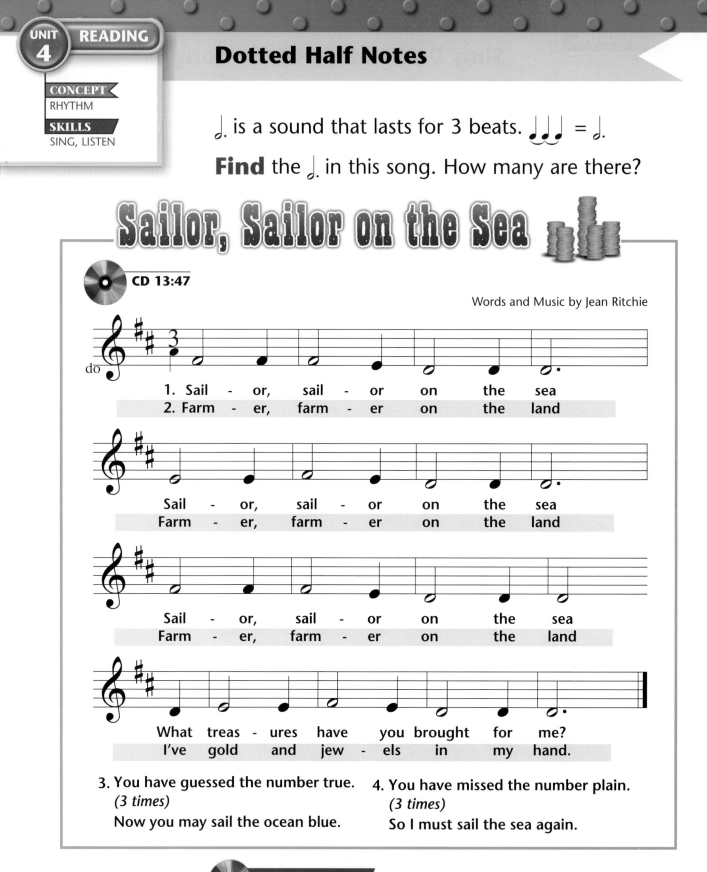

Sailor, Sailor on the Sea

CD 13:47

Words and Music by Jean Ritchie

do

1. Sail - or, sail - or on the sea
2. Farm - er, farm - er on the land

Sail - or, sail - or on the sea
Farm - er, farm - er on the land

Sail - or, sail - or on the sea
Farm - er, farm - er on the land

What treas - ures have you brought for me?
I've gold and jew - els in my hand.

3. You have guessed the number true.
   (3 times)
   Now you may sail the ocean blue.

4. You have missed the number plain.
   (3 times)
   So I must sail the sea again.

LISTENING   CD 13:50

Sérénade by Cécile Chaminade

Listen to "Sérénade" and sway on each strong beat.

A Pentatonic Song

Penta means five. *Tonic* means tones, or pitches. Pentatonic songs have five tones, or pitches. Sing up and down the pentatonic ladder. Say this pattern with the song.

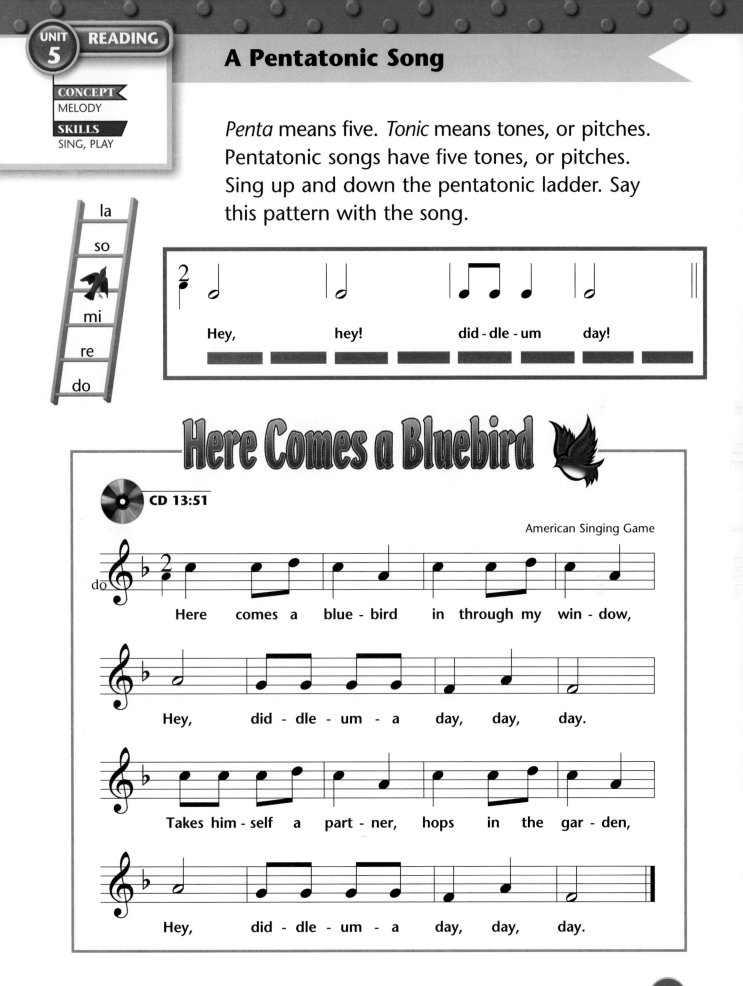

Hey,   hey!   did - dle - um   day!

Here Comes a Bluebird

CD 13:51

American Singing Game

Here comes a blue - bird in through my win - dow,

Hey, did - dle - um - a day, day, day.

Takes him - self a part - ner, hops in the gar - den,

Hey, did - dle - um - a day, day, day.

263

Pentatonic Pitches

Sing with pitch syllables then with words.

Dance Together

CD 14:1

American Folk Song

do

Dance to - geth - er one by one, two by two;

Live - ly mu - sic calls to me, calls to you.

Read and play this rhythm with the song.

Bow, Wow, Wow

CD 14:4

Mother Goose Rhyme

do

"Bow, wow, wow!" "Whose dog art thou?"

"Lit - tle Tom - my Tuck - er's dog. Bow, wow, wow!"

Read These Songs

Find the pitches and sing the songs.

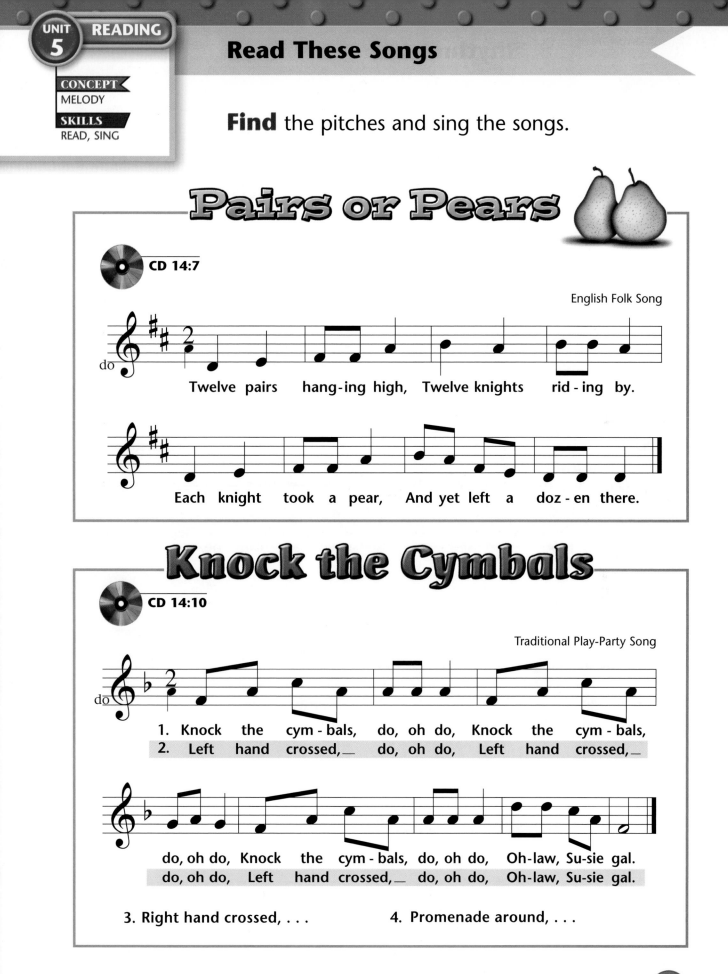

Pairs or Pears

CD 14:7

English Folk Song

Twelve pairs hang-ing high, Twelve knights rid-ing by.

Each knight took a pear, And yet left a doz-en there.

Knock the Cymbals

CD 14:10

Traditional Play-Party Song

1. Knock the cym-bals, do, oh do, Knock the cym-bals,
2. Left hand crossed,___ do, oh do, Left hand crossed,___

do, oh do, Knock the cym-bals, do, oh do, Oh-law, Su-sie gal.
do, oh do, Left hand crossed,___ do, oh do, Oh-law, Su-sie gal.

3. Right hand crossed, . . .   4. Promenade around, . . .

Rhythms in 𝄢2.

A dot after a note makes it longer.

In 2. each of these rhythms gets one beat.

Sing this song and play the game.

CD 14:13

American Folk Song

Solo

1. I see, as plain as can be,

Some-thing that starts with "P."_____ Pen - cil.

Solo

2. . . . "D." Desk.
3. . . . "R." Ruler.
4. . . . "T." Table.

LISTENING CD 14:19

Merry-Go-Round by Georges Bizet.

Listen for rhythms in 2.

Read in ²/. ·

Read and sing this pentatonic song in ²/. · meter.

Merry-Go-Round

CD 14:16

Music by Marilyn Copeland Davidson
Words by Dorothy Baruch

I climbed up on the mer-ry-go-round And
I climbed up on a big___ brown horse and

it went 'round and 'round.
it went up and down.

'Round and 'round and up and down, I sat high up on a

big brown horse And rode a-round on the mer-ry-go-round And

rode a-round on the mer-ry-go-round. I rode a-round on the

mer-ry-go-round, A-round and 'round and 'round.

Game Songs in $\frac{2}{\cdot}$ Meter

Read the rhythms of these songs in $\frac{2}{\cdot}$ meter.

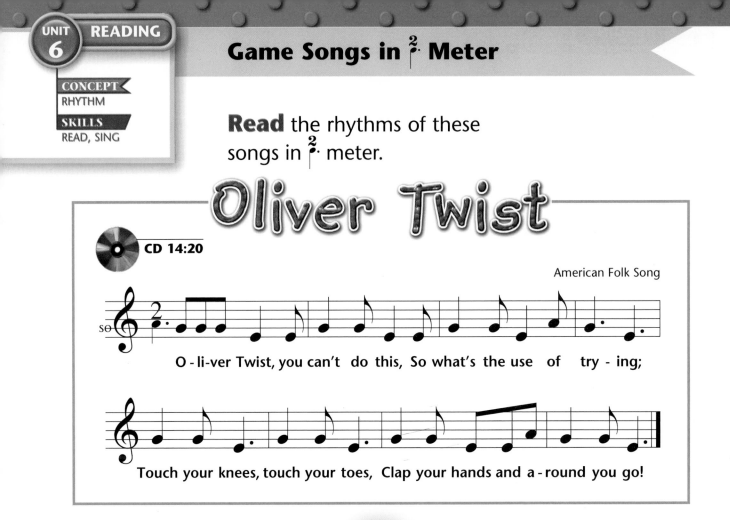

CD 14:20

American Folk Song

O - li-ver Twist, you can't do this, So what's the use of try - ing;

Touch your knees, touch your toes, Clap your hands and a - round you go!

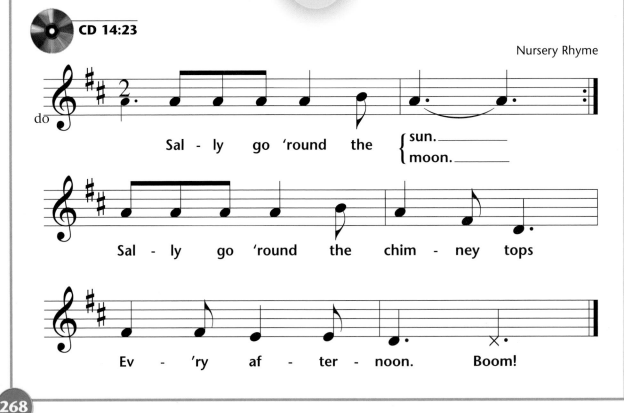

CD 14:23

Nursery Rhyme

Sal - ly go 'round the { sun._____ { moon._____

Sal - ly go 'round the chim - ney tops

Ev - 'ry af - ter - noon. Boom!

Listen for ⅜ Patterns

Gigue is the French word for jig. A jig is a quick dance in ⅜ meter.

 **LISTENING** CD 14:26

Gigue
by Johann Sebastian Bach

Listen for these ⅜ patterns and follow the listening map.

Listening Map for Gigue

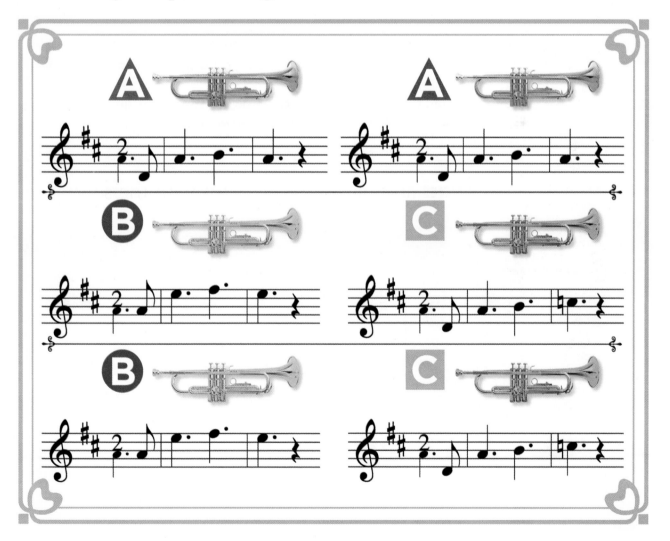

Read and Play 2. Rhythms

Sing this song and learn the game.

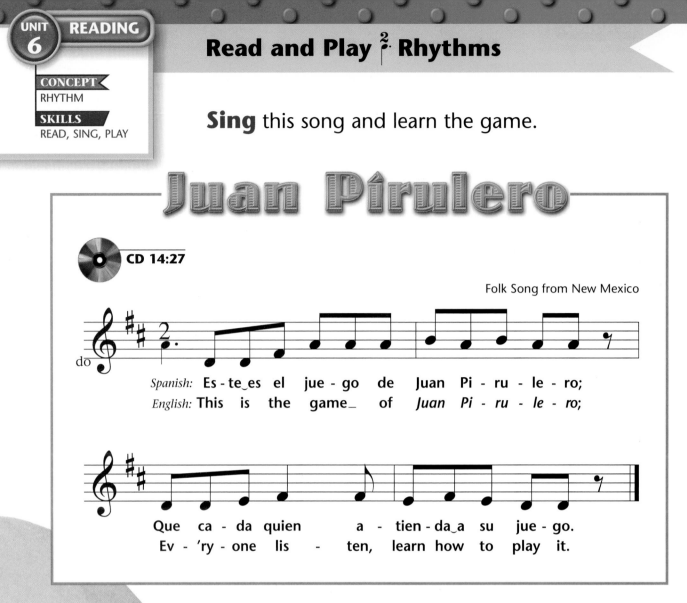

Juan Pírulero

CD 14:27

Folk Song from New Mexico

Spanish: Es - te es el jue - go de Juan Pi - ru - le - ro;
English: This is the game_ of *Juan Pi - ru - le - ro;*

Que ca - da quien a - tien - da a su jue - go.
Ev - 'ry - one lis - ten, learn how to play it.

Read and play these patterns with the song.

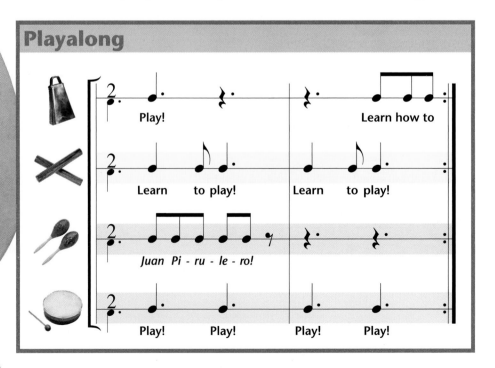

Playalong

Play!
Learn how to

Learn to play!
Learn to play!

Juan Pi - ru - le - ro!

Play! Play! Play! Play!

270

A Bird Sings in ♩.

Read this poem with rhythms.

♩.   ♫♫   ♩♪

I Heard a Bird Sing

I heard a bird sing,
In the dark of December
A magical thing
And sweet to remember,
"We are nearer to spring
Than we were in September."
I heard a bird sing in the dark of December.
— *Oliver Herford*

Create a melody for the poem,
using *do re mi so la.*
Who will sing the solo bird part?

Art Gallery

The Magpie by Claude Monet

271

Spotlight on Performance

Spotlight on Performance

Spotlight on Performance

Broadway For Kids

MTI's BROADWAY junior

SEUSSICAL

Mini musicals specifically designed for classroom study and presentation, featuring scenes and songs from the musical Seussical Junior.

ADMIT ONE 0596033

Music by Stephen Flaherty
Lyrics by Lynn Ahrens
Book by Lynn Ahrens and Stephen Flaherty
Co-Conceived by Lynn Ahrens, Stephen Flaherty, and Eric Idle
Based on the Works of Dr. Seuss

Musical Numbers

Oh, the Thinks You Can Think!

Horton Hears a Who!

Horton Hears a Who! Two

It's Possible

Green Eggs and Ham

Seussical Mega-Mix

About Rehearsals

You are about to begin rehearsals for a mini production of *Seussical Junior*. **Rehearsing** means learning and practicing something. Below are some words actors use during rehearsals.

Upstage

The area farthest away from the audience.

Stage right

The area to the actor's RIGHT as she or he faces the audience.

Stage left

The area to the actor's LEFT as she or he faces the audience.

Downstage

The area onstage closest to the audience.

About the Script

CHARACTER NAMES are colored **RED**

DIALOGUE is colored **BLUE**

STAGE DIRECTIONS are colored *GREEN*

Script

Scene: The World of Dr. Seuss

NARRATOR: It's great to learn something
new and exciting
So we'd like to present
something fun and inviting;
With rhymes running wild and
out on the loose,
Of course they were written
by—who?

KIDS: DR. SEUSS!

Oh, the Thinks You Can Think!

CD 14:31

Music by Stephen Flaherty
Lyrics by Lynn Ahrens

Oh, the Thinks you can think! Oh, the Thinks you can think

if you're will-ing to try.___ Think in-vis-i-ble ink!

Or a Gink with a stink! Or a stair to the sky!___

If you o-pen your mind, oh, the Thinks you will find

276

lin-ing up to get loose.... Oh, the Thinks you can think

when you think a - bout Seuss!

NARRATOR: *(To the KIDS)*
We'll take a few stories and
cook up a stew.
Which Dr. Seuss story
would you like to do?

KIDS (Group 1): "If I Ran the Zoo."

KIDS (Group 2): Or "Solla Sollew."

KIDS (Group 3): How about Horton who heard
the small Who?

NARRATOR: "Horton Hears a
Who!" is a
great idea.

CHILDREN: HURRAY!

(NARRATOR reads from a book.)

Helen Hayes Youth Theatre, Nyack, NY

NARRATOR: On the eleventh of May
In the Jungle of Nool
In the heat of the day
In the cool of the pool
He was splashing.

KIDS: Splash!

277

NARRATOR: Enjoying the jungle's great joys
When Horton the Elephant
Heard a small noise.

KID 1: Help! Help!

NARRATOR: So Horton stopped splashing.
He looked toward the sound.
"That's funny," thought Horton,
"There's no one around."
Then he heard it again!
Just a very faint yelp
As if some tiny person
    were calling for help.

KID 2: Help! Help!

NARRATOR: "I'll help you," said Horton,
"But who are you, and where?"
He looked and he looked.
He could see nothing there
But a small speck of dust
Blowing past, through the air.
"I say! How confusing! I've never
    heard tell
Of a small speck of dust
    that is able to yell.
So you know what I
    think? Why I
    think that there must
Be someone on top of that
    small speck of dust.
Some poor little person
    who's shaking with fear
That he'll blow in the pool!
He has no way to steer!"

KID 3: He's alone in the universe!

NARRATOR: And Horton the Elephant said:

Horton Hears a Who!

CD 14:32

I'll just have to save him be-cause af-ter all, a

per-son's a per-son, no mat-ter how small. A

per-son's a per-son, no mat-ter how small._____

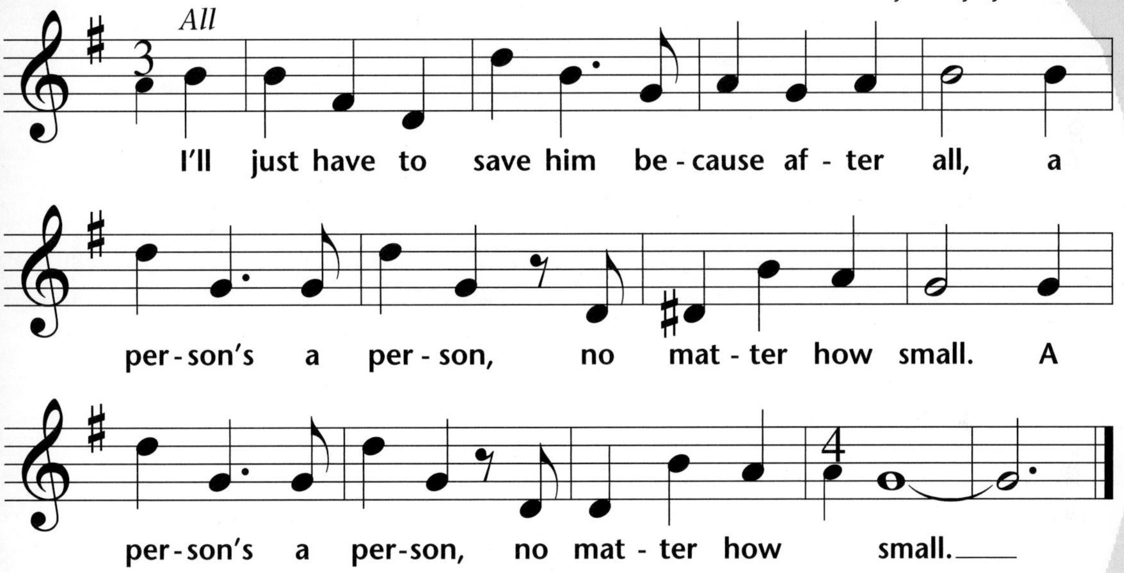

NARRATOR: So, gently and using the greatest
of care
The elephant stretched his great
trunk in the air
And he lifted the dust speck
and carried it over
And placed it down safe
on a very soft clover.

KIDS: Thank you!

NARRATOR: I won't let you down. No, I won't
let you fall.

279

Horton Hears a Who! Two

Music by Stephen Flaherty
Lyrics by Lynn Ahrens

I'll just have to save him be-cause, af - ter all, a per-son's a per-son, no mat - ter how small. A per-son's a per-son, no mat - ter how small.___ Whooo...!

NARRATOR: Now open your minds—you've got quite a tool.
Let's all take a dive in McElligot's pool.

It's Possible

Music by Stephen Flaherty
Lyrics by Lynn Ahrens

All

This might be a pool, like I've read of in books, con-

nec-ted to one of those un-der-ground brooks! An

un-der-ground riv - er that starts here and flows right

Kid 4   *All*

un - der the bath - tub! And then... who knows? It's

pos-si-ble. An-y-thing's pos-si-ble! It

might go a - long down where no one can see, right

un - der State High - way Two - Hun-dred-and - Three! Right

un - der the wag - ons! Right un-der the toes of

More

281

Kid 5 ... *All*

Mis-sus Um-bro - so who's hang-ing out clothes! It's pos-si-ble.___

An - y-thing's pos - si - ble!_____ This

might be a riv - er, now might-n't it be, con -

nec-ting Mc - El - li-got's pool___ with the sea! Then

may-be some fish___ might be swim-ming, swim-ming toward me!___

Oh, the sea is so full___ of a

num-ber of fish. If a fel-low is pa - tient, he might get his wish! And

that's why I think_ that I'm not such a fool when I

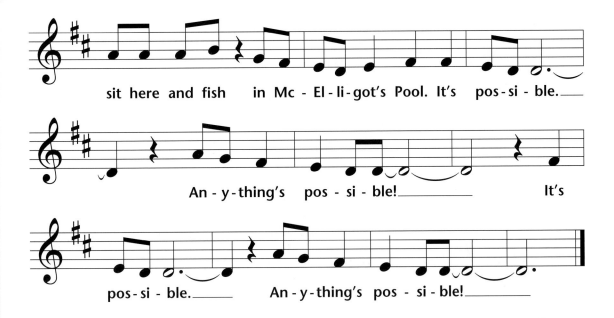

sit here and fish in Mc-El-li-got's Pool. It's pos-si-ble.____

An-y-thing's pos-si-ble!_____ It's

pos-si-ble.____ An-y-thing's pos-si-ble!_____

NARRATOR: What have we learned so far from Dr. Seuss?

KID 6: A person's a person, no matter how small.

KID 7: Anything's possible.

KID 8: I hate green eggs and ham?

NARRATOR: How did you learn that? We haven't had green eggs and ham.

KIDS (Group 1): Let's have them now!

KIDS (Group 2):
(Pinching their noses) Yuck!

Helen Hayes Youth Theatre,
Nyack, NY

283

Green Eggs and Ham

CD 14:35

Music by Stephen Flaherty
Lyrics by Lynn Ahrens

Group 2

I do not like green eggs and ham._ I

do not like them Sam-I - Am._ I do not like them

here or there._ I do not like them an-y-where. Not

in a house. Not with a mouse. Not here or there. Not

an-y-where. I do not like green eggs and ham! I

Group 1

do not like them, Sam - I - Am! Could_

NARRATOR: *(To audience)* That was a
wonderful story, I say,
But that's all the time that we
have for today.
All kinds of wonderful lessons
were taught
Filling our thinkers with barrels
of thought.
And just to be sure that his
poetry sticks
Let's all sing a big Dr. Seuss
Mega-Mix.

Helen Hayes Youth Theatre, Nyack, NY

Seussical Mega-Mix

CD 14:36

Music by Stephen Flaherty
Lyrics by Lynn Ahrens

Oh, the Thinks you can think! Oh, the Thinks you can think

if you're will-ing to try.___ Think in-vis-i-ble ink!

Or a Gink with a stink! Or a stair to the sky!___

If you o-pen your mind, oh, the Thinks you will find

lin-ing up to get loose...___ Oh, the Thinks you can think

when you think a-bout Seuss!

I'll just have to save him be-cause, af-ter all, a

per-son's a per-son, no mat-ter how small. A per-son's a

per-son, no mat-ter how small.

Oh, and that's why I think__ that I'm

not such a fool When I sit here and fish in Mc-

El - li-got's Pool. It's pos - si - ble!_____ An - y-thing's

pos - si - ble!_____ I

do not like green eggs and ham.__ I do not like them

Sam-I - Am.__ I do not like them here or there.__ I

do not like them an - y-where. Not in a house. Not

with a mouse. Not here or there. Not an-y-where. I

do not like green eggs and ham! I do not like them,

Sam-I-Am! Seuss! Seuss!

Seuss! I do not like green eggs and ham!

⭐ CURTAIN CALL

Meet the Musicians

Lynn Ahrens and **Stephen Flaherty** are the composers of *Seussical*. They have written many different Broadway musicals. Their musicals have won many awards. They also composed the music for the movie *Anastasia*. When Lynn and Stephen decided to compose *Seussical*, they took ideas from many different Dr. Seuss stories. They put them together and created a great new Broadway show!

Disney Favorites

Do you have a favorite Disney song? It is not easy to choose! Here are five Disney songs you might know.

THE GREAT OUTDOORS

CD 14:49

Words and Music by
George Wilkins

If ya just been wish-in' 'bout go-in' fish - in' and you're

still on the shore,___ grab your camp-in' gear___ and

meet us right here, got all kinds a fun in

store. It's time for a va-ca - tion, for some

rest and re-lax-a - tion. For-get your cares 'n'

290

The Country Bears

"Hakuna Matata" is a song from the movie *The Lion King*. In Swahili *hakuna matata* means "no worries." In the movie, Timon and Pumbaa become good friends with Simba. Friends can always help you cheer up.

HAKUNA MATATA

CD 15:1

from the movie
The Lion King

Music by Elton John
Lyrics by Tim Rice

Ha - ku - na ma - ta - ta,

what a won - der - ful phrase!

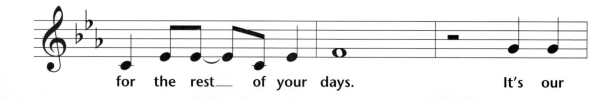

Ha - ku - na ma - ta - ta, ain't no pass - ing

2nd time to Coda

craze. It means no wor - ries

for the rest___ of your days. It's our

prob-lem - free___ phi - los - o - phy.___

D.C. al Coda

Ha - ku - na ma - ta - ta._____

Coda

It means no wor-ries for the rest___ of your

days. It's our prob-lem - free___

phi - los - o - phy.___

Ha - ku - na ma - ta - ta._____

Ha - ku - na ma - ta - ta.

In the song "Part of Your World," a young mermaid named Ariel wants to leave the sea and live on land. Did you ever wonder what it would be like to live in a different world? If you lived underwater, you could be friends with sea animals like an octopus and a starfish!

Part of Your World

from the movie *The Little Mermaid*

CD 15:4

Music by Alan Menken
Lyrics by Howard Ashman

run,   up where they   stay   all   day   in   the

sun.   Wan - der - in'   free,   wish   I   could

be   part of that world.   Up where they

world.   Out of the   sea,   wish I could

be   part of that   world._____

295

CONCEPT
MELODY
SKILLS
SING

Everyone has someone special that he or she can count on. It might be a friend, a relative, or even a pet. When times are tough, you can be a special person for someone else, too.

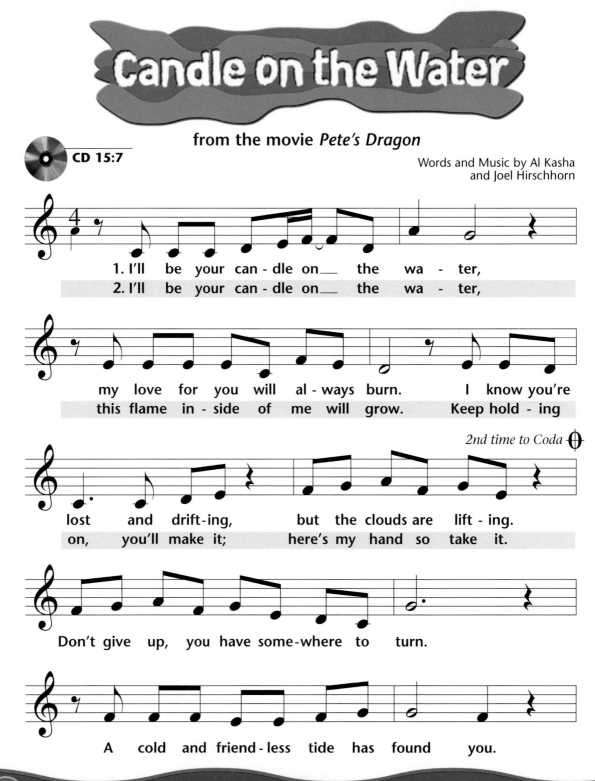

Candle on the Water

from the movie *Pete's Dragon*

Words and Music by Al Kasha
and Joel Hirschhorn

CD 15:7

1. I'll be your can-dle on___ the wa - ter,
2. I'll be your can-dle on___ the wa - ter,

my love for you will al - ways burn. I know you're
this flame in - side of me will grow. Keep hold - ing

2nd time to Coda

lost and drift-ing, but the clouds are lift - ing.
on, you'll make it; here's my hand so take it.

Don't give up, you have some-where to turn.

A cold and friend - less tide has found you.

Don't let the storm-y dark-ness pull you down.

I'll paint a ray of hope a-round you,

D.C. al Coda

cir-cling in the air, light-ed by a prayer.____

Coda

Look for me reach-ing out to show, as sure as riv-ers

flow, I'll nev-er let you go.

I'll nev-er let you go. I'll nev-er let you go.

297

CONCEPT
MELODY
SKILLS
SING

"It's a Small World" is one of the best-known Disney songs. It reminds you that people may look different on the outside, but they share many of the same feelings.

It's a Small World

CD 15:10

Words and Music by Richard M. Sherman
and Robert B. Sherman

Verse

Sing 3 times

It's a world of laugh - ter, a world of

tears; it's a world of hopes and a

world of fears. There's so much that we

share, that it's time we're a - ware, it's a

small world af - ter all.

Zoo-Rific!

Have you ever been to a zoo?
Let's take a trip to a musical
zoo. We will see birds, bats,
horses, elephants, and
even little crabs. It will
be zoo-rific!

SKILL BUILDER: Eye Contact and Posture

When you are standing on stage
at a concert, there are many
interesting things to watch. To
be a good performer, keep your
eyes on your teacher and stand
up straight.

When you sing, try to:

- Stand with your feet shoulder-
  width apart.
- Keep your back straight.
- Place your hands at your sides.

Let's stop first at the petting zoo. Four pretty white horses are standing in the barn. Here is a great song from the Caribbean we can sing for them!

Four White Horses

CD 15:13

Caribbean Folk Song
Collected by Lois Choksy

Four white hors - es on the riv - er,

Hey, hey, hey, up to - mor - row,

Up to - mor - row is a rain - y day.

Come on up___ to the shal - low bay.

Shal - low bay___ is a ripe ba - nan - a,

Up to - mor - row is a rain - y day.

CONCEPT
MELODY
SKILLS
SING

This zoo has many different kinds of birds. There are parrots, peacocks, ostriches, eagles, and ducks. One little bird is singing her song alone. Sing "Chíu, chíu, chíu" along with her song.

Chíu, chíu, chíu

CD 15:16

Chirp, Chirp, Chirp

MAP

UNITED STATES

URUGUAY

Uruguayan Folk Song
English Version by MMH

Verse

Spanish: Can-ta, can-ta, pa-ja - ri - to.___ Can-ta, can - ta tu can-
English: *Can-ta, can-ta, pa-ja - ri - to.___* Sing the songs that cheer me

ción. Mi - ra que la vi-da es tris - te y tu can-
so. See, my life is full of sor-row, your mer-ry

tar me a - le - gra el co - ra - zón. Chí - u, chí - u, chí - u,
sing - ing sets my heart a - glow. *Chí - u, chí - u, chí - u,*

chí - u,___ chí - u, chí-u, chí-u, chí - u.___ Can - ta, can-ta pa-ja -
chí - u,___ chí - u, chí-u, chí-u, chí - u.___ Can - ta, can-ta pa-ja -

ri - to   que   tu can - tar me_a - le - gra_el co - ra - zón.
ri - to.   Your mer - ry   sing - ing sets my heart a - glow.

Refrain

Con tus gor - je - os,___ con   tu tri - nar,   des - pier - ta_el
Your mer - ry chirp - ing;___ your roun - de - lay,   You bring the

al - ba,   la no - che   ya   se va.   Con   tus gor -
dawn - ing, the shad - ows fade a - way,   Your mer - ry

je - os,_____ con tu tri - nar,_____ des - pier - ta_el
chirp - ing;_____ your roun - de - lay._____ You bring the

al - ba,   la   no - che   ya   se   va.
dawn - ing,   the shad - ows fade a - way.

CONCEPT
MELODY
SKILLS
SING

One building at the zoo is very dark inside. There is something furry hanging upside down from the ceiling. What is it?

Leatherwing Bat

CD 15:20

Appalachian Folk Song

1. "Hi!" said the lit - tle leath - er - wing bat,
(Refrain) How - did - dle - dow - dee did - dle - um - day,

"I'll tell you the rea - son that,
How - dee - dow - dee did - dle - um day.

The rea - son that I fly__ by night
Dee - how - dee - dow - dee - did - dle - um - day.

Is be - cause I lost____ my heart's de - light."__
And - a - hey - dee - lee - lee - lye - dee - low.____

2. "Hi!" said the redbird, sitting on a chair,
   "Once I loved a lady fair,
   But she got sassy and from me fled
   And ever since my head's been red."

Refrain

304

A big favorite at the zoo is the elephant. This song is about an elephant from the country of India.

The Elephant

CD 15:23

Words and Music by T. Santhalakshmi

Tamil: யா னை யா னை யா னை
English: Ya - nai, Ya - nai, Ya - nai,

யா னை பெ ரி ய யா னை
In - di - an e - le - phant Ya - nai.

யா னை மு கத் தில் தும் பிக் கை
Ro - yal look - ing as a ra - ja,

அ து வே அ தற் கு கை கை கை
Grand and glo - ri - ous as the Taj.

Coda

யா னை யா னை யை னை
Ya - nai, Ya - nai, Ya - nai.

305

CONCEPT
MELODY
SKILLS
SING

Can you name an animal that can live underwater and walk on land? It is the crab! Here is a song from Brazil about the crab.

The Crab

CD 15:27

MAP

UNITED STATES

BRAZIL

Brazilian Folk Song
English Words by María Luisa Muñoz

Portuguese: 1. Ca - ran - gue - jo não é pei - xe,
English: 1. When a crab is in the o - cean,

ca - ran - gue - jo pei - xe é _____
With an un - du - la - ting mo - tion,

Ca - ran - gue - jo não é pei - xe na - da.
He is ve - ry much at home with all the

San - tu da ma - ré.
crea - tures of the sea.

¡Pal - ma! pal - ma! pal - ma!
Swish, swish, swish, he swish - es,

¡Pé_____ Pé_____ Pé, Pé!
Down a - mong the fish - es.

Ca - ran - gue - jo só é pei - xe na en -
Oh, a crab is not a fish and yet a

chen - te da ma - ré.
fish he seems to be.

2. Should he take a crabby notion To go walking by the ocean,
He appears to be no fish at all while crawling on the sand.
Click, click, click, he's clicking, With his sidewise kicking.
Oh, a crab is not a fish because no fish can swim on land.

 **LISTENING** CD 15:31

Batuque na cozinha by Martinho da Vila

Listen to samba music by Martinho da Vila. He is from Brazil, which is where samba music comes from. The rhythm of the drums in samba music makes people want to dance!

What would happen if all the animals at the zoo could sing? They would make a super silly group! But no matter how well they could sing, they would all have a place in the choir.

A Place in the Choir

CD 15:32

Words and Music by Bill Staines

Refrain

All God's crit - ters got a place in the choir,

Some sing low, Some sing high - er,

some sing out loud on the tel - e - phone wire,

And some just clap their hands

Fine

or paws or an - y - thing they got now.

Verse

1. Lis - ten to the bass, it's the one on the bot-tom
2. Lis - ten to the top where the lit - tle birds___ sing___
3. It's a sim - ple song of liv - ing sung ev - 'ry - where_

where the bull - frog croaks, and the hip - po - pot - a - mus
On the mel - o - dies with the high notes ring-ing. The
By the ox and the fox and the griz - zly bear, __ The

moans and groans with a big to - do,
hoot owl holl-ers o - ver ev - 'ry - thing
grum-py al - li - ga - tor and the hawk a - bove,

3rd time - D.C. al Fine

And the old cow just goes moo. The
And the jay - bird dis - a - grees.
The sly ra - coon and the dove.

dogs and the cats, they take up the mid - dle,
Sing-in' in the night time, sing - in' in the day __

while the hon - ey - bee hums and the crick - et fid - dles,
The __ lit - tle duck quacks, then he's on his way. __

The don - key brays and the po - ny neighs,
The 'pos - sum ain't got __ much to say

To Refrain

and the old coy - o - te howls.
And the por - cu - pine talks to him - self.

309

Food, Glorious Food!

What is your favorite food? Have you ever been so happy to eat it that you felt like singing? Here are five fun food songs that you can sing anytime, whether you are hungry or not.

VOICE BUILDER: Take a Breath

Good singers make sure they control their breathing. You can learn to control your breathing. Follow these steps:

• Imagine you are holding a giant balloon.
• Pretend to suck all the air slowly out of it.
• Now fill the balloon back up.

OPEN

GROCERY STORE

LISTENING CD 16:4

Food, Glorious Food by Lionel Bart

Listen to this song. What do these children get to eat?

When you are hungry, the best place to go is the grocery store. You can find many kinds of food there. Next time you visit the grocery store, you can sing this song.

CD 16:1

American Folk Song

There were beans, beans, e - nough to feed ma-rines in the

store, in the store. There were beans, beans, e -

nough to feed ma-rines in the cor-ner gro-cery store. My

eyes are dim, I can-not see. I have not brought my

specs with me. I have not brought my specs with me!

311

CONCEPT
MELODY
SKILLS
SING

Hooray, look what's for dinner! It is spaghetti, topped with big meatballs and cheese.
Oh no! A meatball rolled off the table.

CD 16:5

American Folk Song
Words by Tom Glazer

1. On top of spa - ghet - ti _____
(2.) gar - den _____
(3.) cov - ered _____

All cov - ered with cheese, _____
And un - der a bush, _____
With beau - ti - ful moss; _____

I lost my poor meat - ball _____
And then my poor meat - ball _____
It grew love - ly meat - balls _____

When some - bod - y sneezed.
Was noth - ing but mush.
And to - ma - to sauce.

312

It rolled off the ta - ble
The mush was as tast - y
So if you eat spa - ghet - ti

And on - to the floor,
As tast - y could be,
All cov - ered with cheese,

And then my poor meat - ball
And ear - ly next sum - mer,
Hold on to your meat - balls

1., 2.

Rolled out of the door.
It grew in - to a tree.
And don't ev - er

2. It rolled in the
3. The tree was all

3.

sneeze.   A - choo!

CONCEPT
RHYTHM
SKILLS
SING

The artichoke is a strange vegetable. It does not look friendly, with all those spikes on its leaves! But when it is cooked and dipped in butter, it tastes good enough to sing about!

ARTICHOKES

CD 16:8

Words and Music by Malvina Reynolds

Refrain

Ar - ti-chokes   Mmm mmm   Ar - ti-chokes

(2nd time to Verse 2)
Fine

Mmm mmm   Ar - ti-chokes   Mmm mmm

Verse

1. Down   in Mon - ter-rey   the   ar - ti-chokes grow,

Tow - sy head - ed ar - ti-chokes   row   af-ter   row,

they grow   in Mon-ter-rey 'cause it's com - for-ta - ble there,

they   like   the san - dy bot - tom and the cool   salt   air.

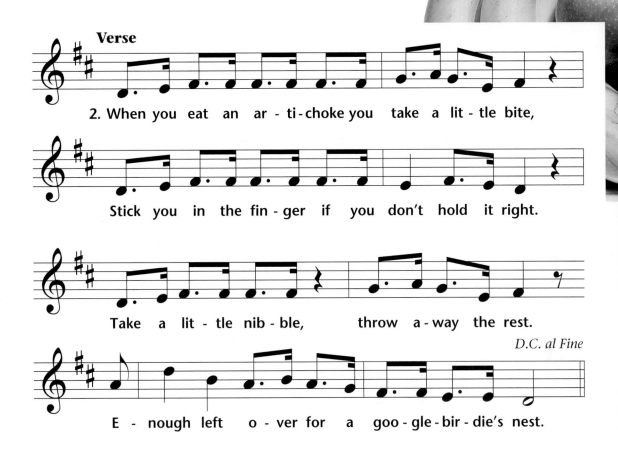

2. When you eat an ar - ti - choke you take a lit - tle bite,

Stick you in the fin - ger if you don't hold it right.

Take a lit - tle nib - ble, throw a - way the rest.

D.C. al Fine

E - nough left o - ver for a goo - gle - bir - die's nest.

Piggy

For breakfast I had ice cream
With pickles sliced up in it;
For lunch, some greasy pork chops
Gobbled in a minute;
Dinner? Clams and orange pop,
And liverwurst, slicked thick—
And now, oops! Oh pardon me!
I'm going to be sick!
—*William Cole*

CONCEPT
RHYTHM
SKILLS
SING

People in different parts of the world enjoy different foods. In Croatia, children and adults enjoy eating watermelons.

Ja posejah lubenice

I Planted Watermelons

CD 16:11

MAP

UNITED
STATES
CROATIA

Croatian Folk Song
English Version by MMH

Verse

Croatian: 1. Ja po - se - jah___ lu - be - ni - ce,
English: 1. I am plant - ing___ wa - ter - mel - ons,

Po - kraj vo - de stu - de - ni - ce,
By the riv - er cool and___ flow - ing,

Refrain

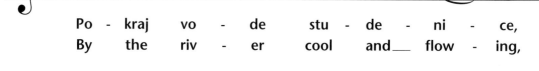

Se - no, sla - ma, se - no, sla - ma.
Hay___ and straw,___ hay___ and straw,___

Zob, zob, zob, zob, zob, zob.
Oats, oats, oats, oats, oats, oats.

2. Seven fields of wheat and barley,
   Nine more fields of corn are planted. *Refrain*

CONCEPT
MELODY
SKILLS
SING

Oranges taste great, and are good for you, too! In Sri Lanka, oranges are a tasty treat. People from Sri Lanka are proud of the oranges they grow.

Me gase boho

MAP

UNITED STATES

SRI LANKA

CD 16:15

Orange Tree

Sinhala Folk Song
English Version by Mary Lu Walker

Sinhala: මේ ග - සේ බො - හෝ පැ - ණි දො -
English: Or - ange tree bends low. Branch - es are

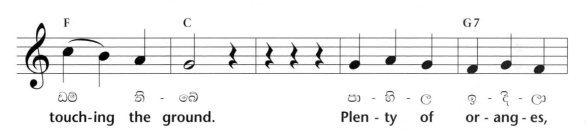

ඩම් ති - බේ පා - හි - ල ඉ - දි - ලා
touch-ing the ground. Plen - ty of or - ang - es,

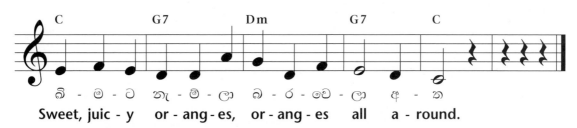

බී - ම - ට නැ - මි - ලා බ - ර - වෙ - ලා අ - ත
Sweet, juic - y or - ang - es, or - ang - es all a - round.

CONCEPT
FORM
SKILLS
SING

Do you know all of the foods in this song? Which food in it is your favorite? Singing about all of these foods can make you hungry. It must be time to eat!

The Food Song

CD 16:19

Words and Music by Jackie Silberg

1. Cap - el - li - ni, fet - tu - ci - ni, es - car - got and bok choy.
2. Wie - ner schnitz - el, salt - ed pret - zels, sau - er - kraut and bok choy.

Jam - ba - lay - a and pa - pay - a, ter - i - yak - i, bok choy.
Moo goo gai pan, en - chi - la - da, sau - er - brat - en, bok choy.

Her - ring, kip - pers, gua - ca - mo - le, krep - lach, crum - pets, rav - i - o - li,

gy - ros, gum - bo, su - shi, cur - ry, poi, bok choy.

318

Ta - cos,_____ bak - la - va, egg rolls,

french fries,_____ ru - ma - ki, Sal - ly Lunn.

Brat - wurst,_____ la - sa - gna, won ton,

chow mein,__ ce - vi -che, crab ran-goon.   crab ran-goon.

Trip to the Tropics

Pretend you are in the warm tropics in a rain forest. What sounds do you hear? You might hear the sounds of birds, rain, or insects in the forest. Would you like to visit? Pack your bags, because we are taking a musical trip to the tropics!

VOICE BUILDER: Listening

Did you know listening is very important when you sing? Here are some things you need to listen for when you sing. Can you think of any others?

- Instructions from your teacher
- Your own voice
- Other people's voices around you

Jamaica is an island country in the Caribbean Sea. A tree called the banyan tree grows in Jamaica. Banyan trees have roots that grow down from their branches.

Banyan Tree

CD 16:22

Moderately

Jamaican Folk Song

1. Moon shine to - night; come make we dance an' sing.
2. La - dies make curt - sy; gen - tle - men make bow.
3. Then we join hands an' dance a - roun' an' roun'.

Moon shine to - night; come make we dance an' sing.
La - dies make curt - sy; gen - tle - men make bow.
Then we join hands an' dance a - roun' an' roun'.

Me da rock so, you da rock so, un - der ban - yan tree.

Me da rock so, you da rock so, un - der ban - yan tree.

CONCEPT
METER
SKILLS
SING

Fiji is an island country in the Pacific Ocean. In Fiji the water is sky blue and there are many beautiful white-sand beaches. Herons live along streams in Fiji. They are birds with long legs.

MAP

UNITED STATES

FIJI

Na belo

CD 16:25

Little Heron

Fijian Folk Song
English Words by Linda Worsley

Fijian: Na be - lo na be - lo___ lai___ lai.
English: Lit - tle her - on came fly - ing to me.

Vu - ka vo - li mai, Va - ka - mu - ri wai. Lai ro
Lit - tle her - on flew down a - long the stream. Then it

i - na ta - ba - ni ti - ri wai. Lai ro!
land - ed a - way up in a tree, Her - on!

(Click, click, click) Lai ro! (Click, click, click)
(Click, click, click) Her - on! (Click, click, click)

CONCEPT
MELODY
SKILLS
SING

People came from all over the world to live in the tropics of Latin America. This is a song some of them sang to celebrate the good things in their lives.

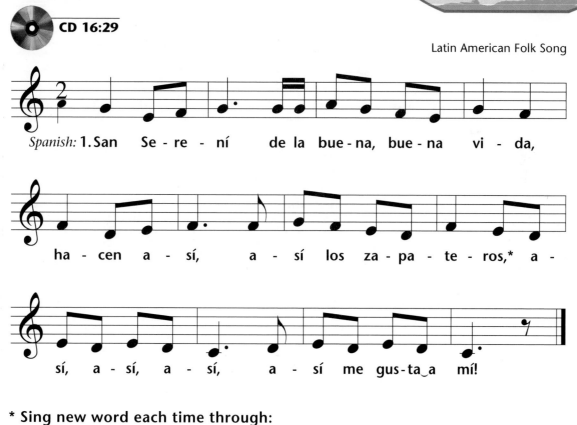

San Sereni

CD 16:29

MAP

UNITED STATES   LATIN AMERICA

Latin American Folk Song

Spanish: 1. San Se - re - ní de la bue - na, bue - na vi - da,

ha - cen a - sí, a - sí los za - pa - te - ros,* a -

sí, a - sí, a - sí, a - sí me gus-ta a mí!

* Sing new word each time through:

1. los zapateros   (the cobblers)
2. las bailadoras   (the folk dancers)
3. los carpinteros   (the carpenters)
4. las pianistas   (the pianists)
5. los campañeros   (the bell ringers)
6. las costureras   (the seamstresses)

CONCEPT
MELODY
SKILLS
SING

Wouldn't it be neat if all birds could talk? If you visit the Tiki Room, you will meet some feathered friends who love to sing and play.

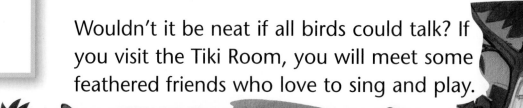

The Tiki Tiki Tiki Room

CD 16:33

Words and Music by Richard M. Sherman
and Robert B. Sherman

In the Ti - ki Ti - ki Ti - ki Ti - ki

Ti - ki Room,__ in the Ti - ki Ti - ki Ti - ki Ti - ki

Ti - ki Room,___ all the birds sing words and the

flow-ers croon_ in the Ti - ki Ti - ki Ti - ki Ti - ki

2nd time to Coda 𝄌 *Fine*

Ti - ki Room.__

Wel-come to our trop-i-cal hide a-way,___ you

luck-y peo-ple you!___ If we

were-n't in the show start-ing right a-way,___ we'd be

in the aud - i-ence, too. All to-geth-er!

Coda

The bird of par-a-dise is an el-e-gant bird.___ It

likes to be seen and it loves to be heard.

Most lit-tle bird-ies will fly a-way,___ but the

D.C. al Fine

Ti - ki Room birds are here ev-'ry day.

For the last stop on our musical trip, we need to take a train. We are going to a city called Caracas in the country of Venezuela. We will travel through the mountains, singing the whole way!

MAP

UNITED STATES

VENEZUELA

El tren

 CD 16:36

The Train

Venezuelan Folk Song

Spanish: "Pá Ca - ra - cas" di - ce el tren cuan - do
English: "To Ca - ra - cas," says the train when it's

vie - ne de Los Te - ques. "Pá Ca - ra - cas" di - ce el
com - ing from Los Te - ques. "To Ca - ra - cas," says the

tren cuan - do vie - ne de Los Te - ques. Pá Ca -
train when it's com - ing from Los Te - ques. To Ca -

ra - cas, pá Ca - ra - cas, siem - pre lle - ni - to de
ra - cas, to Ca - ra - cas, al - ways ver - y full of

gen - te pa - sa_a ve - ces por un
peo - ple, some - times pass - ing through a

tu - nel y_o - tras ve - ces por un puen - te.
tun - nel, some - times pass - ing o - ver bridg - es.

2. When it's going through a tunnel,
   it goes very, very slowly.
   (Repeat)

   Very gently, very slowly,
   so the people won't be frightened.
   (Repeat)

3. When it crosses over bridges,
   it begins to go much faster.
   (Repeat)

   Hurry, hurry, hurry, hurry,
   we're arriving in Caracas!
   (Repeat)

LISTENING CD 17:1

Railroad Blues by Freeman Stowers

Sometimes people make their instruments
sound like something else. "Railroad Blues," by
Freeman Stowers, was recorded a long time
ago. He makes his harmonica sound like a train.

CONCEPT
RHYTHM
SKILLS
PLAY

Play the music patterns after you read two lines of the poem.

by Betsy Franco

Beep, honk, step on the brake.
City traffic makes us wait.

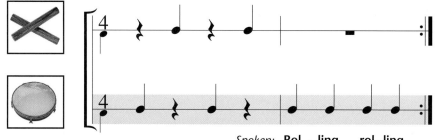

Taxis dodging here and there.
Cars and vans are everywhere.

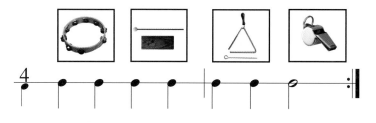

Buses pick up girls and boys.
Trucks look like they're giant toys.

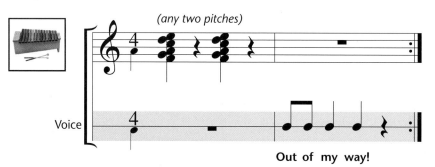

Blinking stoplights flash and glow.
City traffic's stop and go.

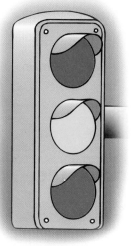

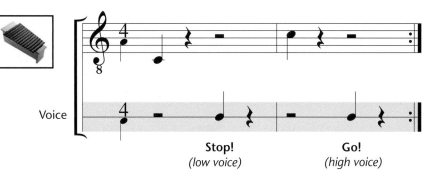

Voice

Stop!
(low voice)

Go!
(high voice)

Pull to the right for the siren sound.
Fire trucks are all around.

Traffic stops while a car gets towed.
Lots of people cross the road.

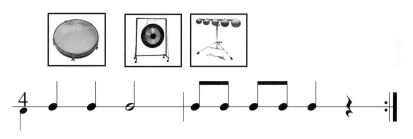

City traffic's really cool,
but I hope that I'm not late for school!

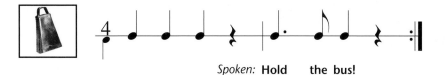

Spoken: **Hold   the bus!**

Señor Coyote

Adapted by MMH from the Mexican Folk Tale as retold by Pleasant DeSpain

Play the musical part when you see a symbol in the story.

One day Señor Rattlesnake was resting on the nice, warm sand enjoying the sun.

He was almost asleep when a great rock rolled down the hill and landed on top of him.

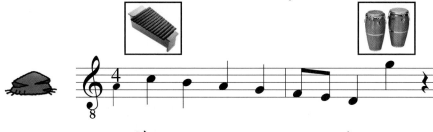

He wiggled and he jiggled but he could not get out from under it.

"Help! Help!" he whispered. It was so tight he could hardly breathe. A rabbit hopped by and saw the poor snake.

The rabbit had a kind heart, so he pushed the rock and freed the snake.

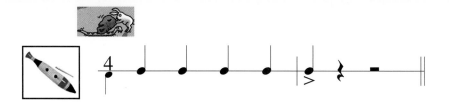

But when Señor Rattlesnake was free, he opened his mouth to swallow the rabbit for his supper.

"Wait! I just saved you!" cried the rabbit.

"Rabbits-s-s are my favorite treat. You should know better!" laughed Señor Rattlesnake.

While they were talking, Señor Coyote walked over the hill.

Ah - ooo!

"What is going on here?" asked Señor Coyote. The rabbit and the snake started talking at once.

"Wait, wait," said Señor Coyote. "Take turns talking. Let me judge who is right."

"Señor Rattlesnake was trapped under a rock," explained the rabbit. "I pushed off the rock to help him. Now he wants to eat me!"

"How funny," laughed Señor Rattlesnake. "I was-s-s hiding under the rock to trick the rabbit into helping me. I caught him fair and s-s-square."

"Let's see," said Señor Coyote. "Señor Rattlesnake, show me how you were hiding."

"You must push the rock on top of me s-s-so I can show you," hissed the snake. The rabbit and Señor Coyote pushed the heavy rock back on top of the snake.

"Now do you s-s-see? Help me out now," whispered the snake.

"No, Señor Rattlesnake," said Señor Coyote. "You must learn a lesson about being cruel to those who help you." And they left the rattlesnake there to think about it!

The Drumming Spider

This story is told in many countries in West Africa. **Play** the music when you see the symbol in the story.

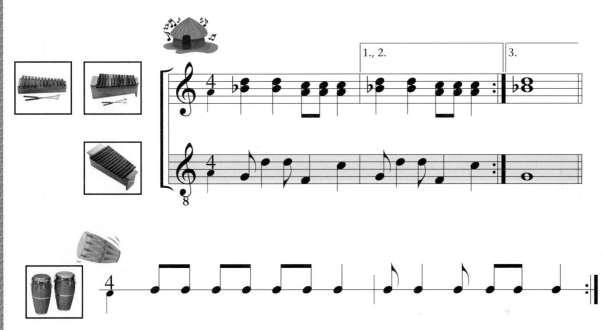

Once upon a time, there was a village where animals and people lived together. The animals could talk, sing, and even play music.

The village had many parties. Spider came to every party. With his eight legs, he could play the most wonderful music on his drums.

But the people in the village did not like to invite Spider and his family. They ate all the food and left nothing for the rest of the guests.

333

So, when the village chief planned a party for his son's wedding, he did not invite Spider and his family. But Spider's wife found out. She ran home to tell him.

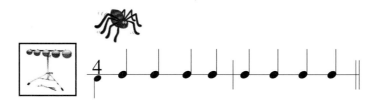

"What? Am I not the best musician at every party?" said Spider. "I'll show them."

On the night of the big party, Spider and his family hid by the stream. Spider brought his drums. And Spider had a plan.

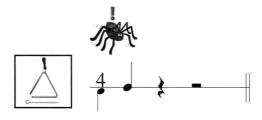

Back at the party, the chief asked a girl to fetch some water at the stream.

When she arrived at the stream, Spider and his family began to play the drums. The girl felt a magic rhythm in her heart. She began to dance and dance. She finally fell to the ground completely worn out.

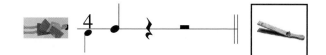

Back at the party, the chief ordered a boy to go find the girl. When the boy got to the stream, Spider and his family began to play the drums. The boy felt the magic rhythm in his heart and began to dance.

This time, the villagers heard the music and came running to the stream. One by one they all felt the magic rhythm beating in their hearts and began to dance. Spider and his family came out from the bushes. The villagers begged them to stop playing, but they would not.

After a long time, the villagers fell to the ground and crawled home to bed. They had never been so tired. From then on, Spider was invited to all the village parties. And he and his family always ate as much as they wanted!

Spotlight on
Celebrations

Spotlight on Celebrations

Spotlight on Celebrations

PATRIOTIC

CONCEPT
RHYTHM

SKILLS
SING, LISTEN

Songs of Our Country

People sing songs to show pride in their country. Sing "America" to show your pride in the United States.

CD 17:2

Music by Henry Carey
Words by Samuel F. Smith

My coun - try 'tis of thee, Sweet land of

lib - er - ty, Of thee I sing. Land where my

fa - thers died, Land of the Pil - grim's pride,

From ev' - ry___ moun - tain-side Let___ free-dom ring.

LISTENING CD 17:5

Washington Post
by John Philip Sousa

Listen to this piece written for a band.

339

CONCEPT
RHYTHM
SKILLS
SING

Some patriotic songs are about our history. "Yankee Doodle" helps us remember our first president, George Washington.

Yankee Doodle

CD 17:6

Traditional Melody
Words by Dr. Richard Shuckburgh

Verse

1. Fath'r and I went down to camp a
2. Yan - kee Doo - dle went to town, a

long with Cap - tain Good - in', and there we saw the
rid - ing on a po - ny, He stuck a feath - er

men and boys as thick as hast - y pud - din'.
in his cap and called it mac - a - ro - ni.

Refrain

Yan - kee Doo - dle keep it up, Yan - kee Doo - dle dan - dy,

Mind the mu - sic and the step, and with the girls be han - dy.

3. There was Captain Washington upon a slapping stallion, a-giving orders to his men; I guess there were a million. *Refrain.*

Pat with the steady beat.

There Are Many Flags in Many Lands

Composer Unknown
Words by M.H. Howliston

CD 17:9

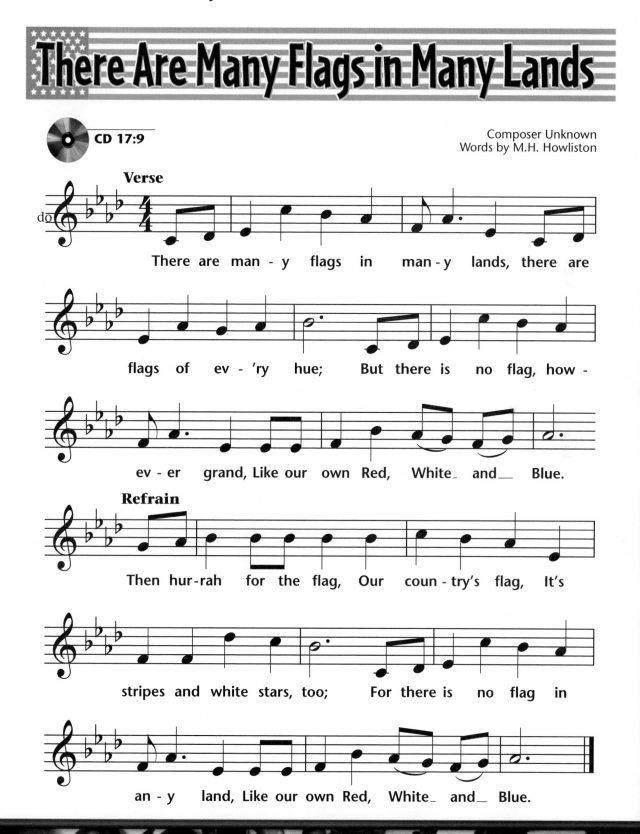

Verse

There are man - y flags in man - y lands, there are

flags of ev - 'ry hue; But there is no flag, how -

ev - er grand, Like our own Red, White_ and_ Blue.

Refrain

Then hur-rah for the flag, Our coun-try's flag, It's

stripes and white stars, too; For there is no flag in

an - y land, Like our own Red, White_ and_ Blue.

Harvest

In autumn, leaves fall everywhere! This is also the season when the crops are gathered.

CD 17:12

Georgia Folk Song

1. Time to gath - er har - vest.__ Oh, Em-ma, oh!____

You turn a-round, dig a hole in the ground,_ Oh, Em - ma, oh!

2. Digging sweet potatoes . . .
3. Digging rutabagas . . .
4. Digging big fat parsnips . . .

The apple harvest is in autumn.

How many kinds of apples do you see in your grocery store?

Apple Picker's Reel

CD 17:15

Words and Music by Larry Hanks

Hey! Ho! Don't you feel so fine, Look-ing
out a-cross the or-chard in the bright sun-shine.
Hey! Ho! Don't you feel so free,
Stand-ing on the top of the ap - ple tree.

Christopher Columbus sailed across the ocean over 500 years ago.

Find the names of Columbus's three ships in this song.

CD 17:18

Words and Music by Margaret Campbelle-Holman

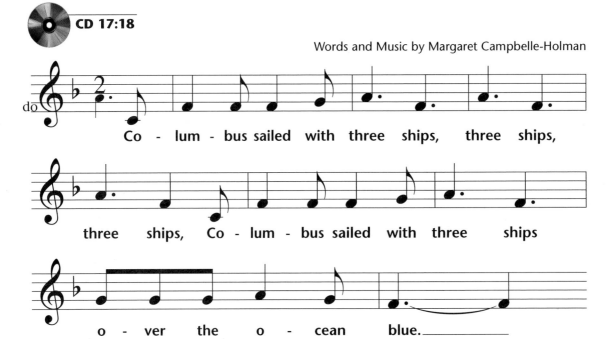

do

Co - lum - bus sailed with three ships, three ships,

three ships, Co - lum - bus sailed with three ships

o - ver the o - cean blue._____

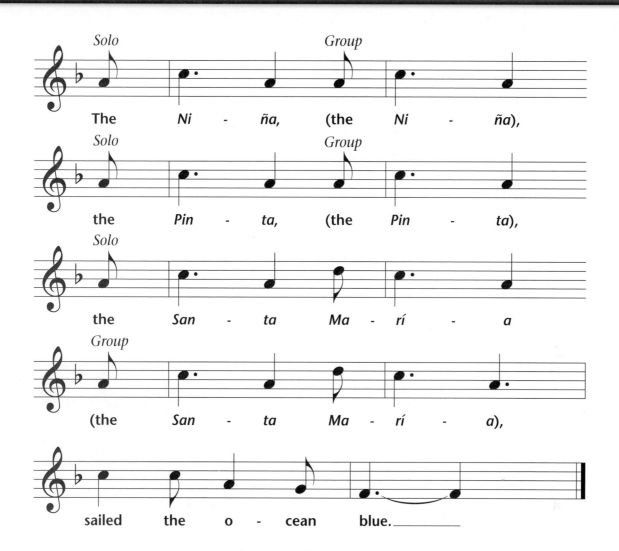

Solo The Ni - ña, *Group* (the Ni - ña),

Solo the Pin - ta, *Group* (the Pin - ta),

Solo the San - ta Ma - rí - a

Group (the San - ta Ma - rí - a),

sailed the o - cean blue._____

Halloween is a time when it is fun to pretend.

This Is Halloween

CD 17:21

Eerily

Words and Music by Teresa Jennings

do

1. Crea - tures!   Mon - sters!   Wit - ches! } Hal - low - een!
2. Spook - y!   Eer - ie!   Creep - y! }

{ Spi - ders!   Gob - lins! } This is Hal - low - een!
{ Scar - y!   Hair - y! }

1.

(Ghosts moaning)

2.   *Shout:*

(Wolves howling)   **Boo!**

Create new spooky words.

 **LISTENING** CD 17:24

In the Hall of the Mountain King
from *Peer Gynt Suite* by Edvard Grieg

Describe when the music gets louder.

Some pumpkins are used for decorating. Other pumpkins are used to make pumpkin pie!

Pick a Pumpkin

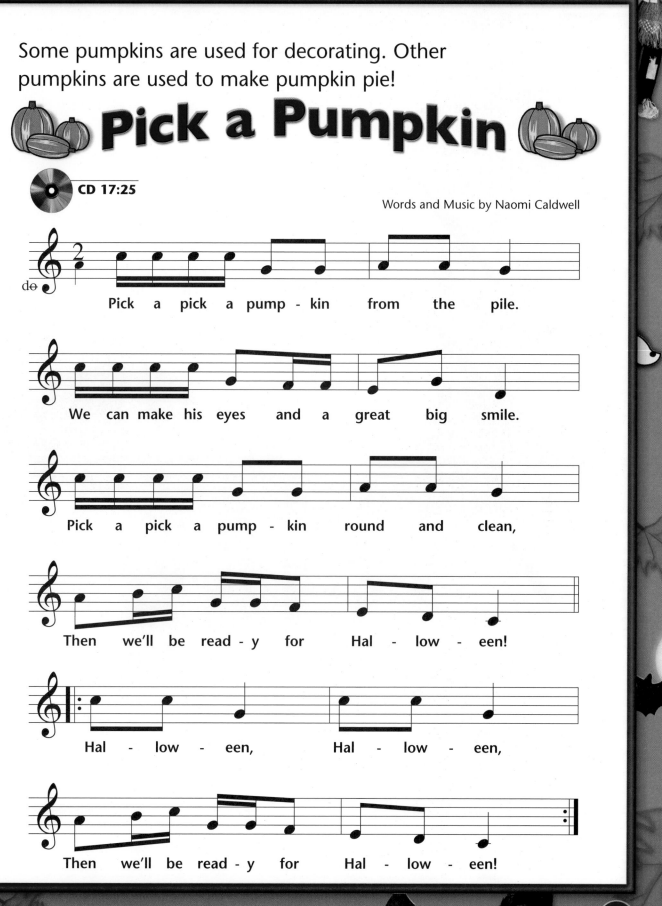

CD 17:25

Words and Music by Naomi Caldwell

Pick a pick a pump - kin from the pile.

We can make his eyes and a great big smile.

Pick a pick a pump - kin round and clean,

Then we'll be read - y for Hal - low - een!

Hal - low - een, Hal - low - een,

Then we'll be read - y for Hal - low - een!

Thanksgiving is here! We gather around the table and share food. We give thanks for family and friends.

Listen to an old American song.

 **LISTENING** / CD 17:28

Turkey in the Straw (American folk song)

This fiddle tune became a favorite dance.

At Thanksgiving we are thankful for many things.
Name some things you are thankful for.

Find the rhyming words in this song.

CD 17:29

Music by Franz Schubert

Thank You for the world so sweet,

Thank You for the food we eat,

Thank You for the birds that sing,

Thank You, God, for ev - 'ry - thing.

Seasonal Songs

Snow and ice bring winter fun!

Slide your hands to the steady beat in this song.

CD 17:32

Words and Music by Lynn Freeman Olson

Glid - ing,   glid - ing,   Skat-ing a-round the   ice.

See how my feet are   fly - ing, Noth-ing could be   so nice!

Watch   me   turn - ing   smooth   and   free.

When I am skat-ing   I   am   hap-py as I can be!

Winter Landscape with a Bird Trap
by Pieter Brueghel

This painting was created more than 450 years ago. It shows a winter scene in a village.

Describe what people are doing in this scene.

CONCEPT
TONALITY
SKILLS
LISTEN

Hanukkah is a holiday of lights. It lasts for eight days. A *menorah* holds nine candles. There is one candle for each of the eight nights, and one candle to light the others.

In the Window

CD 17:35

Hebrew Folk Song
English Words by Judith Eisenstein

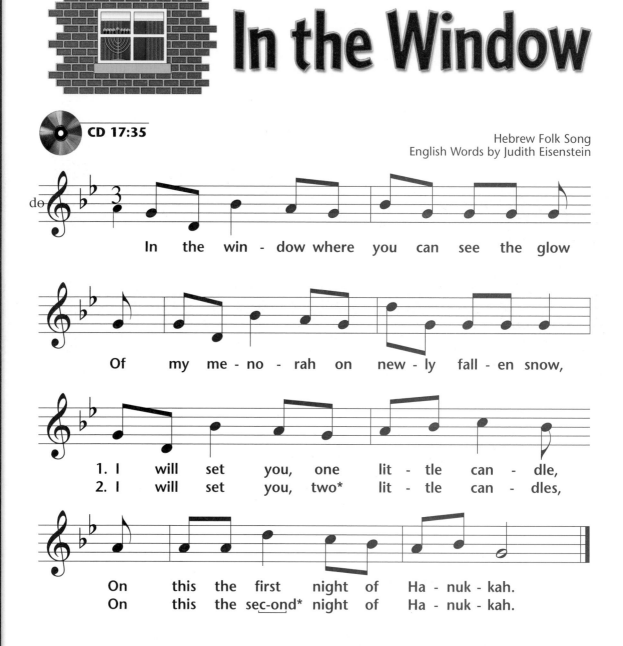

In the win - dow where you can see the glow

Of my me - no - rah on new - ly fall - en snow,

1. I will set you, one lit - tle can - dle,
2. I will set you, two* lit - tle can - dles,

On this the first night of Ha - nuk - kah.
On this the sec-ond* night of Ha - nuk - kah.

*For each of the nights of Hanukkah, sing the correct number. On the eighth verse, sing the word "last."

352

At Hanukkah children play with a special top called a *dreidel*.

My Dreidel

Music by S.E. Goldfarb
Words by S.S. Grossman

CD 18:1

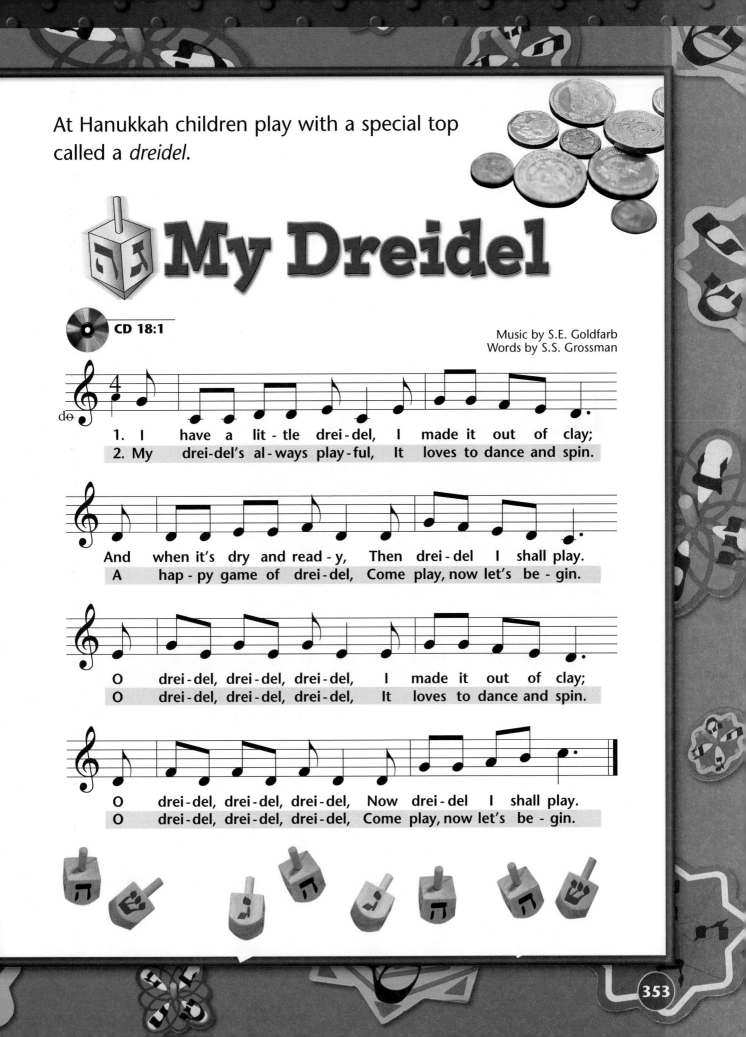

1. I have a lit-tle drei-del, I made it out of clay;
2. My drei-del's al-ways play-ful, It loves to dance and spin.

And when it's dry and read-y, Then drei-del I shall play.
A hap-py game of drei-del, Come play, now let's be-gin.

O drei-del, drei-del, drei-del, I made it out of clay;
O drei-del, drei-del, drei-del, It loves to dance and spin.

O drei-del, drei-del, drei-del, Now drei-del I shall play.
O drei-del, drei-del, drei-del, Come play, now let's be-gin.

CONCEPT
TONE COLOR
SKILLS
LISTEN

Holidays often have special music.

LISTENING CD 18:8

Chinese Dance from *The Nutcracker Suite* by Piotr Ilyich Tchaikovsky

The ballet *The Nutcracker* is a Christmas story. Clara dreams of adventures with her Nutcracker doll, a Mouse King, a Snow Queen, and others.

Listen to the music of this famous ballet.

Listening Map for Chinese Dance
from *The Nutcracker*

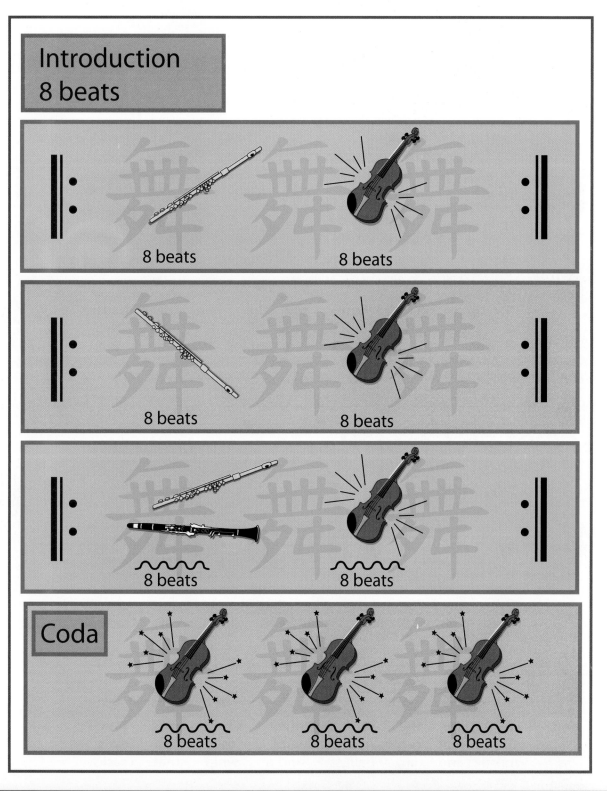

Introduction
8 beats

8 beats   8 beats

8 beats   8 beats

8 beats   8 beats

Coda

8 beats   8 beats   8 beats

CONCEPT
FORM
SKILLS
SING, PLAY

Pat with the beat as you sing this song.

Find the rhyming words.

Up on the Housetop

CD 18:9

Words and Music by Benjamin T. Hanby

A Verse

do

1. Up on the house-top the rein-deer pause,
2. First comes the stock-ing of lit-tle Nell,
3. Look in the stock-ing of lit-tle Bill,

Out jumps good old San-ta Claus;
Oh, dear San-ta, fill it well.
Oh, just see what a glor-ious fill!

Down through the chim-mey with lots of toys,
Give her a dol-ly that laughs and cries,
Here is a ham-mer and lots of tacks,

All for the lit-tle ones' Christ-mas joys.
One that can o-pen and shut its eyes.
Whis-tle and a ball and a whip that cracks.

B Refrain

Ho, ho, ho, Who would - n't go?

Ho, ho, ho, Who would - n't go? _____

Up on the house - top, click, click, click,

Down through the chim - ney with good Saint Nick.

Play the rhythm patterns for each section.

Tambourine **A**

Jingle bells **B**

CONCEPT RHYTHM
SKILLS LISTEN, READ

At Christmas time people like to sing for their neighbors. This is an old carol from England.

We Wish You a Merry Christmas

MAP
UNITED STATES   ←ENGLAND

English Carol

CD 18:12

1. We wish you a mer - ry Christ - mas,
2. Now bring us some fig - gy pud - ding,
3. For we love our fig - gy pud - ding,

We wish you a mer - ry Christ - mas,
Now bring us some fig - gy pud - ding,
For we love our fig - gy pud - ding,

We wish you a mer - ry Christ - mas,
Now bring us some fig - gy pud - ding,
For we love our fig - gy pud - ding,

And a hap - py New Year.
And___ bring it out here.
So___ bring some out here.

4. We won't go until we get some,
   We won't go until we get some,
   We won't go until we get some,
   So bring some out here.

5. We wish you a merry Christmas,
   We wish you a merry Christmas,
   We wish you a merry Christmas,
   And a happy New Year.

This carol tells the story of a special boat trip.

I Saw Three Ships

CD 18:15

English Carol

1. I saw three ships come sail - ing in,
2. And what was in those ships all three,
3. 'Twas Jo - seph and his fair la - dy,
4. Then all the bells on earth shall ring,

On Christ-mas Day, on

Christ - mas Day;
I saw three ships come sail - ing in,
And what was in those ships all three,
'Twas Jo - seph and his fair la - dy,
Then all the bells on earth shall ring,

On

Christ - mas Day in the morn - ing.

This song tells the story of Christmas.

Mary Had a Baby

CD 18:18

Swing (♪♪ = ♪♪)

African American Spiritual

do

1. Ma - ry had a ba - by,
2. What did Ma - ry name him?
3. Ma - ry named him Je - sus,
4. Where was Je - sus born?____

Yes,   Lord,

Ma - ry had a ba - by,
What did Ma - ry name him?
Ma - ry named him Je - sus,
Where was Je - sus born?____

Yes,   my   Lord,

Ma - ry had a ba - by,
What did Ma - ry name him?
Ma - ry named him Je - sus,
Where was Je - sus born?____

Yes,   Lord,

The peo - ple keep a-com - ing and the train has gone.

5. Born in lowly stable . . .
6. Where did Mary lay him? . . .
7. Laid him in a manger . . .

On Christmas Eve in Mexico, people eat something sweet called *buñuelos*. Buñuelos are flavored with honey and spices.

Ésta sí que es Nochebuena

This Is Christmas Eve

CD 18:21

Mexican Folk Song

Spanish: És - ta sí que es No - che - bue - na, No - che - bue - na,
English: **Christ-mas Eve is real - ly here now, real - ly here now!**

no - che de co - mer bu - ñue - los.
It's a night to eat *bu - ñue - los.*

Y en mi ca - sa no los ha - cen, no los ha - cen
But in my house we can't make them, we can't make them,

por fal - ta de ha - ri - na y hue - vo.
for we have no egg or flo - ur.

CONCEPT
FORM
SKILLS
SING, PLAY

Kwanzaa is a holiday that lasts seven days. Many African American families and friends get together to share stories of their history and culture. They eat traditional foods and sing songs from their culture and other African cultures.

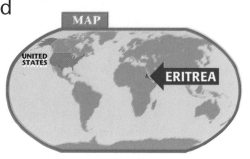

MAP

UNITED STATES

ERITREA

HASHEWIE

Going Round

CD 18:25

Eritrean Folk Song
Words by Hidaat Ephrem

Tigrinya: Ha - shew - i - e_____ } Shew - i - e. { Ha - e.
English: Go round and round_ } Shew - i - e. { Go e.

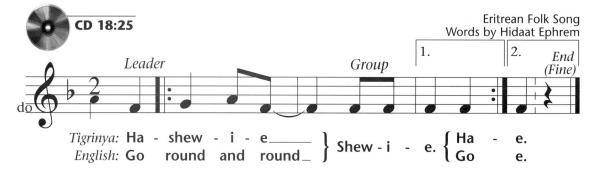

Bi-ha - de ha - bir - na } Shew - i - e.
All to - geth - er round } Shew - i - e.

Ha-shew - ie e - na - bel - na } Shew - i - e.
Say - ing round and round } Shew - i - e.

Leader

Group

A - lem kit-fel - to } Shew - i - e.
So the world would know } Shew - i - e.

Leader

Group

Ku-lu - me - nin - et - na } Shew - i - e.
Know___ who we are } Shew - i - e.

Leader

Group

Ha-shew - i - e ni - bel } Shew - i - e.
Let us say out loud } Shew - i - e.

Leader

Group

Ne-fa - lit - a - di - na } Shew - i - e.
This is who we are } Shew - i - e.

Go back to the beginning and sing to the End.
(Da Capo al Fine)

Leader

Group

Bi-ha - de ha - bir - na } Shew - i - e.
All to - geth - er round } Shew - i - e.

CONCEPT
RHYTHM

SKILLS
SING, PLAY

Martin Luther King, Jr., was a great American leader. He had a dream of freedom for everyone.

Martin Luther King

CD 18:29

Words and Music by Mary Donnelly
Arranged by George L.O. Strid

Mar - tin Lu - ther King.___ Mar - tin Lu - ther King.___

He had a dream_ for A - mer - i - ca.___

Mar - tin Lu - ther King.___

He was a man who want - ed jus - tice
He was a man who loved his coun - try,

more than an - y - thing.___
now his name we sing.___

He was a man who died for free - dom.
He taught us how to make a dif - 'rence.

Mar - tin   Lu - ther   King. _____

Mar - tin   Lu - ther   King. _____

_____ Ev' - ry - bod - y sing!   Mar - tin   Lu - ther   King! _____

Mar - tin   Lu - ther   King! _____   Sing,   Mar - tin   Lu - ther,

Mar - tin   Lu - ther,   Mar - tin   Lu - ther   King!

Play these patterns with the song.

Chinese people celebrate the New Year in late January or early February. It is a celebration of family and friends, gift giving, and special food.

LISTENING   CD 18:32

Dragon Dance (Chinese folk music)

The dragon means good wishes to Chinese people. During the New Year celebration, there is music in the streets. Groups of people wear big dragon costumes and move through the streets.

Use *World Instruments* **CD-ROM** to learn more about Asian instruments.

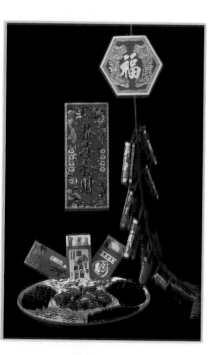

Sing this song about the Chinese New Year.

MAP

UNITED STATES   CHINA

Bei Fang Chre
North Wind Blows

CD 19:1

Chinese New Year Festival Song
Collected and Transcribed by Kathy B. Sorensen
English Words by Linda Worsley

Mandarin: 北 风 那 个 吹   雪 花 那 个 飘   雪

English: The north wind_ blows,___ the north wind_ blows.___ And

花 那 个 飘   年 来 到

snow - flakes are fly - ing, the new year has_ come.

CONCEPT
RHYTHM, MELODY
SKILLS
SING, READ

Valentine's Day is a time of fun!
What would you send your Valentine?

Skinnamarink

CD 19:5

Tin Pan Alley Song

Skin-na-ma-rink a-dink a-dink, skin-na-ma-rink a-doo,

I love you; Skin-na-ma-rink a-dink a-dink,

skin-na-ma-rink a-doo, Yes, I do.

I love you in the morn-ing and in the af-ter-noon,

I love you in the eve-ning, 'neath the sil-v'ry moon.

Skin-na-ma-rink a-dink a-dink, skin-na-ma-rink a-doo,

I love you.

You Are My Sunshine

CD 19:8

Words and Music by
Jimmie Davis and Charles Mitchell

do

You are my sun - shine,____ my on-ly sun - shine.____

You make me hap - py____ when skies are gray.____

You'll nev-er know, Dear,____ how much I love you,____

Please don't take my sun - shine a - way.____

CONCEPT
TONE COLOR
SKILLS
LISTEN, SING

George Washington fought for freedom. He became the first President of our country.

LISTENING CD 19:11

Washington's Birthday by Charles Edward Ives

Charles Edward Ives was an American composer. He played the drums in his father's band when he was 12 years old. This music celebrates Washington's birthday.

Move your hands up when you hear this instrument.

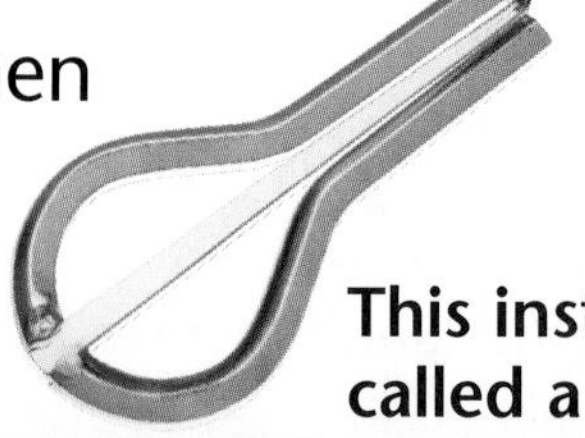

This instrument is called a jaw harp.

Sing a song about George Washington.

Who Chopped the Cherry Tree Down?

CD 19:12

Words and Music by Ruth Norman

Solo
Hide your eyes and you will see who chopped down the cher - ry tree.

All
Who chopped the cher - ry tree down?

Who chopped the cher - ry tree down? Who did? I did!

All *Solo* *All*
Who did? I did! { He / She } chopped the cher - ry tree down.

371

CONCEPT
FORM
SKILLS
SING, LISTEN

Purim is a day of rejoicing for the Jewish people.
Children make up plays about brave Queen Esther.
She saved the Jewish people a long time ago.

Ani Purim

Purim

MAP

UNITED
STATES

ISRAEL

CD 19:15

Music by Nachum Nardi

Hebrew: אַ - נִי פוּ-רִים אַ - נִי פוּ-רִים מַ - ח מוּ - בְּ - דֵ - ח

English: A - ni Pu-rim, A - ni Pu-rim, it comes but once a year.

ה - לָ רָק פָּ - עַם בְּ - שָׁ - נָה אַ - בּוֹא לְ - הִתְ - רָ - ח

We all dress up and cel - e - brate, We sing and dance and cheer.

Hoo - ray for Mor-de-chai! Hoo - ray for Es - ther!

Hoo - ray for hol - i - days! At last it's here!

372

Cherkassiya (Israeli folk dance)

Children in Israel wear costumes on Purim. How many parts does this Israeli dance have?

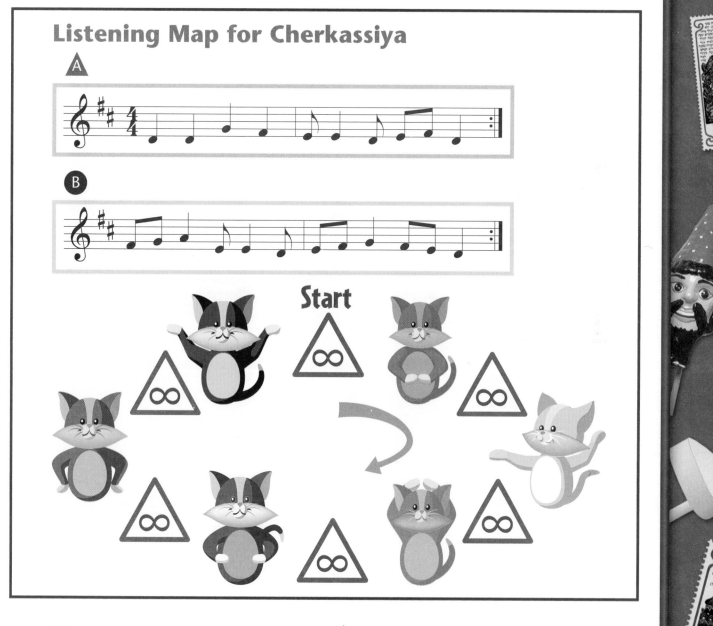

Move the same way for each ▲. Copy your cat leader during ⬤.

The shamrock is the symbol of Ireland. It is a tradition to wear green on St. Patrick's Day.

 **LISTENING** CD 19:20

St. Patrick's Day (Irish folk music)

On St. Patrick's Day, there are parades all over the country. Bands play Irish music.

Listening Map for St. Patrick's Day

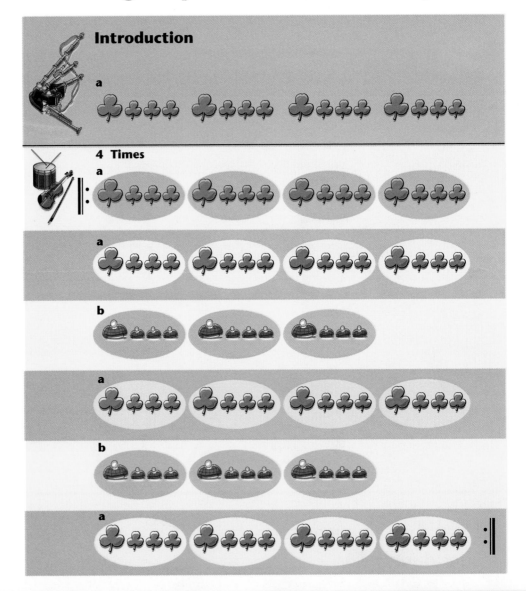

This song is about an Irishman who can do many kinds of jobs.

Find Irish words in this song.

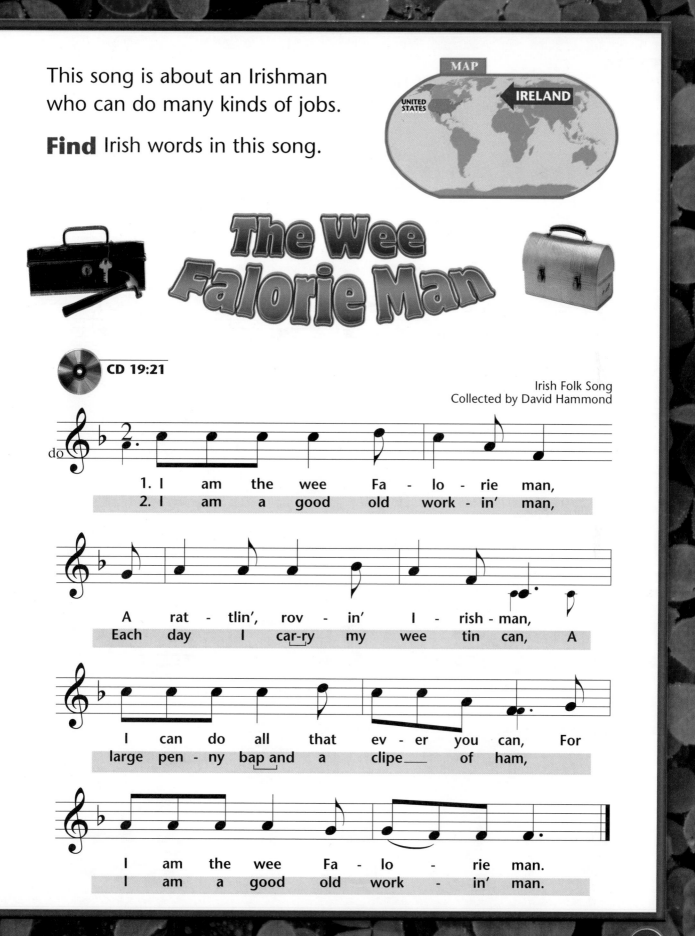

MAP

IRELAND

UNITED STATES

CD 19:21

Irish Folk Song
Collected by David Hammond

1. I am the wee Fa - lo - rie man,
2. I am a good old work - in' man,

A rat - tlin', rov - in' I - rish - man,
Each day I car-ry my wee tin can, A

I can do all that ev - er you can, For
large pen - ny bap and a clipe___ of ham,

I am the wee Fa - lo - rie man.
I am a good old work - in' man.

375

SPRING

CONCEPT
RHYTHM

SKILLS
SING, READ

Earth Day

Earth is our home. How does your neighborhood celebrate Earth Day?

Big Beautiful Planet

CD 19:24

Words and Music by Raffi

Refrain

do

There's a big beau-ti-ful plan-et in the sky,

And it's my home, It's where I live.

You and man-y oth-ers live here too.

The earth is our home, It's where we live.

Verse

1. We can feel the pow-er of the noon-day sun,
2. We can feel the spir-it of a blow-ing wind,

A blaz-ing ball of fire___ up a-bove.
A might-y source of pow-er in our lives.

Shin-ing light and warmth e-nough for ev-ery-one,
Of-fer-ing an-oth-er way to fill our needs,

Sing Refrain after each verse.

A gift to ev-'ry na-tion from a star.
Na-ture's gift to help us car-ry on.

CONCEPT
DYNAMICS
SKILLS
LISTEN, SING

In spring the weather starts to get warmer.
It is a time of changes.

🔊 **LISTENING** CD 19:27

Appalachian Spring

by Aaron Copland

Aaron Copland was a famous
American composer. He composed
this music for a great dancer,
Martha Graham. It is a celebration
of spring.

Welcome Is the Month of May

🔊 CD 19:28

Words and Music by Mary Donnelly
and George L.O. Strid

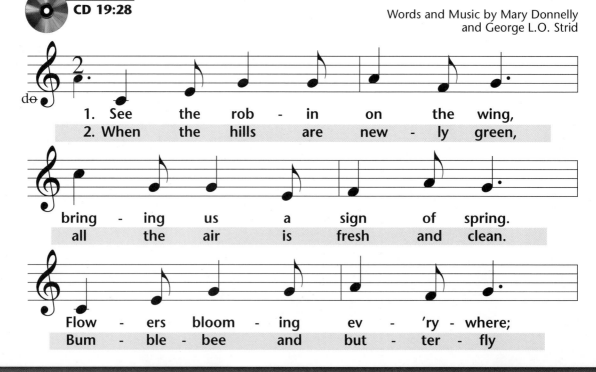

1. See the rob - in on the wing,
2. When the hills are new - ly green,

bring - ing us a sign of spring.
all the air is fresh and clean.

Flow - ers bloom - ing ev - 'ry - where;
Bum - ble - bee and but - ter - fly

sweet per - fume____ will fill the air.
flit and flut - ter a - cross the sky.

Gone, the win - ter's bit - ter chill;
Gone, the win - ter's ice and snow.

time for tu - lip and daf - fo - dil. }
Time for flow - ers to bloom and grow. }

Sing a cheer - ful roun - de - lay.

Wel - come is____ the month of May!

What signs of spring can you find in
"Welcome Is the Month of May"?

CONCEPT
RHYTHM
SKILLS
LISTEN, SING

More than 130 years ago, Mexicans won a major battle. Today they celebrate that victory with a holiday called *Cinco de Mayo*.

 **LISTENING** CD 19:31

Sones de mariachi by Blas Galindo

Blas Galindo was a Mexican composer. He liked to use folk music to create new music.

EL PALOMO Y LA PALOMA
The Doves

CD 19:32

Mexican Folk Song
Adapted by José-Luis Orozco
English Words by Linda Worsley

Verse

Spanish: El pa - lo - mo y la pa - lo - ma se sa - lie - ron
English: Mis - ter Dove and Miss Dove, they went out one day to

a pa - sear. El pa - lo - mo le de -
fly a - round. Mis - ter Dove said, "Miss Dove,

cí - a ven - te que voy a bai - lar.
would you dance with me? Let's go on down."

Refrain

El pa - lo - mo_y la pa - lo - ma los dos fue - ron a bai - lar,
Both of them came fly - ing down to land and dance up - on the ground.

y_el pa - lo - mo le de - cí - a
Mis - ter Dove soon had to stop; he

1.
yo ya quie - ro des - can - sar. El pa - sar.
said, "I'm just too tired to hop." Both of

2.
hop."

See **music.mmhschool.com**
to research Mexican music.

SUMMER

CONCEPT
BEAT, METER

SKILLS
SING, READ

Summer is a good time to grow fruits and vegetables. In the Philippines there are two seasons, rainy and dry. The rainy season is hot. It is a good time to plant.

Name the vegetables you sing about in this song.

Bahay Kubo

My Nipa Hut

MAP

UNITED STATES

PHILIPPINES

CD 19:36

Filipino Folk Song
from the Tagalog Province
English Version by John Higgins

Tagalog: 1.,3. Ba - hay ku - bo ka - hit mun - ti
English: 2. My ni - pa hut may look quite small,

ang ha - la - man do - on ay sa - ri sa - ri.
but the plants in my gar - den grow big and tall.

Sing - ka - mas at ta - long, si - ga - ril - yas at ma - ni,
There are tur - nips there are pea - nuts, there are beans all in a row.

si - tao, ba - tao pa - ta - ni._____
So man - y plants that I grow._____

What sights and sounds from summer
can you find in the poem?

The Sun Is First to Rise

Up in the morning early,
The sun is first to rise;
The little birds begin to sing,
The farmers rub their eyes.
The rabbits hop down roads of dew,
The newborn baby cries,
And the gray kitten runs and leaps,
Chasing white butterflies.

Away to bed with darkness
The sun is first to go;
Across the fields with heavy wings
There flaps a shiny crow;
The children put away their toys,
Their steps are dragging slow;
And in the woods the spotted fawn
Lies close beside the doe.

—*Elizabeth Coatsworth*

Glossary of Instruments

accordion a keyboard instrument. It is a hand-held organ that is played by pressing buttons while air is forced through the instrument. It is often played while standing and held by straps over the shoulders, **178 CD 21:10**

bagpipe a member of the woodwind family. It is played by blowing air through a tube into the bag and then pressing the bag so that the air is forced out through the pipes, **CD 21:11**

banjo a member of the string family. It is played by plucking or strumming the strings, **191 CD 21:20**

bass drum a member of the percussion family. It is a very large drum that gives a deep sound when hit, **229 CD 20:32**

bassoon a member of the woodwind family. It is played by blowing into the reed while covering holes along the body with fingers, **228 CD 20:15**

C

cello the second-largest member of the string family in an orchestra. It is held between the knees and played by bowing or plucking the strings, **97 CD 20:6**

clarinet a member of the woodwind family. It is played by blowing into the mouthpiece while covering holes along the body with fingers, **70 CD 20:12**

conga a Latin American percussion instrument. It is a drum that has a low-pitched sound when struck, **24 CD 21:30**

cymbals members of the percussion family. These dish-shaped instruments are often played by hitting one against another to make a clashing sound, **29 CD 20:37**

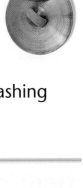

D

djembe a West African percussion instrument. It is a drum made from pottery or wood that is played with the hands, **CD 21:2**

double bass the largest instrument in the string family in an orchestra. It is held upright and played by bowing or plucking the strings, **97 CD 20:7**

Glossary of Instruments   385

flute a member of the woodwind family. It is played by blowing across a hole at one end while covering holes along the body with fingers, **228 CD 20:10**

French horn a member of the brass family. It is played by buzzing the lips into the mouthpiece while pressing keys with fingers, **72 CD 20:20**

güiro a Latin American percussion instrument. It is a gourd with a bumpy surface that is scraped with a stick to make a sound, **20 CD 21:33**

guitar a popular member of the string family. It is played by plucking or strumming the strings, **61 CD 21:13**

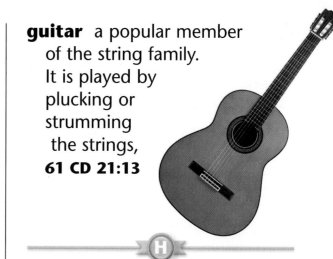

harp one of the oldest members of the string family. It is played by plucking or strumming the strings with fingers, **229 CD 20:8**

koto a long, flat, Japanese string instrument. It is played by plucking its 13 strings, **23 CD 21:53**

mandolin a member of the string family. It is similar to a guitar, but it has a different bodyshape and 8 metal strings, **CD 21:16**

maracas members of the percussion family. The pair of Latin American rattles is played by shaking when held at the handles, **20 CD 21:35**

oboe a member of the woodwind family. It is played by blowing into the reed while covering holes along the body with fingers, **127 CD 20:13**

piano a member of the percussion family. It is played by pressing the keys on the keyboard, **17 CD 20:41**

piccolo one of the smaller members of the woodwind family. It is a small flute that plays high pitches, **228 CD 20:11**

saxophone a member of the woodwind family. It is played by blowing into the mouthpiece while pushing the keys along the body with fingers, **70 CD 20:16**

shekere an African percussion instrument. It is a hollow gourd covered with a net of beads or seeds and is played by shaking, **CD 21:8**

slit drum a percussion instrument used in Africa, Asia, and the South Pacific. It is formed by hollowing a tree trunk through a slit on one side and played by hitting with sticks, **CD 21:9**

snare drum a member of the percussion family. It is played by hitting the top of the drum with drumsticks, **229 CD 20:35**

spoons a common object used as a percussion instrument. They are played by holding two together and hitting them against the body, **37 CD 21:23**

taiko drum a member of the percussion family. It is a barrel-shaped, Japanese drum that is played with sticks, or bachi, **23 CD 21:51**

tambourine a member of the percussion family. It is a small, hand-held drum that has metal disks attached loosely around the rim, and it is played by shaking or hitting it with the hand, **24 CD 20:36**

timpani members of the percussion family. They are a set of large kettle-shaped drums that are played with mallets, **229 CD 20:26**

trombone a large, low-pitched member of the brass family. It is played by buzzing the lips into the mouthpiece while moving the slide in and out, **72 CD 20:21**

trumpet the smallest, highest-pitched member of the brass family. It is played by buzzing the lips into the mouthpiece while pressing keys with fingers, **61 CD 20:18**

tuba the largest, lowest-pitched member of the brass family. It is played by buzzing the lips into the mouthpiece while pressing keys with fingers, **72 CD 20:22**

viola a member of the string family. It is held under the chin and played by bowing or plucking the strings, **97 CD 20:5**

violin the smallest member of the string family in an orchestra. It is held under the chin and played by bowing or plucking the strings, **70 CD 20:4**

xylophone a member of the percussion family. It is played by hitting the wooden bars with small wooden hammers, or mallets **30 CD 20:30**

Glossary of Terms

A

accelerando gradually getting faster, **168**

aria a solo in an opera, **217**

B

ballet a story that is told through dance and music, **25**

beat a steady pulse felt in most music, **6**

brass family metal instruments such as trumpet, French horn, trombone, and tuba that are played by buzzing the lips into the mouthpiece, **228**

C

concerto music written for a solo performer and orchestra, **73**

crescendo (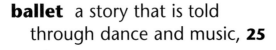) getting louder little by little, **103**

D

D.S. al Fine Italian words that tell you to go back to the sign (𝄋) and keep going until you see the word *Fine*, **75**

decrescendo (⟍) getting softer little by little, **110**

dotted half note (𝅗𝅥.) a musical note that shows a sound that is three beats long, **128**

dotted quarter note (𝅘𝅥.) a note equal to one quarter note plus one eighth note, **167**

downstage the area on the stage closest to the audience, **275**

dynamics the loudness or softness of music, **26**

E

eighth notes () musical notes that show two sounds to a beat, **14**

F

fanfare a short piece of music to honor an important person or to announce an important event, **86**

fermata (⌢) a symbol placed over a note to show that it should be held longer than its normal value, **222**

fine an Italian word that means "the end," **75**

folk song a song that emerged from the culture of a group of people, usually of unknown authorship, **151**

form the order of phrases or sections, or the plan, of a piece of music, **67**

forte (*f*) loud, **26**

half note (♩) a musical note that shows a sound that is two beats long, **87**

leap one way a melody moves; to move higher or lower by jumping over two or more pitches, **230**

melody several pitches that are sounded one after the other to make a tune, **12**

meter signature the symbol that tells how many beats are grouped in each measure, **49**

note a sign for a sound in music, **12**

opera a story told through music, **152**

pentatonic having five pitches, **171, 263**

percussion family instruments such as drum, rattle, and bell that are played by striking, scraping, or shaking, **228, 229**

piano (*p*) soft, **26**

pitch the highness or lowness of a sound, **12**

quarter note (♩) a musical note that shows one sound to a beat, **14**

quarter rest (𝄽) a musical sign that shows a beat with no sound, **14**

 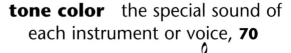

Acknowledgments, continued

Four White Horses, from *120 Singing Games and Dances for Elementary School,* by Lois Chosky and David Brummitt. Copyright © 1987 by Prentice-Hall Inc. International Copyright Secured. All Rights Reserved.

Garden Song, Words and Music by Dave Mallett. Copyright © 1975; Renewed 2003 Cherry Lane Music Publishing Company, Inc. (ASCAP) and Dimensional Music Of 1091 (ASCAP). Worldwide Rights for Dimensional Music Of 1091 Administered by Cherry Lane Music Publishing Company, Inc. International Copyright Secured. All Rights Reserved.

Great Outdoors, The, from Disneyland and Walt Disney World's COUNTRY BEAR JAMBOREE, Words and Music by George Wilkins. Copyright © 1988 Walt Disney Music Company, Inc. All Rights Reserved. Used by Permission.

Green Eggs and Ham, From MTI's Broadway Junior Broadway for Kids SEUSSICAL Junior. Music by Stephen Flaherty. Lyrics by Lynn Ahrens. Copyright © 2001 by Warner Chappell Publishing Co., Inc., Hillsdale Music, Inc., Pen and Perseverance, Inc.

Hakuna Matata, from Walt Disney Pictures' THE LION KING, Music by Elton John. Lyrics by Tim Rice. Copyright © 1994 Wonderland Music Company, Inc. All Rights Reserved. Used by Permission.

Hashewie (Going Round), from *Roots & Branches.* Eritrean Folk Song. Words by Hidaat Ephrem. Copyright © Hidaat Ephrem/World Music Press (ASCAP). World Music Press, P.O. Box 2565, Danbury, CT 06813-2565, www.worldmusicpress.com. All Rights Reserved.

Hello, Hello There, Words by Betty Comden and Adolph Green. Music by Jule Styne. Copyright © 1956 by Stratford Music Corporation. Copyright Renewed. All Rights Administered by Chappell & Co. International Copyright Secured. All Rights Reserved.

Horton Hears a Who!, From MTI's Broadway Junior Broadway for Kids SEUSSICAL Junior. Music by Stephen Flaherty. Lyrics by Lynn Ahrens. Copyright © 2001 by Warner Chappell Publishing Co., Inc., Hillsdale Music, Inc., Pen and Perseverance, Inc.

Horton Hears a Who! Two, From MTI's Broadway Junior Broadway for Kids SEUSSICAL Junior. Music by Stephen Flaherty. Lyrics by Lynn Ahrens. Copyright © 2001 by Warner Chappell Publishing Co., Inc., Hillsdale Music, Inc., Pen and Perseverance, Inc.

It's a Small World, from "it's a small world" at Disneyland Park and Magic Kingdom. Words and Music by Richard M. Sherman and Robert B. Sherman. © 1963 Wonderland Music Company, Inc. Copyright Renewed. All Rights Reserved. Used by Permission.

It's Possible, from MTI's Broadway Junior Broadway for Kids SEUSSICAL Junior. Music by Stephen Flaherty. Lyrics by Lynn Ahrens. Copyright © 2001 by Warner Chappell Publishing Co., Inc., Hillsdale Music, Inc., Pen and Perseverance, Inc.

Joy, from THE FEEL OF MUSIC. Words and Music by Hap Palmer. Copyright © 1976 by Hap-Pal Music, Inc., www.happalmer.com. International Copyright Secured. All Rights Reserved.

Jugaremos en el bosque (We'll Be Playing in the Forest), from *Lirica infantil de Mexico,* by Vicente T. Mendoza. Copyright © 1980 by Fondo De Cultura Economica, Av. de la Universidad 975, 03100 Mexico, D.F. International Copyright Secured. All Rights Reserved.

Let's Go Fly a Kite, from Walt Disney's MARY POPPINS. Words and Music by Richard M. Sherman and Robert B. Sherman. © 1963 Wonderland Music Company, Inc. Copyright Renewed. All Rights Reserved. Used by Permission.

Mama Paquita, Brazilian Carnival Song. English Version by Merrill Staton. Copyright © 1986 by ROCKHAVEN MUSIC. International Copyright Secured. All Rights Reserved.

Martin Luther King, Words and Music by Mary Donnelly and George L.O. Strid. Copyright © 2002 by HAL LEONARD CORPORATION. International Copyright Secured. All Rights Reserved.

Merry-Go-Round, Words by Dorothy Baruch. Arranged by Marilyn Davidson. Copyright © 1952, 1961 (Renewed 1980, 1989) by Scott Foresman & Company, International Copyright Secured. All Rights Reserved.

My Dreidel, from *Songs We Sing.* Words by S.S. Grossman. Music by S.E. Goldfarb. Edited by Henry Coopersmith. Copyright © 1950 (Renewed) by the Board of Jewish Education of Greater New York. International Copyright Secured. All Rights Reserved.

Oh, the Thinks You Can Think!, from MTI's Broadway Junior Broadway for Kids SEUSSICAL Junior. Music by Stephen Flaherty. Lyrics by Lynn Ahrens. Copyright © 2001 by Warner Chappell Publishing Co., Inc., Hillsdale Music, Inc., Pen and Perseverance, Inc.

Oma Rapeti (Run, Rabbit), New Zealand Folk Song collected and transcribed by Kathy Sorensen. © 1991 Kathy B. Sorensen. All Rights Reserved.

On Top of Spaghetti, Words and Music by Tom Glazer. Copyright © 1963, 1965 by Songs Music Inc. Copyright Renewed. International Copyright Secured. All Rights Reserved.

Orff Instruments, by Donna Otto and Janet Graham. Use by permission.

Part of Your World, from Walt Disney's THE LITTLE MERMAID. Lyrics by Howard Ashman. Music by Alan Menken. © 1988 Walt Disney Music Company and Wonderland Music Company, Inc. All Rights Reserved. Used by Permission.

Pick a Pumpkin, Words and Music by Naomi Caldwell. Copyright © 1965, 1970 (Renewed 1993, 1998) by Ginn & Company. International Copyright Secured. All Rights Reserved. Used by Permission of Silver, Burdett & Ginn, Inc.

Place in the Choir, A, Words and Music by Bill Staines. © 1978 Mineral River Music (BMI). Rights Administered by Bug Music Inc. International Copyright Secured. All Rights Reserved.

Puff, the Magic Dragon, Words and Music by Lenny Lipton and Peter Yarrow. Copyright © 1963; Renewed 1991 Honalee Melodies (ASCAP) and Silver Dawn Music (ASCAP). Worldwide Rights for Honalee Melodies Administered by Cherry Lane Music Publishing Company, Inc. Worldwide Rights for Silver Dawn Music Administered by WB Music Corp. International Copyright Secured. All Rights Reserved.

Red Rover, Traditional English Rhyme. Music by Denise Bacon. Copyright © 1974 (Renewed) by Boosey & Hawkes Co., Inc. International Copyright Secured. All Rights Reserved.

Sailor, Sailor on the Sea, Words and Music by Jean Ritchie. Copyright © by Jean Ritchie/Geordie Music Publishing Co. International Copyright Secured. All Rights Reserved. Used by Permission.

San Sereni, from *Roots & Branches.* Latin American Folk Song . Copyright © World Music Press (ASCAP). World Music Press, P.O. Box 2565, Danbury, CT 06813-2565, www.worldmusicpress.com. All Rights Reserved.

Seeds and Seasons, Words and Music by Jim Walters. Copyright © by JIM WALTERS. International Copyright Secured. All Rights Reserved.

Seussical Mega-Mix, from MTI's Broadway Junior Broadway for Kids SEUSSICAL Junior. Music by Stephen Flaherty. Lyrics by Lynn Ahrens. Copyright © 2001 by Warner Chappell Publishing Co., Inc., Hillsdale Music, Inc., Pen and Perseverance, Inc.

Sheep in the Meadow, from *Anna Banana: 101 Jump Rope Rhymes.* Compiled by Joanna Cole. Copyright 1989 by Joanna Cole. Used by permission of HarperCollins Publishers.

Shrimp Boats, Words and Music by Paul Mason Howard and Paul Weston. © 1951 Walt Disney Music Company. Copyright Renewed 1979 Walt Disney Music Company and Hanover Music Corporation. All Rights Reserved. Used by Permission.

Sing! Sing! Sing!, Words and Music by Branice McKenzie. Copyright © 2002 by EUNICE MUSIC. International Copyright Secured. All Rights Reserved.

Acknowledgments, continued

CREDITS

Illustration Credits: Martha Avilés: 54, 55. Rose Mary Berlin: 303. Ken Bowser: 330, 331, 332. Carlos Caban: 231. Carly Castillon: 46, 47, 79. Mircea Catusanu: 333, 334, 335. Jack Crane: 306, 307. Lynn Cravath: 326, 327. Renee Daily: 379. Molly Delaney: 126, 127. Sarah Dillard: 310. Angela Donato: 167. Drew-Brook-Cormack Assoc.: 91, 146, 147. Kathi Ember, 271. Leslie Evans: 316, 317. Ruth Flanigan: 214, 215. Felipe Galindo: 116, 117. Jo Gershman: 232, 233. Dara Goldman: 134, 135. Oki Han: 22. Judy Hand: 210, 211. Greg Harris: 304. Eileen Hine: 236, 237. Phyllis Hornung: 26, 27. John Hovell: B, C, F, G, N, O, R, U, W. Nicole in den Bosch: 1, 168, 169, Spotlight on Concepts (2). Jui Ishida: TAB 4, 337. Aleksey Ivanov: 108, 109. Holly Jones: 100. John Kanzler: 180, 181. Virg Kask: 207. Dave Klug: 293. Erin Eitter Kono: 246. Peter Lacalamita: 290, 291. Fran Lee: 313. Stephen Lewis: 253. Susan Lexa: 170, 171. Bryan Liedahl: 259. Margaret Lindmark: 138, 139. Amy Loeffler: 204, 205. Loretta Lustig: 14, 15. Lyn Martin: 324, 325. Deborah Maze: 142, 143. Lucinda McQueen: 76, 77. Cheryl Mendenhall: 50, 51. Ashley Mims: 243. Gosia Mosz: 156, 157. Keiko Motoyama: 136, 137, 213. Kathleen O'Malley: 273, Spotlight on Performance (2). Page O'Rourke: 222, 223. Donna Perrone: 226, 227. Gary R. Phillips: 90, 188, 189. Mindy Pierce: 133. Trevor Pye: 328, 329. Mary Reaves-Uhles: 300. Adam Rogers: 20. Nicole Rutten: 173. Janet K. Skiles: 112, 113. Jamie Smith: 84, 85. Karen Stormer Brooks: 6,7,8. Susan Swan: 2, 33, 241, 320, Spotlight on Reading (2). Maggie Swanson: 102, 103. Andrea Tachiera: 320, 321. Bruce Van Patter: 225. Laura Watson: 124, 125. Jody Wheeler: 196, 197. Toby Williams: 18, 19. Marsha Winborn: 130, 131. Anna Wodecki: 74, 75.

Photography Credits: all photographs are by Macmillan/McGraw-Hill (MMH) except as noted below.

Allan Landau/MMH: cover. i. iv-vii: (tcr tr). A-H: (bcl tl br). 2-3. 4. 18. 38. 42-43. 44. 45. 48: (tl). 49: (c b). 51. 63. 68. 71. 86. 91: (cr). 95. 103. 122-123. 131. 143. 145: (tr). 148. 158: (l r). 162-163. 198: (br). 202-203. 204-205. 221. 228: (bcr). 388: (cl bl). 389: (tl).

iv-vii: (t tc tcl tl b bcl bl) C Squared Studios/Getty Images; (tr r cr br) Royalty-Free/Corbis. A-H: (bl) PhotoDisc/Getty Images; (tl cl) Rubberball; (b) Comstock; (tcr) Barbara Penoyar/Getty Images; (tr) Royalty-Free/Corbis. C: (cl) Stockbyte; (tl) Royalty-Free/Corbis; (tr) Image Club. D: (t) PhotoDisc. E: (bkgd) MetaCreations/Kai Power Photos; (c) Comstock. G: (l) Scenics of America/PhotoLink/Getty Images; (tr) R. Morley/PhotoLink/Getty Images. G-H: (bkgd) Royalty-Free/Corbis; (c) PhotoLink/Getty Images. H: (bkgd) Royalty-Free/Corbis. 4-5: (bkgd) Tamara Studios/MMH. 8: (t) Dorling Kindersley/Getty Images; (tr) Rob Chapple/Taxi/Getty Images; (bl) Michael J. Doolittle/ The Image Works. 8-9: (bkgd) Michael J. Doolittle/The Image Works. 9: (l) Dorling Kindersley/Getty Images. 10: (l) IT Stock Int'l/eStock Photo/ PictureQuest/ Jupiterimages; (r) Robert W. Ginn/PhotoEdit. 10-13: (bkgd) Corel. 11: (b) Steve Cole/Getty Images. 12: (b) Scott T. Smith/Corbis. 13: (b) Smithsonian American Art Museum, Washington, DC/Art Resource, NY. 16-17: (bkgd) Ric Ergenbright/Corbis. 17: (tl) Bettmann/Corbis. 20: (bl) Adam Rogers. 20-21: (bkgd) Tony Arruza/Corbis. 21: (br) Reuters NewMedia/Corbis. 23: (tr) Kenneth Hamm/Photo Japan; (br) Jay Syverson/Corbis; (c) Jack Fields/Corbis; (l) Kelly-Mooney Photography/Corbis. 24: (7 11) C Squared Studios/Getty Images; (bkgd 8 10 14) Royalty-Free/Corbis. 25: (c) "The photo of Wendy Whelanin "Mozartiana" is used with the permission of New York City Ballet. "Mozartiana", choreography by George Balanchine, The George Balanchine Trust. BALANCHINE is a trademark of the George Balanchine Trust. Photo by Paul Kolnik; (r) Philadelphia Museum of Art/ Corbis. 29: (tr) Royalty-Free/Corbis; (bc) LWA/Sharie Kennedy/Blend Images/Getty Images; (bl) Michael S. Yamashita/Corbis; (br) Rob Lewine/Corbis. 30: (t) Lebrecht Music & Arts. 30-31: (bkgd) Bill Bachmann/ Index Stock Imagery/PictureQuest. 31: Courtesy Sonor Instruments a Division of Hohner, HSS. 34: (l) Myrleen Ferguson Cate/ PhotoEdit. 34-35: (b) Steve Vidler/ SuperStock. 34-35: (t) R.F. Elliott/Robertstock.com. 36: (t b) Courtesy Clancy Dennehy/ Scrap Arts Music. 36 37: (bkgd) PhotoDisc/Getty Images. 39: (l r) Courtesy Sonor Instruments a Division of Hohner, HSS. 40: (b) C Squared Studios/Getty Images. 41: Jim Powell/ MMH. 47: (b) Rico D' Rozario/Redferns/Getty Images. 48: (tr) Dave G. Houser/Corbis; (b) Mark Adams. 48-49: (bkgd) Royalty-Free/Corbis. 49: Mark Adams. 52-53: (bkgd) Royalty-Free/Corbis. 53: (br) 2003 Board of Trustees, National Gallery of Art, Washington, DC. 56-57: C Squared Studios/Getty Images. 57: (tc) Elsa/Getty Images; (tl tr) Reuters NewMedia/ Corbis. 58: (tr) Gerard Brown/Getty Images; (cr) Gerard Lacz/Animals Animals. 59: (tc) Tim Davis/Photo Researchers; (tl) Royalty-Free/Corbis; (tr) David Young-Wolff/PhotoEdit. 60: (l) Gary Conner/Index Stock/Photolibrary; (b) David Seawell/ Corbis. 61: (r) Gary Conner/Index Stock/Photolibrary; (tl) Corbis. 62: (c) Lew Robertson/Getty Images. 64: (bkgd) Corbis; (tl) Hideo Haga/HAGA/The Image Works; (bl) Richard Glover/ Corbis; (br) Matthew McKee/Eye Ubiquitous/Corbis; (cl) www.mikeclare.com. 65: (b) Eastcott/Momatiuk/The Image Works. 66: (r) Danny Lehman/Corbis. 66-67: (t) Victoriene Parsons Mitchell/Bridgeman Art Library/Getty Images. 67: (tr) Cummer Museum of Art and Gardens, Jacksonville, FL, USA/Bridgeman Art Library. 68-69: (t) Victoriene Parsons Mitchell/Bridgeman Art Library/Getty Images. 69: (bkgd) Siede Preis/PhotoDisc/Getty Images. 70: Susan Varick/Maxwell Street Klezmer Band, Chicago. 72: (c cl) C Squared Studios/Getty Images. 72: (cr) PhotoDisc Collection/Getty Images. 73: (br) Music Museum, Bologna, Italy/A.K.G., Berlin/SuperStock; (c cr) C Squared Studios/ Getty Images; (cl) Barros & Barros/The Image Bank/Getty Images. 73: (r) Jeffrey Ufberg/ WireImage/Getty Images. 75: (bkgd) Kindra Clineff/Index Stock/Photolibrary. 77: (b) Color woodcut, 36.3 x 24 cm, Fine Arts Museums of San Francisco, Achenbach Foundation for Graphic Arts. 80: (b) Royalty-Free/Corbis. 81: (b) C Squared Studios/Getty Images. 82: (t) Paul Chesley/Stone/Getty Images. 82-83: (b) Lawrence Manning/Corbis. 83: (t) Angelo Cavalli/Image Bank/Getty Images; (br) Billy Hustace/Stone/Getty Images. 84: (tr) Hulton-Deutsch Collection/Corbis; (bl) Lawrence Manning/ Corbis. 86-87: (t) Royalty-Free/Corbis. 87: (bkgd) C Squared Studios/Getty Images. 88-89: (bkgd t) Royalty-Free/Corbis. 89: (tr) Saelon Renkes; (bl) Patti Murray/Animals Animals; (br) Ron Sanford/Corbis. 91: (bkgd) Paul Thompson/Eye Ubiquitous/Corbis. 92: (tr) Bettmann/Corbis. 92-93: (bkgd) MetaCreations/Kai Power Photos. 93: (tr) Hinata Haga/HAGA/ The Image Works. 94: (bc) C Squared Studios/Getty Images; (br) North Carolina Museum of Art/Corbis; (c) David Redfern/ Redferns/Getty Images; (l) Jason Lauré/The Image Works. 94-95: (bkgd t) Dorling Kindersley/Getty Images. 96: (c) Imapress/Vario Press/The Image Works. 96-97: (bkgd t) Dorling Kindersley/Getty Images. 97: (4) Jim Powell/ MMH; (5) Royalty-Free/Corbis; (tr) General Photographic Agency/ Hulton Archive/Getty Images. 98-99: (bkgd) Corel. 99: (tr cr) Xinhua/Sovfoto; (bl cl) Ingrid Booz Morejohn/PictureWorks/ Link; (br) Peter Parks/AFP Photo/Getty Images. 101: (bkgd) Chris Lisle/Corbis; (t) Werner Forman/Art Resource, NY; (br) Whitworth Art Gallery, The University of Manchester, UK/ Bridgeman Art Library. 102-105: (t) Royalty-Free/Corbis. 104: (tr) Hideo Haga/HAGA/The Image Works. 104-105: (bkgd) Steve Vidler/SuperStock; (c) PhotoLink/Getty Images. 105: (tr) Austrian Archives/Corbis. 106-107: (bkgd) Corbis. 107: (tl) Prenzel Photo/Animals Animals; (bc) Tierbild Okapia/ Photo Researchers; (tr bl) PhotoDisc/Getty Images; (br) Royalty-Free/Corbis. 108-109: (bkgd) Trans-World Photos/SuperStock. 109: (tr) Brian Flintoff. 110-111: (bkgd) Jonathan and Angela/ Taxi/Getty Images; (t) Bob Krist/Corbis. 111: (tl) E.R. Degginger/Alamy; (tr) Bryan & Cherry Alexander Photography/Alamy; (b) George D. Lepp/Photo Researchers; (cl) D. Puleston/Photo Researchers; (cr) Gregory G. Dimijian/ Photo Researchers. 112: (tc) Corbis; (tl) Tim Davis/Corbis; (tr) John Conrad/ Corbis. 112-113: (t) Bob Krist/Corbis. 113: (tr) Tim Davis/Corbis; (c) Ralph A. Clevenger/Corbis; (cr) John Conrad/Corbis. 114-115: (bkgd) PhotoDisc/Getty Images. 115: Shane Morgan/MMH. 117: (tl) Dallas and John Heaton/ Corbis; (tcl bc bl) Royalty-Free/Corbis; (br) Diamar Portfolios; (tcr) Gavin Hellier/Robert Harding World Imagery/Getty Images; (tr) Volkmar Wentzel/ National Geographic Stock. 118: (br cr) C Squared Studios/Getty Images. 120: (c) C Squared Studios/Getty Images. 121: (r) David Farrell/Lebrecht Music & Arts Photo Library. 128-129: (bkgd) Danny Lehman/ Corbis. 130: (c) C Squared Studios/Getty Images. 132: (tr) Jules Frazier/Getty Images. 134-137: (t) PhotoLink/Getty Images. 136: (c) Archivo Iconografico, S.A./Corbis. 140-141: (bkgd) Nigel Hillier/Stone/Getty Images. 141: (t) Alexander Hubrich/Stone/Getty Images; (cr) Courtesy Morriston Orpheus Choir; (b) Wolfgang Meier/Corbis. 142-143: (t) Royalty-Free/Corbis. 144: (r) Scala/Art Resource, NY. 144-145: (bkgd) Bettmann/Corbis; (t) Royalty-Free/Corbis. 146-147: (t) Corbis. 147: (tc) Shane Morgan/MMH. 148-149: (bkgd) Royalty-Free/Corbis; (t) Corbis. 149: (tr) Cpl. M. Trent Lowry/ USMC; (bc) Michael S. Yamashita/Corbis. 150-151: (bkgd) Royalty-Free /Corbis. 151: (tr) Archivo Iconografico, S.A./Corbis; (b) George D. Lepp/Corbis. 152: (tr b) Ron Scherl. 152-153: (bkgd) Doug Mazell/Index Stock/ Photolibrary. 153: (t) Music Lovers Society, Vienna/ A.K.G., Berlin/SuperStock; (b) Lelli & Masotti/AP Images. 154: (tr) Kit Breen. 154-155: (bkgd) Wolfgang Kaehler/Corbis. 155: (tr) Kevin R. Morris/Corbis; (cr) Joseph Amadeus Fleck/ Private Collection/Bridgeman Art Library. 157: (tr b) Larry Engelhart/Deja Views. 158: (br) Jim Powell/MMH. 161: (r) C Squared Studios/Getty Images. 165: (t) Bob Daemmrich/ PhotoEdit 166-167: (bkgd) Corel; (t) Corbis. 168: (tr) C Squared Studios/Getty Images; (bl) Vittoriano Rastelli/Corbis. 168-169: (t) Corbis. 171: (tr) SuperStock. 174: (c) Doug Pearson/Alamy; (br) The British Museum/ Topham-HIP/The Image Works. 174-175: (bkgd) Hugh Sitton/Stone/Getty Images; (t) Corel. 175: (b) Topham/ The Image Works; (cr) Chris Hellier/Corbis. 176-177: (bkgd t) Corel. 177: (t) Shane Morgan/MMH; (c) C Squared Studios/Getty Images. 178-179: (bkgd b) Philip Gould/Corbis. 182: (tc tr) Courtesy Sonor Instruments a Division of Hohner, HSS; (bc bl br) Shane Morgan/MMH; (cl) Royalty-Free/Corbis. 182-183: (bkgd) Corel. 184: (t) Digital Vision Ltd; (b) Courtesy Orff-Zentrum München; (c) Hannelore Gassner. 184-185: (bkgd) Corel. 185: (t) Courtesy Sonor Instruments a Division of Hohner, HSS; (b) Erich Lessing/Art Resource, NY. 186: (tr) Michael Fogden/Animals Animals. 186-187: (bkgd) Harald Sund /Image Bank/Getty Images. 187: (bl) Wolfgang Kaehler/ Wolfgang Kaehler Photography; (br) Ludovic Maisant/Corbis; (c) Steve Vidler/SuperStock. 190-191: (bkgd) Artville LLC. 191: (b) Daniel Templeton/Alamy; (cl) Frost School of Music, University of Miami, Coral Gables, FL/University of Miami; (cr) Bob Daemmrich/The Image Works. 192: (t) C Squared Studios/Getty Images; (b) Nathan Bilow/Allsport Concepts/ Getty Images. 192-193: (bkgd) Patrick Bennett/Corbis. 194-195: (bkgd) C Squared Studios/Getty Images. 195: Shane Morgan/ MMH. 198: (tr) C Squared Studios/Getty Images. 201: (cl) Paul Nestor/Operation Respect. 206-207: (bkgd) Jack Kurtz/The Image Works; (t) Corel. 207: (br) Comstock/ Jupiter Images. 208-209: (bkgd) Guy Cali/Corbis; (t) Corel. 209: (t) Diego Rivera/São Paulo Art Museum Brazil/Dagli Orti/Art Archive. 210: (tr) Charles Belle/Denise Cade Gallery/ 2005 Artists Rights Society (ARS), New York/ ADAGP, Paris. 212: (b) Brown & Bigelow; (t) Royalty-Free/ Corbis. 214-215: (t) Corel. 216-217: (bkgd t) Corel. 217: (t) Beatriz Schiller/ Time Life Pictures/Getty Images. 218: (br) Peter Davidson/ Private Collection/Bridgeman Art Library. 218-219: (bkgd) PhotoLink/Getty Images; (t) Setboun/Corbis. 220-221: (bkgd) African Designs from Traditional Sources. Geoffrey Williams. (Toronto: Fover Publications, 1971.). 222-223: (t) Corel. 223: Shane Morgan/MMH. 224: (t) Suzie Maeder/Lebrecht Music & Arts; (br) ChicagoTribune photo by Terrence Antonio James. 224-225: (t) Corel. 225: (tr) PhotoDisc/Getty Images; (br) Archivo Iconografico, S.A./Corbis. 228: C Squared Studios/ Getty Images; (c) Fox Model 500 English horn, photo Courtesy Fox Products Corporation, South Whitley, IN. 228-229: (b) C Squared Studios/Getty Images. 229: C Squared Studios/Getty Images; (tcr) Jules Frazier/PhotoDisc Green/Getty Images; (tl) Brand X Pictures/PunchStock. 230: (bc) PlaceStockPhoto.com. 230-231: (bkgd) Marilyn Angel Wynn/Nativestock Pictures; (t) Corel. 231: (cr) PlaceStockPhoto.com. 232: (b) Stan Funk/Courtesy Stephen Hatfield/Funk Art Publications. 232-233: (t) Corel. 234: (c) Courtesy African Children's Choir. 234-235: (bkgd) David Samuel Robbins/ Corbis. 235: Courtesy African Children's Choir. 236: (r) The London Art Archive/Alamy. 244: (b) Tony Hamblin/ Frank Lane Picture Agency/Corbis. 246: (l) Jules Frazier/ Getty Images. 247: (t) Ali Meyer/Corbis; (b) Jules Frazier/ Getty Images. 250-251: PhotoDisc/Getty Images. 255: (cl) C Squared Studios/Getty Images. 256 260 264: (b) PhotoDisc/Getty Images. 270: (bl) C Squared Studios/ Getty Images. 271: (b) Réunion des Musées Nationaux/Art Resource, NY. 274: (cl) Corel; (l) C Squared Studios/Getty Images. 275: (br tc) Corel. 277: (r) MTI; (br) Corel. 283: (b) MTI; (br) Corel. 284: (t) PhotoDisc/ Getty Images. 286: (c) MTI; (l) Corel. 289: (br) MTI; (cr) PhotoDisc. 291-295 297: Walt Disney Pictures/The Kobal Collection. 291 293 295 297 299 301 303 305 307-309: (tr) PhotoDisc/Getty Images. 299: (bkgd) Jim Zuckerman/ Corbis. 300: (b) Shane Morgan/ MMH. 307: (b) Bruno Veiga/Tyba/BrazilPhotos. 308: (bl) PhotoDisc/Getty Images. 311 313: (tr) John A. Rizzo/Getty Images. 314: (t) Comstock/Jupiter Images. 315: (bc) Comstock/Jupiter Images; (bl) Corel; (br) C Squared Studios/Getty Images; (br tr) John A. Rizzo/Getty Images. 317: (tr) John A. Rizzo/ Getty Images. 318: (c) Comstock/ Jupiter Images; (l) C Squared Studios/Getty Images. 318-319: (c) John A. Rizzo/Getty Images. 319: (tr) John A. Rizzo/Getty Images; (bl br) Comstock/Jupiter Images. 321: (tc) Joanna McCarthy/SuperStock; (tr) PhotoDisc/Getty Images. 322: (cr) Wayne Lawler/Ecoscene/Corbis; (tr) Dave G. Houser/ Corbis. 323 325 327: (tr) PhotoDisc/Getty Images. 327: (br) C Squared Studios/Getty Images. 329: (1) Jim Powell/MMH. 330: (2) Jim Powell/MMH. 333: (3) Jim Powell/MMH. 338: (tl tr) Image Club. 338-339: (1 2) Image Club; (3 5) Steve Cole/ Getty Images; (4) C Squared Studios/Getty Images. 339: C Squared Studios/Getty Images; (b) Kevin Fleming/Corbis; (tr) Corbis. 340-341: (bkgd) PhotoLink/Getty Images. 342: (bc) Burke Triolo Productions/Getty Images; (tc bcl) Siede Preis/ Getty Images; (tr bl) John A. Rizzo/Getty Images; (br) Stockdisc/PunchStock. 342-343: (1) MetaCreations/ Kai Power Photos; (2) Steve Cole/Getty Images. 343: (tl bc) Comstock/Jupiter Images; (bl) PhotoDisc; (tr br) C Squared Studios/Getty Images. 344: (bl) Bettmann/ Corbis; (br) Richard T. Nowitz/Corbis. 344-345: (1) Comstock/ PunchStock; (2) Comstock Images/Alamy; (3) Artville; (4) Comstock/Jupiter Images; (5) MetaCreations/ Kai Power Photos. 345: (b) Bettmann/Corbis. 346-347: (bkgd) Steve Cole/Getty Images. 348: (b) Michael Newman/PhotoEdit; (bl) Comstock/Jupiter Images; (br) John A. Rizzo/Getty Images; (cl) MetaCreations/Kai Power Photos; (cr) Steve Cole/Getty Images. 349: (tl) PhotoDisc/ Getty Images; (tr) Jules Frazier/ Getty Images. 350: (tl tr) C Squared Studios/Getty Images. 350-351: (bkgd) Royalty-Free/Corbis. 351: (t) Scala/Art Resource, NY; (bl) David Tose/Getty Images; (br) C Squared Studios/Getty Images. 353: (tr) PNC/Brand X Pictures/Getty Images; (b) MetaCreations/Kai Power Photos. 354: (bl) PhotoDisc/Getty Images; (tl br) Jack Vartoogian/ FrontRowPhotos; (tr) Siede Preis/Getty Images. 354-355: (bkgd) Siede Preis/ Getty Images; (t bl l) Steve Cole/Getty Images. 356-357: (1 2) Steve Cole/Getty Images; (3) Image Club. 357: (bl br) Steve Cole/Getty Images. 358-359: (bkgd b) C Squared Studios/Getty Images. 360-361: (bkgd) Annie Reynolds/PhotoLink/Getty Images. 361: (tr) Siede Preis/ Getty Images. 362: (tl) Jules Frazier/Getty Images. 363: (bl) Inti St. Clair/Getty Images; (br) John Burke/ JupiterImages/Getty Images. 365: (b) Francis Miller/Time Life Pictures/Getty Images. 366: (bl) Brian Jackson/Mira; (br cl) C Squared Studios/Getty Images; (cr) Francisco Cruz/SuperStock. 366-367: (bkgd) MetaCreations/Kai Power Creations. 367: (bl) Lawrence Migdale/Mira; (br) Peter/Georgina Bowater/Mira. 367: (t) C Squared Studios/Getty Images. 368: (tr) Jules Frazier/Getty Images. 368-369: (bkgd) MetaCreations/Kai Power Photos. 370: (br cl) C Squared Studios/Getty Images; (c) Artville; (cr) The Granger Collection, NY; (tr) Wildside Press. 370-371: (1) Image Club; (2) C Squared Studios/Getty Images; (3) Steve Cole/Getty Images. 371: (tl) Siede Preis/ Getty Images; (tr) Wildside Press. 374-375: (bkgd) Royalty-Free/ Corbis. 375: (tl tr) PhotoDisc/Getty Images; (l) Corel; (r) C Squared Studios/Getty Images. 376: (bcl) PhotoLink/ Getty Images; (bl) Royalty-Free/Corbis; (br) MetaCreations/Kai Power Creations. 376-377: (bkgd) Royalty-Free/Corbis. 377: (bc) Diamar Portfolios; (bl) PhotoLink/Getty Images; (br) Jeremy Hoare/Life File/Getty Images. 378: (tr) The Granger Collection, NY. 378-379: (bkgd) PhotoLink/Getty Images. 381: (b c) David Young-Wolff/PhotoEdit. 382-383: (bkgd) PhotoLink/Getty Images. 384: (bl) PhotoDisc/Getty Images; (tl br) C Squared Studios/Getty Images. 385: (br) Jules Frazier/PhotoDisc Green/Getty Images; (cl cr) C Squared Studios/ Getty Images. 386: (tl br) C Squared Studios/Getty Images. 387 388: (tl) C Squared Studios/Getty Images. 389: (br cl) C Squared Studios/Getty Images.

All attempts have been made to provide complete and correct credits by the time of publication.

Classified Index

Alphabetical Index

Pronunciation Key

Simplified International Phonetic Alphabet
VOWELS

ɑ	father	o	obey	æ	cat	ɔ	paw
e	chaotic	u	moon	ɛ	pet	ʊ	put
i	bee	ʌ	up	ɪ	it	ə	ago

SPECIAL SOUNDS

β	say *b* without touching lips together; *Spanish* nueve, haba
ç	hue; *German* ich
ð	the; *Spanish* todo
n̩	sound n as individual syllable
ö	form [o] with lips and say [e]; *French* adieu, *German* schön
œ	form [ɔ] with lips and say [ɛ] *French* coeur, *German* plötzlich
ɾ	flipped r; butter
r̄	rolled r; *Spanish* perro
ǂ	click tongue on the ridge behind teeth; *Zulu* ngcwele
ü	form [u] with lips and say [i]; *French* tu, *German* grün
ʊ̈	form [ʊ] with lips and say [ɪ]
x	blow strong current of air with back of tongue up; *German* Bach, *Hebrew* Hanukkah, *Spanish* bajo
ʒ	pleasure
ʼ	glottal stop, as in the exclamation "uh, oh!" [ʼʌ ʼo]
~	nasalized vowel, such as *French* bon [bõ]
¬	end consonants *k*, *p*, and *t* without puff of air, such as sky (no puff of air after *k*), as opposed to *kite* (puff of air after *k*)

OTHER CONSONANTS PRONOUNCED SIMILAR TO ENGLISH

ch	cheese	ny	onion; *Spanish* niño
g	go	sh	shine
ng	sing	ts	boats

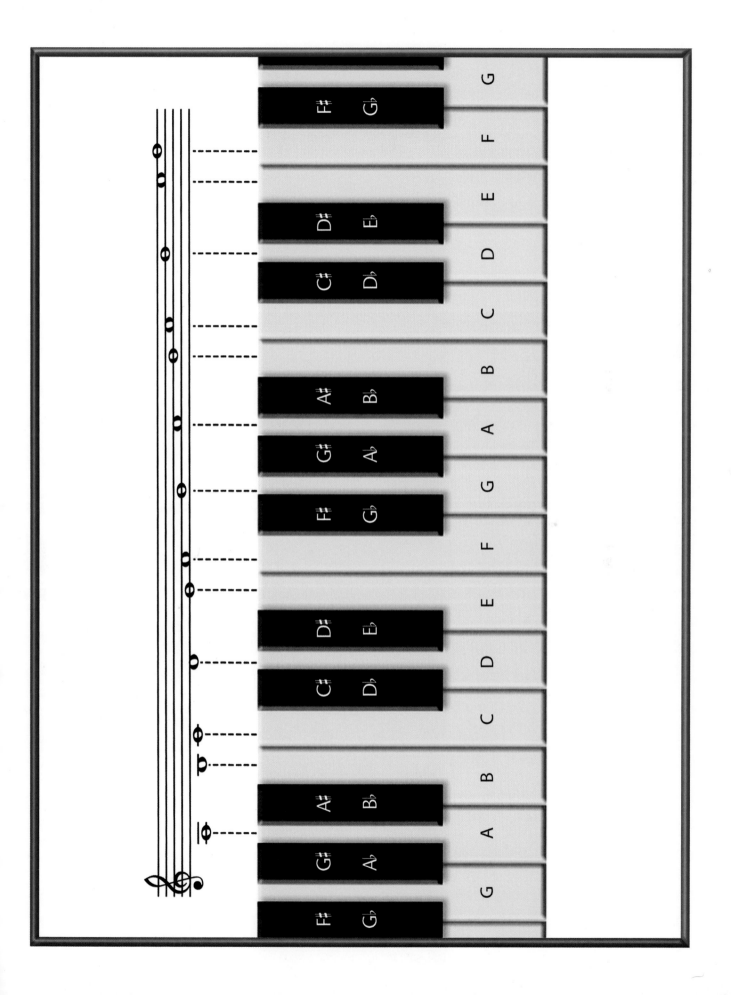